OCEAN CITY'S
WESTSIDE

Breaking Barriers, Building Bridges

Published by Indelible Ink, LLC.
Marmora, New Jersey
Amazon Kindle Direct Publishing

Copyright © 2024 by Loretta Thompson Harris
All rights reserved.

Editing and book design by Michelle Harris Anderson and Angela Harris Moore

Cover Images
    Front Top – L-R:
- *Cape May County Municipal Utilities Authority installation by S. W. Thompson & Sons, Inc.*
- *The Lomax House*
- *Al Jolson in blackface from the 1927 film 'The Jazz Singer'*

    Front Bottom – L-R:
- *Ocean City Beach Patrol: Samuel Martin, Henry Skipwith, Archie Harris, Alvin Thompson*

    Back: *Sailor Roger K. Williams*

Images not otherwise credited courtesy of the Thompson family collection

First published 2024
Manufactured in the United States
979-8-9879843-1-4

For general or ordering information contact Indelible Ink at:
E-Mail: IndelibleInkOC@gmail.com

This book is dedicated to yesterday's childhood friends, today's senior citizens -- revered sages blessed with countless untold stories of the past just waiting to be told.

OCEAN CITY'S
WESTSIDE

Breaking Barriers, Building Bridges

Loretta Thompson Harris

CONTENTS

FOREWORD

Many people from Philadelphia and suburbs took respite from the sweltering asphalt-reflected heat "down the shore" which means at the New Jersey shore. Towns like Cape May, the Wildwoods, Sea Isle, Ocean City, Longport, Margate, Ventnor, Atlantic City, and Long Beach Island hosted refugee families from Philly seeking sea breezes and a leisurely pace of life.

Ocean City, New Jersey was a pristine summer resort, originally a Methodist town, and still "dry" which means without bars, nightclubs, or liquor stores. Ocean City in the 1960's was so clean that even the dirt was clean. Its boardwalk and neat, orderly thoroughfares like Asbury Avenue and Bay Avenue offered an Andy-of-Mayberry contrast to the thoroughfares of the big city. The long drawbridge, the Ninth Street Bridge, and its honeycombed steel drawbridge road sections was the entry to the island from Route 9 or the Garden State Parkway.

Rounding the traffic circle in Somers Point by Tony Mart on the north and the Circle Liquor Store to the south, the bay air odor and the odd noise of automobile tire on honeycomb grate confirmed that one was now within the realm of the ocean. The rowdy, raucous laugh of the hovering gulls said hello to a place where life was slow. The shore was always perhaps fifteen degrees cooler than the city and never without at least a modest breeze. Nights demanded a sweater or jacket. Heavy dew covered everything in the early morning. Sometimes, one was treated to a dense blanket of fog that hushed the island into an otherworldly state of tranquility.

With the stern specter of the Methodist founders gazing on, businesses on the island were all closed on Sunday. After the summer crowd left, eventually, the streetlights were turned off and covered in burlap bags. The miniscule winter volume of traffic did not warrant lights. In winter, one could stroll along the boardwalk completely alone without another soul in sight. Moments like that were priceless.

Printed with the permission of Robert A. Butler, author.
December 2021

Robert Butler is a step-great grandson of Virginia native John Sylvester Pye and grandson of Maryland native Fannie Waters Gillis Pye. John Pye arrived in Ocean City in the early 1920s. Since that time, six generations, from Mamie to Emilio, have enjoyed the quiet, slow-paced lifestyle found in Ocean City. The Butler brothers, Robert, Donovan, and Whitney, hold fond memories of visiting their great grandfather "down the shore" during the 1960s and 1970s.

ACKNOWLEDGEMENTS

My sincere thanks to cousin William "Bill" Griffin, the keeper of the Thompson Bible, family photographs and clippings since the passing of his mother, Mable Thompson Griffin.

William Griffin, OCHS Class of 1963   Mable Thompson Griffin (1920-2009)

Editing and book design by Michelle Harris Anderson and Angela Harris Moore

Michelle Harris Anderson   Angela Harris Moore

The Westside community is indebted to William "Billy" Mitchell, an Ocean City High School graduate who relocated to Philadelphia but made timely trips to the shore to visit relatives and friends and photograph Westside clients. While most photographs of the Westside and its residents have faded, disintegrated, or been destroyed by floods and fires, some of Mitchell's professional work survives. In this book, it is attributed to him whenever identifiable.

A special posthumous thank you to Dr. Ray Giron, a historian, antique dealer, Civil War expert, actor, and costumer for the movie "Glory" who helped unlock secrets of Springtown, the Greenwich Township, Cumberland County community where runaway slaves landed and sought refuge with sympathetic Native Americans and Quakers after crossing the Delaware River.

Many thanks to the researchers, historians, archaeologists, and archivists who helped in this pursuit of truth. A debt of gratitude is owed to national, state, and local archives and to repositories for meticulously maintaining the old records that have proven to be invaluable. Included are:

Civic and Community Organizations
- The African American Heritage Museum of Southern New Jersey
- Ocean City Historical Museum
- The Church of Jesus Christ of Latter-day Saints
- Ocean City Free Public Library

Historical Societies
- Atlantic County Historical Society
- Cape May County Historical and Genealogical Society
- Cumberland County Historical Society
- The Historical Preservation Society of Upper Township
- Margate Historical Society
- Millville Historical Society
- Salem County Historical Society
- Somers Point Historical Society

My thanks are also extended to several people whose contributions to the research and oral histories helped enrich the content of this book.

- R. Barry Banks
- Barbara Potts Bonaparte
- Butler Brothers (Robert, Whitney, and Donovan)
- Janet Motley Cline
- Nathan and Emma Davis
- Samuel Ellis Ford, III
- Tyree Harmon Lawson Eason
- Theodore Ford
- Marion E. Harmon
- Sonia Henry
- Irene and Joanne Rolls
- Vivian M. Strawberry
- George Walker Williams family

INTRODUCTION

Everybody has a story. *The Westside - Ocean City in True Color* unveiled the early history of the Westside community and introduced the people of color who braved the unknown with a sense of excitement and determination, toiling long hours in hopes of laying the foundation for a better life for later generations. The final chapter is devoted to histories of Westside churches and their religious leaders, the early spiritual and moral guidance for the visionaries who stepped out on faith when they ventured off to Ocean City.

Ocean City's Westside – Breaking Barriers, Building Bridges brings to light the daily life of new arrivals as they managed to eke out a living and slowly improve their lot, making their neighborhood a more promising place for those who followed. No book about Ocean City's people of color would be complete without a truthful look at racism and its effect on the community. Discrimination and segregation were a part of daily life and came in many forms and to many degrees. This book takes a brave step forward as it talks about the issue.

While a conscious effort has been made to confine the impact of race to one chapter to avoid shrouding the entire experience of people of color in racism, it must be noted that racism had a profound effect on the community, whether at home, at work, at the beach, or in the military. Westside residents shouldered the extra load occasioned by racism in the daily struggles as they broke down barriers and built bridges.

On the lighter side, the always available beach and bay provided respite from the day-to-day toils of life. From day laborers to business owners, from tenants to homeowners, this book unearths the many human and material treasures found beyond the veil of the Westside.

"A race, like an individual, lifts itself up by lifting others up."
Booker T. Washington

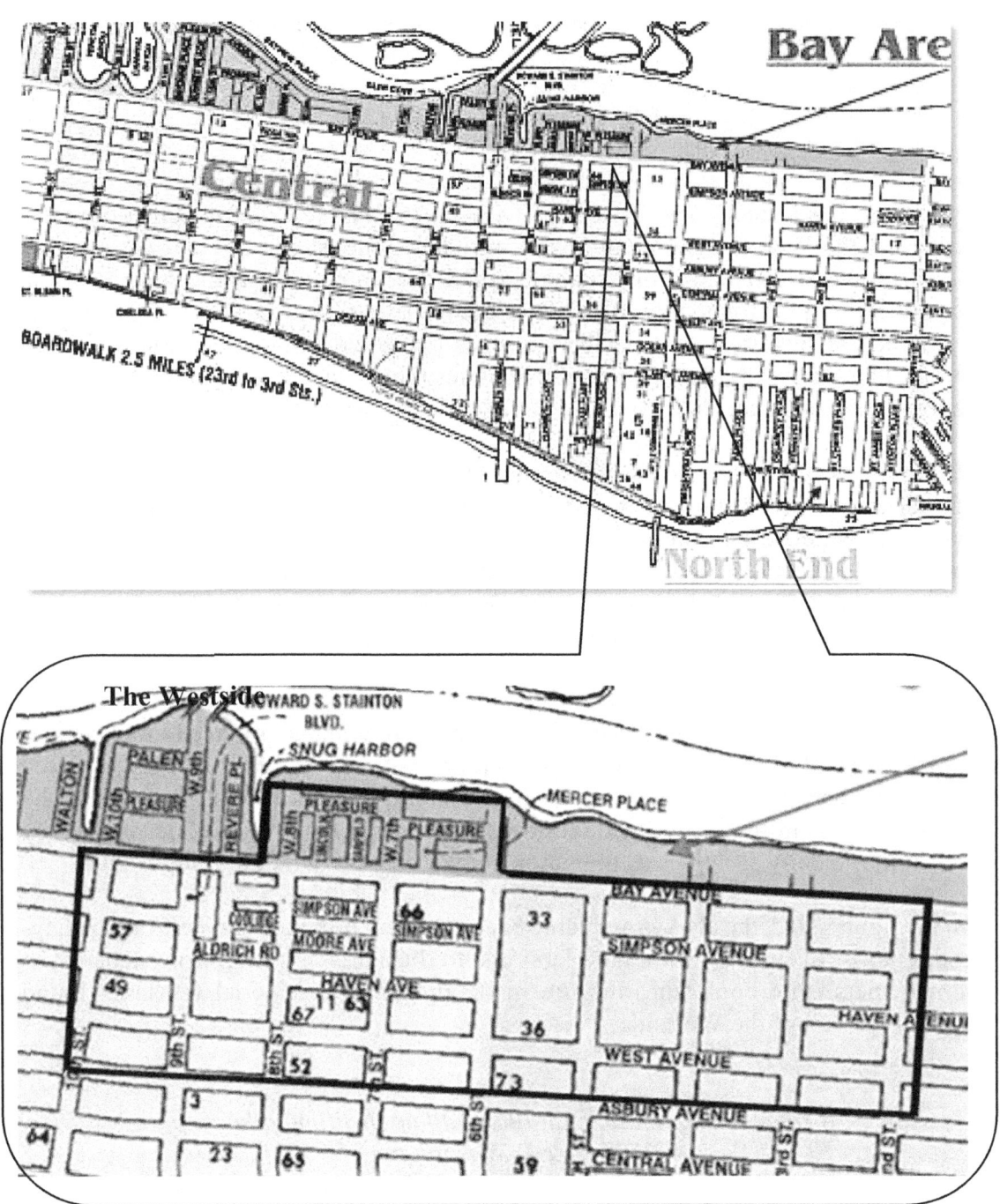

The term "Westside" is a label sometimes used to define the African American neighborhood in Ocean City, loosely bounded by 2nd Street on the North, 10th Street on the South, Asbury Avenue on the East, and Bay Avenue on the West. Occasionally, people of color did live outside this defined area, but that was quite the exception rather than the rule. In time, the easterly boundary pulled back to West Avenue ceding Asbury Avenue to the city's downtown business area. As the community grew it expanded north into the 100 block.

Ocean City Population Schedule
Historical Demographics

Year	Total	Black	% Black
1885	465	3	0.6
1895	879	25	2.8
1900	1,307	41	3.1
1905	1,835	99	5.4
1910	1,950	129	6.6
1915	3,736	366	9.8
1920	2,312	167	7.2
1930	5,525	454	8.2
1940	4,672	236	5.1
1950	6,040	543	9.0
1960	7,618	666	8.7
1970	10,575	815	7.7
1980	13,949	767	5.5
1990	15,512	764	4.9
2000	15,378	663	4.3
2010	11,701	410	3.5
2020	11,065	288	2.6

Compiled by Loretta Thompson Harris 6/1/2020 rev. 10/22/2022[1,2,3,4,5,6,7,8]

Ocean City's resident Black population peaked in 1970. A steady decline ensued as Blacks forsook the town in search of better opportunities eventually leaving the city with less than 300 year-round Black residents in 2020. Ocean City's summertime population traditionally increases tenfold with the influx of tourists, vacationers, and summer help.

***

Flanders Hotel doormen. Photo courtesy Ocean City Historical Museum.

CHAPTER 1
BRINGING HOME THE BACON

Life on the Westside promised new opportunities and unforeseen challenges in uncharted waters as Ocean City developed from a weekend resort into a year-round community. By 1895, several African American and Native American families resided in Ocean City. Finding life sustaining employment and housing were the first challenges confronting new arrivals. Men and women played a vital role in the growth of the town. West Avenue developed as the commercial center for the Westside. Numerous tradesmen, restaurants, corner stores, barber shops, and a variety of other businesses provided goods and services for the growing community.

Service Sector Employment

Much of the service sector employment in the resort town came and went with the seasons. Workers came from north and south to meet the demand as the influx of snowbirds returning home, vacationers, and day trippers exploded the summer population tenfold. Many seasonal workers returned to the same job each summer. Most looked for jobs that allowed them to work enough weeks to earn unemployment benefits in the off season. Ocean City's tourist industry virtually depended on the Westside's people of color for back-of-the-house operations. Chefs, cooks, dishwashers, chambermaids, bellhops, and a few elevator operators formed the backbone of the service sector.

Women also worked as cooks in hotel and guest house kitchens and as waitresses in Westside restaurants. Some stay-at-home women took in laundry, ironing, and cleaning the silverware of wealthier families to augment the family income. Many found work in the commercial laundries that serviced resort hotels. Others were stay-at-home mothers responsible for rearing the children and making the house a home.

A handful of men like resident Willard Drain(e) worked year-round as private butlers to wealthy residents such as portrait artist Elizabeth Rockwell. Women considered domestics were housekeepers for affluent Whites. Ethel Morris Rolls worked as a domestic at the Wesley Avenue home of John and Margaret Kelly, parents of movie star-to-be Grace Kelly.

Ethel Morris Rolls (1898-1986) holding
son Harry. Photo c. early 1930s.
Photo courtesy Joanne Rolls

Kelly home, 26th & Wesley Ave.
Photo credit Associated Press

"My grandmother first worked for the Kelly family here in Ocean City. They loved her and trusted her, so they offered her a permanent job at their home in the East Falls section of Philadelphia. I was a preschooler in the early '50s when my older siblings, Irene and Harry "Buster", and I went to live with our grandparents in Philadelphia. We spent summers back in Ocean City.

I remember Grandmother wearing a grey and white uniform to work. She usually took public transportation, but every now and then the Kellys sent a car for her. The chauffeur's name was Ford. The Kellys also had a chef, gardener, tennis courts, and swimming pool. Many famous people visited Grace Kelly in East Falls after she became a star. Bing Crosby, Alfred Hitchcock, Cary Grant, and Elizabeth Taylor were regular visitors to the home. Our grandmother was protective of the family's privacy and selective about what she shared with us.

Mrs. Kelly sent dresses Grace no longer wanted home to me. Grace asked my grandmother to go work for her in Monaco. Grandmother declined but did work in center city for Grace's brother, John B. Kelly, Jr. "Kell."

My grandfather, Harry A. Rolls, a World War I veteran, died in 1964. The Kelly family paid off the mortgage on the house. When I graduated from high school, the Kellys wanted to send me to Jefferson University to become a doctor, but I was focused on getting back to a certain young man in Ocean City. Our grandmother was in her eighties when she suffered a stroke. We closed down the Philadelphia house and brought her home to Ocean City where she passed the following year."

Joanne Rolls interview. October 19, 2023

Halcyon Hall kitchen crew.

L-R third row: Marion Johnson Thompson and Dorothy Gordon Thompson worked as cooks at the Halcyon prior to marrying brothers Alvin and Sylvester Thompson.

Photo c. early 1930s.

"Excellent Food in a Pleasant Atmosphere"

Halcyon Hall

DONALD B. KELLY, Prop.

Breakfast • **DINING ROOM** ⸢ Dinner

1116 Wesley Ave.   Member of Ocean City Hotel Association   Phone 1365

Polk's Ocean City Directory, 1948

HALCYON HALL HOTEL (Donald B Kelly), "Noted For Its Excellent Food," Centrally Located Near Boardwalk, 1116 Wesley av, Tel 1365, Member Ocean City Hotel Assn (See page 21 Buyers' Guide and right top lines)

Polk's Ocean City Directory, 1948

In the 1940s, Mississippi native Homer Jones left his job at Hogate's Restaurant to work as head chef at Mac's Restaurant, the restaurant with the lobster on the roof known for its seafood and steaks. Each year, the owners of Mac's hired Homer to cook on their annual hunting trip.

Homer Jones (1902-1975), holding granddaughter Dena Preston. Photo c. early 1970s. Photo courtesy Aline Bennett Milligan

Mac's Restaurant, Somers Point. Photo c. 1940s.

Mac's Restaurant Advertisement
Ocean City Sentinel Ledger, June 26, 1930

Homer Jones as cook on the annual hunting trips of the One Buck Gunning Club.
Photo courtesy Aline Bennett Milligan

Hogate's Sea Food Restaurant next to the 9th Street bridge.

Hogate's Restaurant kitchen staff. Unidentified Hogate's chef.
Photo courtesy Ocean City Historical Museum

Curtis McMillan

Curtis McMillan (1904-1960) born in Citrus County, Florida was a cook at Watson's during summers from the 1940s into the 1960s, returning to Lakeland, Florida each year where he worked on the Tampa Bridge and picked oranges and grapefruit.

"Watson's Restaurant and Take-Out, established in 1934, was perhaps the best known of Ocean City's family restaurants. Every year, from June to September, crowds would wait in line just to get a table. The hot, humid weather never dissuaded them. Many believed that Watson's had the best apple pies and scallop dishes in town. It was razed in 1987 to make way for Watson's Resorts."[9]

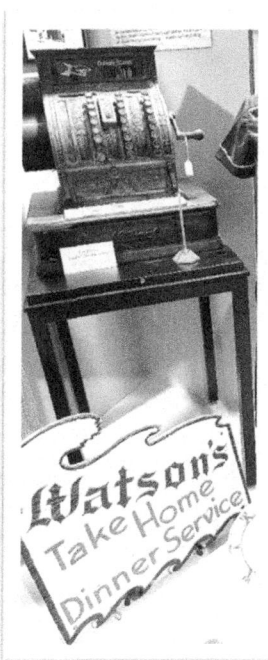

Chris' Seafood Restaurant kitchen staff. c. 1950s
Ocean City, New Jersey. Frank J. Esposito, Robert J. Esposito. Arcadia Pub. 1996

Chris' Seafood Restaurant[10]

Ocean City offered an appealing place to work for those wanting a change from the big city and for students on summer break. John Pye and a long list of extended family members worked in Ocean City each summer as hotel and restaurant cooks, kitchen help, domestics, and chambermaids.

Grace Harris Butler
Philadelphia High School for Girls[11]
Photo credit Donovan Butler, grandson of
Robert Harris

Wife Fannie Pye worked at Hotel Comfort, The Parkside, and had private duty clients in the Gardens. Her daughter Helen worked at The Johnson, Hotel Comfort, the Wesley, Scarborough, and had Gardens clients.

Granddaughter Grace, the apple of Sammy Davis, Jr.'s eye, waitressed at Club Harlem in Atlantic City several summers in the 1940s serving Elvira Sanchez, Jackie Robinson, Billy Eckstine, Count Basie, and Lena Horne. The family found work for her at the less menacing Fleetwood Hotel in Ocean City. She met her future husband at a bus stop in Ocean City.

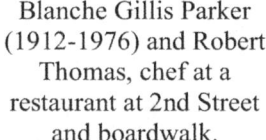

Blanche Gillis Parker (1912-1976) and Robert Thomas, chef at a restaurant at 2nd Street and boardwalk.

Public Sector Employment

Public sector employment opened slowly for people of color with military veterans earning preferential treatment in hiring for public sector jobs. Jobs with the Ocean City Police Department, Fire Department, and Beach Patrol were coveted jobs as were positions with City Administration.

City of Ocean City

Many male Westside residents found employment in the Department of Public Works. Historically, men of color were hired into the Public Works Department and later transferred to other positions as a need arose, i.e., Ocean City Police Department.

> *"Joe Tedesco and I were the only two Whites in Public Works*
> *when I came along. I took the job to earn money for school."*
> *Harry Brown, OCHS Class of 1963*

Ocean City Police Department

Downtown business district, 8th Street and Asbury Avenue, one block outside Westside. Policemen with umbrellas controlled the traffic flow in the busy commercial area. Traffic lights came to Ocean City later in the 1920s. Model T Fords were popular.[12]

Ocean City Police Officers	Service Years	Ocean City Police Officers	Service Years
Clarence S. Turner	1912-1916	Bernard "Mickey" "Sarge" Morris	1959-1989
Joseph Armour Thompson	1919-1924	John Edward Morris	
Abraham Beverly Collins	1928-1941	Robert Conway Bates	c. 1963
William Ivory Spruill	1938	John Phillip Peterson	
Timothy Allen Harris	1940	Daniel L. Money	
Clarence S. Reynolds	c. 1944	William Warren	1966-1978
Aaron Edward Harvey, Jr.	1948	Benjamin Bethea	
Carl Leroy Henry	1952	Fred Alford	1987-2012
Andrew Edward Barton	1953	Tyrone Rolls	1996-2021
Charles Lewis Spence	c. 1954		

Ocean City Police Department. Top row far left William Spruill. Top row far right, Timothy Harris. Second row down far right, Aaron Edward Harvey, Jr. c. 1948.[13]

Ocean City Police Department. Top row Center: Tim Harris. Second row down: Aaron Harvey. Third row down far right: Bill Spruill. c. 1952.[14]

NO IMAGE
AVAILABLE

Clarence S. Turner (1860-1923)
Ocean City's first Black police officer

Born in Miller's Tavern, Essex County, Virginia in 1860, Clarence Turner lived in the City of Salem prior to moving to Ocean City in 1902 to take a job as a driver for Asbury Avenue milk merchant John. P. Fox. The City of Ocean City hired Turner as a laborer the following year.

In 1912, fifty-two-year-old Clarence broke the color line in the Ocean City Police Department when the city reassigned him to the Police Department as summer help on the Westside, a position he held each summer from 1912 until 1916. Thereafter, he worked for the city as a laborer in the Streets Department until his death in 1923.

Bertha Turner, daughter of Clarence Turner

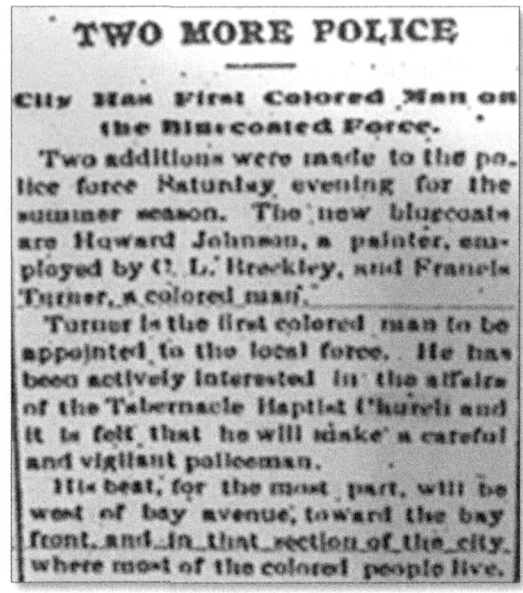

TWO MORE POLICE
City Has First Colored Man on the Blue-coated Force.

Two additions were made to the police force Saturday evening for the summer season. The new bluecoats are Howard Johnson, a painter, employed by C. L. Brackley, and Francis Turner, a colored man.

Turner is the first colored man to be appointed to the local force. He has been actively interested in the affairs of the Tabernacle Baptist Church and it is felt that he will make a careful and vigilant policeman.

His beat, for the most part, will be west of bay avenue, toward the bay front, and in that section of the city where most of the colored people live.

Ocean City Sentinel Ledger, June 6, 1912

Joseph Armour Thompson (1876-1974)
Second Black on Ocean City Police Department
Photo courtesy William Griffin, grandson of
Joseph Armour Thompson

Joseph Thompson was born in Millville, Cumberland County, New Jersey. There he met and married Delaware native, Henrietta Bowman. Joseph worked as a team driver. Henrietta gave birth to two of their six children in Millville. For a brief period in 1905, Joseph joined his parents in Ocean City but returned to Millville. In 1911, he relocated his family to Ocean City permanently and worked as a "laborer" before taking a job as a driver with milk merchant J. P. Fox. The City of Ocean City hired Joseph as a policeman in 1919, a position he held for five years. Thereafter, he was transferred to the Public Works Department.

NO IMAGE
AVAILABLE

Abraham Beverly Collins (1885-1970)

William Ivory Spruill (c. 1905-1979)
Photo courtesy Ocean City Historical Museum

Virginia-born Abe Collins came to Ocean City from New York City where he worked as a pullman car porter. He joined the Ocean City Police Department and quickly became an influential man on the Westside.

"Bill" lived on Widows' Row upon arrival in town from Fishing Creek, North Carolina and worked as a "laborer." The Ocean City Police Department soon hired him into the department as a caretaker. From that position, he advanced to regular policeman. Though he and wife Mary Elizabeth had no children, Bill enjoyed the respected handle "Uncle Bill" from children on the Westside. Sgt. William "Bill" Spruill was inducted into the Exchange Club of Ocean City's Book of Good Deeds in 1968.

Andrew Edward Barton

Barton, a World War II veteran, qualified for police department employment under civil service regulations but was suspended indefinitely for reporting to work late several days and twice calling out sick during his ninety-day probation. Upon return to duty after being out with a knee injury, Acting Chief Smith terminated Barton.

25

Timothy Allen Harris (1895-1959). Photo c. 1948 courtesy Ocean City Historical Museum.

Timothy Allen Harris was from the Pine Top area of Middlesex County, Virginia near the Rappahannock River and Chesapeake Bay area where his father worked as an oysterman before converting to farming. Tim, number eleven or twelve of thirteen children, worked as a farmer in Pine Top. He came to Ocean City around 1930 and found work as a hotel cook. Census records list him as a single man and World War I veteran though a 1905 birth date would make him too young to serve.

By 1940, Tim married and joined the Ocean City Police Department. "Big Tim" as he was known around town or "Uncle Tim" as he was known to neighborhood children, is remembered by local school children as the friendly school crossing officer near Central Avenue Elementary School. After living on West Avenue and 7th Street, Tim and wife Dorothy settled into a home on Pleasure Avenue on the westerly border of the Westside. The couple had no known children.

Clarence Reynolds, better known as "Clanky", was a young child when he and his mother came to Ocean City in 1920. He became an accomplished auto mechanic who worked for William Powell at 12th and Asbury Avenue prior to entering the military during World War II.

NO IMAGE AVAILABLE

Clarence S. Reynolds (1914-1980)

Aaron Edward Harvey, Jr. (1925-1996)

Aaron Harvey grew up in Ocean City. His family has the distinction of living on Mercer Place and Widows' Row, the largest rowhouses on the Westside. After serving two years in the military during World War II, he married his high school sweetheart, Sarah Frances Oliver. Best friends and high school sweethearts Dewitt Harmon and Gloria Henry witnessed the marriage. Aaron joined the police force shortly after marriage.

26

Bernard "Sarge" Morris (1929-2010)
OCHS Class of 1947

Carl Leroy Henry, (1928-2014)
OCHS Class of 1945

Morris served in the New Jersey Army National Guard and the U.S. Army. Neighborhood children loved climbing the landmark willow tree in the front yard of Sarge's West Avenue home.

Ocean City native Carl Henry was the second of fourteen children born to Daniel and Vivian Thompson Henry. Family knew him as "Mikey." He served in the Navy during World War II and then joined the New Jersey Army National Guard. After a brief stint with the Ocean City Police Department, he settled in with South Jersey Gas Company.

John "Big John" Edward Morris (1931-1994)
OCHS Class of 1949. Photo courtesy Ocean City Historical Museum.

Robert Conway Bates (1933-2012)

Charles Lewis Spence (1921-1987)
Pleasantville High School Yearbook

$1,100 Blaze In Restaurant

Building Gutted Early Tuesday

Page 2, please

Fire early Tuesday morning swept through the A. and E. Restaurant, 735 West av., gutting the interior and causing an estimated $1,100 damage to the building and contents.

Deputy Fire Chief William Meenan said the fire was believed to have started from a short circuit, either in a television set or in the wiring connecting it.

J. Edward Williams, proprietor, told police that he and a number of friends were in the establishment Monday night watching the boxing matches on the television set. He said he closed the place around 11 p. m.

Patrolman Charles Spence discovered the fire at 12:50 a. m. while on his tour of duty in the neighborhood. He turned in a box alarm, which fire officials said failed to sound in the city's fire houses.

At about the same time, however, a telephone alarm was received, and apparatus and men responded. When they arrived, firemen found a front plate glass window blown out by the heat, and the flames licking out from beneath the eaves of the roof.

Firemen fought the blaze for almost an hour, and prevented them from reaching nearby frame houses. No one was injured.

The property is owned by William Brinkman, of 604 3rd st., firemen reported.

Ocean City Sentinel Ledger

John Phillip "Pete" Peterson.
OCHS Class of 1957.
600 block of Haven Avenue holding
Michael Thompson.

Benjamin G.
Bethea
OCNJ Daily.
June 9, 2019[15]

William
Warren
OCHS
Class of
1963

On June 7th, the Cape May County Police Academy's 46th Basic Course for Police Officers graduated. Included in the group were three new officers: Class President Officer Benjamin Bethea, Officer Randall Clark, and Officer Jonathan Simonson.

Ocean City native Bill Warren worked for the local Police Department for twelve years before taking an assignment with the Cape May County Narcotics Strike Force. His earliest years were spent on Doctors' Row where his father worked as houseman for Dr. Allen Corson before moving the family to the Westside and opening a restaurant.

Frederick L. Alford (1962-2017),
OCHS Class of 1980

Frederick "Fred" Alford was born in Newnan, Georgia. After graduating from Ocean City High School, Fred joined the Ocean City Police Department where he worked for 25 years, reaching the rank of Sergeant. Fred retired from the Police Department in 2012. He resided in Ocean City until 2005 when he moved to Egg Harbor Township. He was a member of Ocean City PBA Local #61 and enjoyed fishing and motorcycles.

Tyrone Rolls, OCHS Class of 1990.
Photo courtesy Rolls family.

Tyrone Rolls grew up in Ocean City and graduated from Ocean City High School and attended Montclair State University where he excelled in football and track.

Ocean City Fire Department

Bureau of Fire, Ocean City, N.J.[16]

Photo courtesy Ocean City Historical Museum

Oscar James Harmon (1922-2005)
Ocean City's first fireman of color.
See Military chapter for Harmon's life story.

Wallace Gilchrist

Louis Dennis Davis (1938-2020)
OCHS Class of 1956
Ocean City's first Black Fire Captain

Davis demonstrating climbing techniques.
Davis family photos courtesy Nathan Davis, Jr.

Louis Davis was an Ocean City native who attended local schools. He served in the Army for two years after graduating from Ocean City High School. In 1965, the City of Ocean City hired Louis as a fireman, the second person of color known to become a fireman in the city following Oscar Harmon, Jr. who served briefly following World War II. Louis made a career of the Fire Department advancing to Captain in 1991 before retiring in 2003.

Special Mention...
Ocean City Man's Dream Comes True

Eric Jones (1973-2022). OCHS Class of 1991.
Somers Point firefighter.
Photo courtesy Rolls family.

Soft spoken and shy Eric Jones arrived at headquarters for Somers Point Fire Department Company 1 asking how he could become a volunteer firefighter. He offered that he only had one leg. Eric lost a leg to cancer at age twelve or thirteen but never allowed the loss to hold him down. Eric graduated from Ocean City High School where he competed on the wrestling team and rowing team. After graduation from West Virginia State University, Eric worked at engineering firms in Atlantic and Cape May Counties before pursuing his real dream – to be a firefighter. The Somers Point Fire Department hired Eric Jones as a regular fireman. Eric spent twenty-eight years fulfilling his lifelong ambition.[17]

Somers Point firefighters pay "last call" tribute to one of their own.[18]

United States Postal Service

In the late 1940s, the United States Postal Service hired World War II veterans Rayfield Lyles and Richard Grimes as mail carriers in the Ocean City Post Office. Lyles preceded Grimes at the post office and worked at least two years but never completed hiring requirements, making Grimes the first regular, full time Black mail carrier.

In 1950, James Aaron Richardson, a next-door neighbor of Richard Grimes, worked as a mail collector[19]. Grimes hired Nathan Davis as a postal employee for summer work following Davis's graduation in 1955.[20]

United States Postal Service employees. Ocean City, New Jersey.
Nathan Davis and Richard Grimes.[21]

Rayfield Charles Lyles
(1917-1990). First U.S. Post
Office employee in Ocean City

Nathan Davis
OCHS Class of 1955

James Aaron Richardson
(1930-2011)

Richard Grimes (1918-2014)
First full-time, regular
U.S. Post Office employee in
Ocean City

Richard Grimes,
Vice President Ocean City Chapter 1468 NARFE

Private Sector Employment

Men of color who arrived in the sprouting town early in its formation found employment as non-specific "day laborers" performing a variety of odd jobs in exchange for low wages and long hours.[22] Growth of the Westside community attracted contractors, carpenters, blacksmiths, masons, and railroad workers. These day laborers formed the backbone of the construction industry. Construction workers from nearby towns travelled to Ocean City to augment the resident labor force and help build the blossoming town.

In 1900, R. Curtis Robinson, owner and editor of the Sentinel Ledger and Daily Reporter as well as being the local Postmaster, commissioned the construction of a brick building at 744 Asbury Avenue to replace the frame building housing his print shop and the town post office. It would be the second brick building in the city. A handwritten history of the building lists four 'Colored laborers in the Bricklayers' work crew: Isaac M. (Mulford) Harmon (1865-1922) of Millville and Ocean City residents Warren Smith, Simon Frie, and John Brown (1834-1905). Only Harmon and Brown were people of color.[23]

- Isaac Mulford Harmon (1865-1922), a Native American resident of Millville
- Warren Smith (1872-1938), stepson of Simon Frie living on Westside
- Simon H. Frie (1863-Unk.), a German living on the Westside
- John Brown (1934-1905), an African American Ocean City resident.

The building later housed Talese Tailor Shop followed by Talese's Town and Country Shop and still later by Pappagallo's, a women's specialty boutique.

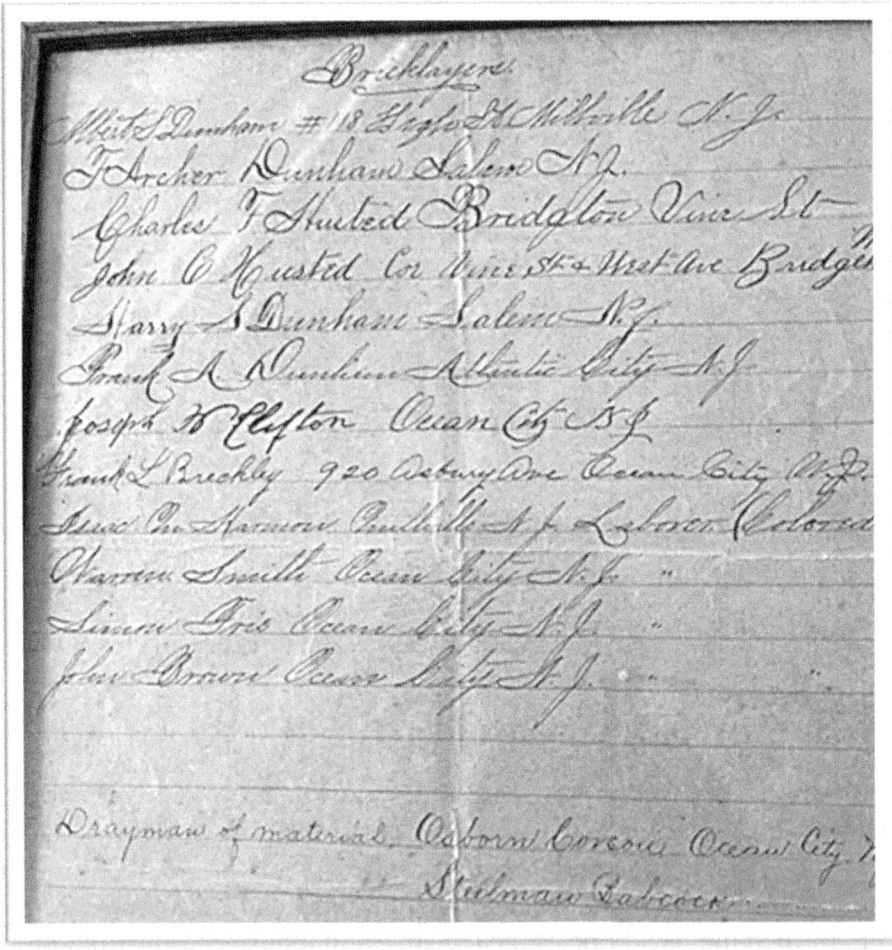

A Concise History of Building 744 Asbury Avenue. Reverse side of original handwritten document in glass frame showing Bricklayers. Photo courtesy Marian Talese, daughter of Guiseppi "Joseph" Talese, owner of Talese's Tailor Shop, 744 Asbury Avenue, August 1, 2023.

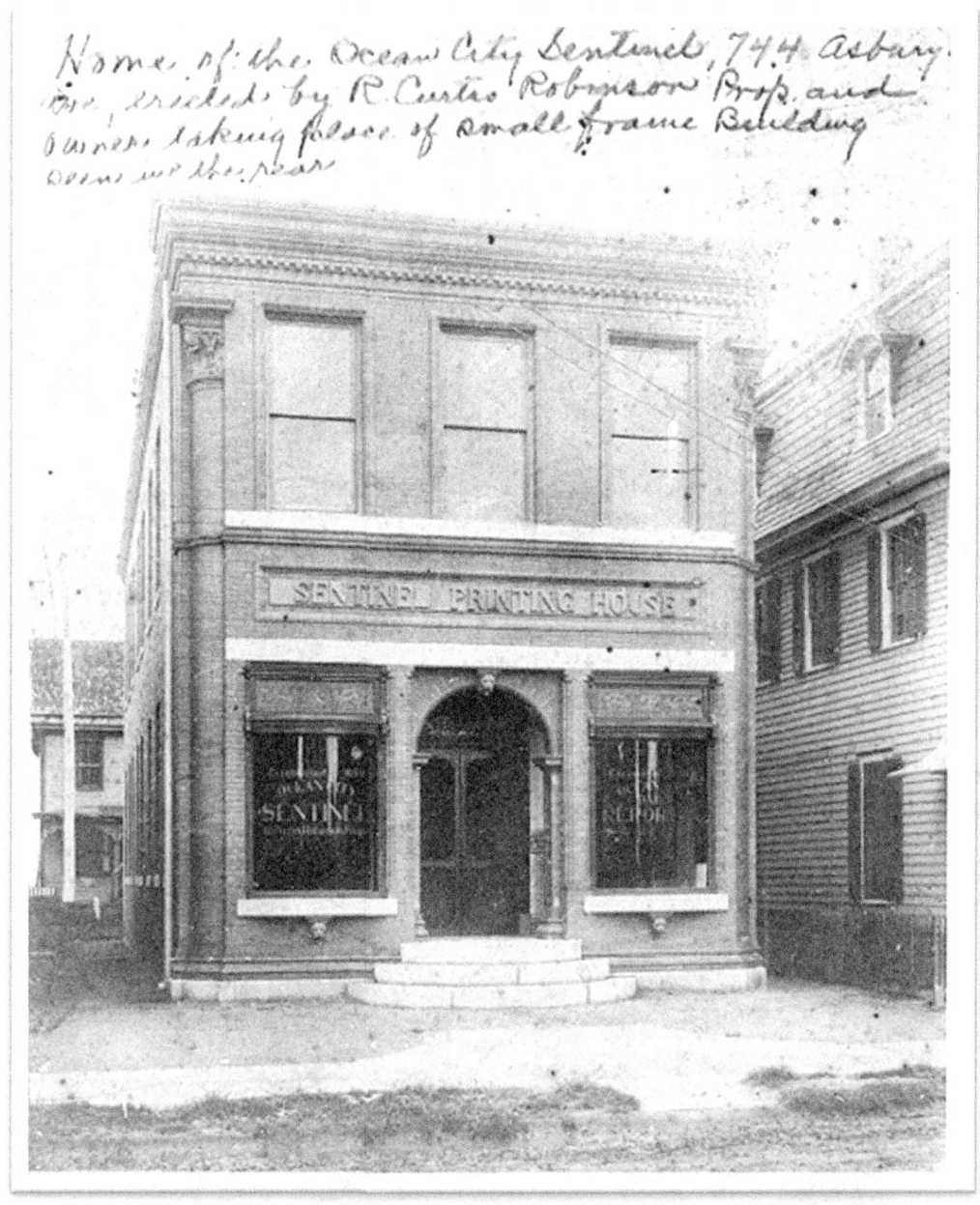

Home of the Ocean City Sentinel, 744 Asbury Ave, erected by R. Curtis Robinson Prop. and Owners taking place of small frame Building seen in the rear

Sentinel Ledger Building c. 1900. Courtesy Ocean City Historical Museum. Talese Collection.

McKendree "Mr. Mack" Casson (1882-1962). Photo c. 1953.

Mr. Mack came to Ocean City from Dover, Delaware around 1910. He worked for the City as a laborer, as a hod carrier (laborer who carried supplies for masons, bricklayers, cement finishers and plasterers), and as a boilerman at Seashore Laundry before going to work for Sylvester W. Thompson, Sr. in the construction business. Mr. Mack stoked the coal fired boilers at Seashore Laundry shoveling soft or hard coal into fiery pits. Stockpiles of coal could be found near commercial establishments. Wessel's Seashore Laundry and Seashore Laundry employed large numbers of Italian Americans who lived on the Westside.

Train 5710 leaving 4th Street station headed south along Haven Avenue.
Photo courtesy Samuel Ellis Ford, III

Wessel's Seashore Laundry, southeast corner 6th Street and Haven Avenue.
Now the site of Shore Siding.

Seashore Laundry Ad

PATRONIZE YOUR HOME
LAUNDRY
USE THE
FRETZ SYSTEM
Sixth Street and Haven Avenue

DAMP WASH   DAILY SERVICE

SPECIALISTS IN HAND IRONING

Rough Dry, 10c lb.   Telephone 117   All Flat Work

Fretz Laundry ad.
Ocean City Sentinel Ledger, 1925

Fretz Surf Laundry, southwest corner 6th Street and Haven Avenue. The manager's house is now a residential rental unit. The remainder of the property, originally a large laundering operation, is now all storage units. Bel-Ford Printing Company, Inc. briefly operated from a portion of this property following the shutdown of the laundry. Photo c. 2022.

Surf Laundry and buildings on 6th Street opposite ball field (now Richard S. Grimes Field)
in background during surf casting contest. L-R: Surf Laundry; roofs of
Irving Carter, J. Richardson, Richard Grimes, Melvin Stevens, Washington Hotel.
Photo c. 1947. Photo courtesy Ocean Historical Museum, Weekly Guide, August 1974

OCEAN CITY LAUNDRY CO., INC.

Rough Dry 10c a Pound. Damp Wash $1.50 a Bag

Including All Flat Work Ironed

HAVEN AVE. and 6th ST.   PHONE 117

Ocean City Laundry Co., Inc. (Fretz).[24]

Announcement

N. E. FRETZ *and* SONS

Ownership Management of

TROY LAUNDRY
295 Congress St.
Ph. 4-3993 — Cape May, N. J.

SURF LAUNDRY
112 6th St.
Ph. 0117 — Ocean City, N. J.

NEW WINTER SERVICE

CLOTHES PICKED UP ON MONDAY & TUESDAY
WILL BE DELIVERED FRIDAY & SATURDAY

- Sheets 12c
- Pillow Cases ... 6c
- Bolster Cases .. 7c
- Dimity Spreads. 15c
- Extra Heavy Spreads 58c

- Hand Towels .. 3c
- Bath Towels ... 6c
- Scarfs 10c
- Shirts 25c
- Table Cloths ... 15c

All Kinds of Family and Hotel Laundry

Satisfaction Guaranteed

We Return Your Clothes Snow-White, Fluff Dried and Sweet Smelling

"OUR LAUNDRIES KEEP CAPE MAY COUNTY CLEAN"

N. E. Fretz and Sons ad[25]

Utilities Employees

Relatively few people of color secured positions with area utilities.

FIFTEEN NEW EMPLOYEES ATTEND ORIENTATION

Another group of new employees attended the day-long orientation session on March 5th in Atlantic City. The new employees and two of the instructors are: left to right, first row — Loretta Thompson, Marylin Heim, Henrietta Fricke, Rita Fullmer, Alice Newkirk, Emma Davis, and Ellen Mawhinney. Second row — John Eaton, Michael Murphy, Joseph Schoenleber, Jr., Frank Mooney, Jr., and Linc Rau, Personnel Director. Back row — Joseph Bell, Henry Braun, William Worsley, Carl Glasser, Jr., and Ken Shales, Director of Training Services.

Atlantic City Electric Company employee orientation, October 1963.

Atlantic City Electric Company

Emma Debnam Davis	Ocean City Business Office
Russell "Genie" Davis	
James Reynolds Gayle	Atlantic City Business Office
Monte Carlton Harmon	Pleasantville Operations
Arthur Gilbert Hopson, III	Cologne Stores
Leroy Robertson	Atlantic City Operations
Alva Thompson	Ocean City Business Office
Loretta Thompson Harris	Atlantic City Operations

New Jersey Bell Telephone Company

Samuel Ellis Ford, III	Marmora Operations
Virginia Gayle	
Wanda Bernedette Money	
Alva Thompson	Marmora Operations

Jersey Central Power & Light

William Lemuel Brown	9th St. & Central Ave., Ocean City

New Jersey American Water

Joan Motley Peterson	Ocean City Business Office

Ocean City Sewer Service Company

Irving Emerson Carter

Ocean City Water Service

Charles A. Quann	Ocean City Office

South Jersey Gas Company

Daniel Carl Henry
Carl Leroy Henry

Emma Debnam Davis, Clerk,
Atlantic City Electric Company,
Ocean City Business Office

Originally from North Carolina, Emma worked at the Ocean City Business Office before becoming a teacher in the Egg Harbor Township school district.

Russell "Genie" Davis
OCHS Class of 1970
Meterman, Atlantic City Electric
Company (Glassboro, Winslow,
Pleasantville and Mays Landing)

James Reynolds Gayle,
OCHS Class of 1970
Customer Service Representative,
Atlantic City Electric Company

Arthur Gilbert Hopson, III
(1940-2013)
Storekeeper A, Atlantic City Electric
Company (Cologne)

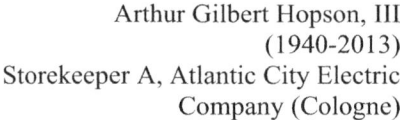

Monte Carlton Harmon,
OCHS Class of 1970
Lineman, Atlantic City Electric
Company (Pleasantville Operations)

Leroy Robertson (1934-2020)
Mechanic, Atlantic City
Electric Company (Atlantic City
Transportation Department)

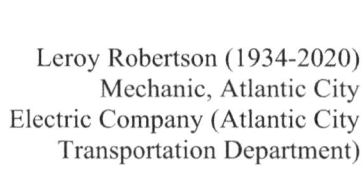

Alva Peggy Thompson,
OCHS Class of 1970,
Cashier and Clerk, Atlantic City
Electric Company (Ocean City
Business Office) & Repair
Service Clerk, Engineering
Department, New Jersey Bell
Telephone Company

Alva's tenure with Atlantic City Electric Company began with an internship at the Ocean City Business Office during her senior year of high school. Each day consisted of one-half day of classroom instruction and one-half day at work at the company's office at 8th Street and Asbury Avenue.

After working at Atlantic City Electric Company several years, Alva accepted a better offer as a Repair Service Clerk with New Jersey Bell Telephone (Ma Bell). During her fifteen years with Ma Bell, she also worked in the Real Estate section of the Engineering Department. In tests for the position, Alva registered the highest retention of numbers rate in the State of New Jersey, a skill set later exhibited by her nephew, Tyrone Thompson, who could retain and calculate numbers with accuracy.

Loretta Thompson Harris, OCHS Class of 1963
Director of Real Estate, Manager Atlantic City External Affairs,
Atlantic City Electric Company

Loretta began her career with Atlantic City Electric as a stenographer in the Personnel Department at Atlantic City Operations. She worked in several capacities during her two tenures with the company while attending evening school and professional institutes. During her combined thirty-two years of service, Loretta advanced through the ranks becoming the only woman and only person of color to head the company's Real Estate Department where she managed multi-million-dollar budgets with responsibility for all real estate activities in the southern third of the state of New Jersey.

The Board of Directors selected Loretta and six others for an unbridled "Save The Company" mission to protect the company against cogeneration competitors. With experience in business and operations, Loretta became the only woman and only person of color to head the company's Atlantic City Office in its 132 years in existence.

UNDERCOVER OPERATION — Bell Telephone repairman Sam Ford shields himself against one of the particular occupational hazards of summer as he splices wires on Route 9 in Mayville, Cape May County, on a ... Staff photo by Tom Kinnemand

Samuel Ellis Ford, III
OCHS Class of 1968
Troubleman, Marmora Operations,
New Jersey Bell Telephone Company

Samuel's career as a Troubleman with the telephone company spanned 42 years. He is shown above splicing cable in the heat of summer shaded by only an umbrella.

Wanda Bernedette Money,
OCHS Class of 1972[26]
New Jersey Bell Telephone Company

William Lemuel Brown (1898-1962)
Plant Operator, Jersey Central Power and Light Company

NO IMAGE
AVAILABLE

World War I veteran William Lemuel Brown was twenty-one when he arrived in Ocean City in 1920 and used his experience at E. I. duPont in Midlothian, Chesterfield County, Virginia to gain employment as a gas company fireman. Work took him to Essex County, New York as a gas maker and back to Ocean City as a gas company civil engineer before becoming plant operator for Jersey Central Power & Light at 9th Street and Central Avenue.

Joan Motley Peterson (1941-2015)
OCHS Class of 1959
Customer Service Supervisor,
New Jersey American Water
Company

Joan attended Glassboro State College before accepting employment with the New Jersey American Water Company where she advanced to Customer Service Supervisor. She retired after thirty years of service.

NO IMAGE
AVAILABLE

NO IMAGE
AVAILABLE

Irving Emerson Carter (1896-1949)
Ocean City Sewer Service Company

Charles A. Quann (1880-1962)
Ocean City Water Service Company

Daniel Carl Henry (1902-1999)
South Jersey Gas Company

Carl Leroy "Mikey" Henry (1928-2014)
South Jersey Gas Company

Jan 1920 census records show Daniel as a 17-year-old teenager employed as a gas company laborer.

Entrepreneurs

Through the years, more than two hundred diverse businesses served the bustling Westside, surrounding neighborhoods, and commercial establishments in town. The Westside was largely self-sufficient with entrepreneurs ranging in scope from rag pickers to general contractors and hotel owners. Working individually and collectively, these risk takers pulled themselves up by the bootstraps and managed to make a decent living. In raw numbers, Ocean City demographics never reached great numbers for people of color, making their success rate as entrepreneurs impressive. The full story of these entrepreneurs unfolds in the pages of *Loretta's Historic Westside Business Directory*.

For newcomers to Ocean City who decided to stay, one viable option was to find an underserved niche and open a business. Thus, the Westside supported hundreds of home-based, owner operated start-ups in all sectors of the economy ranging from barbers, beauticians, and caregivers in the service sector to restaurant owners and caterers in the food industry. In the early 1890s, Mary Jackson and Anna King established laundry businesses while Jacob Still set about establishing a boardwalk confectionery store. Retailers included owners of gas stations, convenience stores, groceries, fish mongers, the ice man, and local hucksters peddling fresh fruits and vegetables. Taxi cabs, hauling companies, and expressmen comprised the transportation sector. Builders, carpenters, a septic system installer, and marine contractor represented the construction industry. Several Westside people invested in real estate and finance.

Entrepreneurial women owned and operated the earliest Westside businesses identified to date. Anna King operated King's American Laundry on Asbury Avenue while widow Mary Jackson owned the Baltimore Laundry on West Avenue. Both advertised their services in local directories in the early 1890s. Confectioner Jacob Still was the first person to bring salt water taffy to Ocean City. He operated his business from Brower's Emporium at 8th Street and the Boardwalk advertising in local directories in 1893. Wealthy Philadelphia caterer and philanthropist John Sheppard Trower brought his business acumen and religious fervor to Ocean City before the turn of the twentieth century. He invested in Ocean City real estate beginning in 1896. Residents and visitors frequented his ice cream parlors on The Square in the 800 block of Asbury Avenue.

Originally from the Indian River area near Millsboro in southern Sussex County, Delaware, Willard Drain(e) came to Ocean City from Philadelphia in 1900. He left a job as a barber in Philadelphia to succeed John Stewart as valet for Ocean City capitalist Sara Myer. Between approximately 1901 and 1905, Drain(e) worked as a butler for banker and mayor Lewis Cresse. He left the Cresses to cook for artist Elizabeth Rockwell for two years before his 1907 marriage to Gouldtown Native

American Florence Pierce. The newlyweds moved to Pennsylvania where Drain(e) returned to barbering. In 1915, the Drain(e)s came back to Ocean City and purchased a large rooming house with wrap-around porches on the corner of 7th Street and West Avenue.[27] There Drain(e) operated a barber shop while also working as a janitor at Tabernacle Baptist Church. Those unaware of the Drain(e)s' and Pierces' Native American ethnicity often mistook them for Whites.[28] The Drain(e)s are buried at Gouldtown Memorial Park in Cumberland County alongside other Native Americans.

West Virginia native Nathan Freeman and wife Frances arrived in Ocean City around 1910. Nathan initially operated a junk dealer business at 222 Bay Avenue. In 1916, the couple purchased 217 Bay Avenue and opened the Bay Villa Laundry. In 1930, they moved their washtub business to 231 Bay Avenue where Nathan died a few years later leaving his much younger wife widowed before age 50.

Proprietor Edward C. Williams owned and operated some of the most popular businesses on the Westside. In 1910, he opened his first business, a pool hall. By 1915, he and his landlord, Mary Hawkins, opened the Williams & Hawkins tailor shop from her home at 721 West Avenue. His auditorium at 722 West Avenue, which opened around 1922, is believed to have housed a pool hall on the lower level and the Silver Slipper dance club on the upper level. Local organizations such as the Elks and Knights of Pythias held meetings in the building.

By 1928, Williams' expanded businesses included real estate, insurance, notary services, and a cigar store. He owned a confectionery store in 1930. Williams lost much of his accumulated wealth during the Great Depression. He owned a restaurant at 716 West Avenue in 1948 while losing his home, the historic Lomax house at 632 Simpson Avenue, to foreclosure that same year. Homer Jones, a chef at Hogate's and Mac's Restaurant, and wife Blanche Mann Jones purchased the house at a sheriff's sale and passed it down to later generations. Williams and his second wife, Alice, settled in at 741 Moore Avenue where Alice hosted regular meetings of the Colored Women's Republican Club.

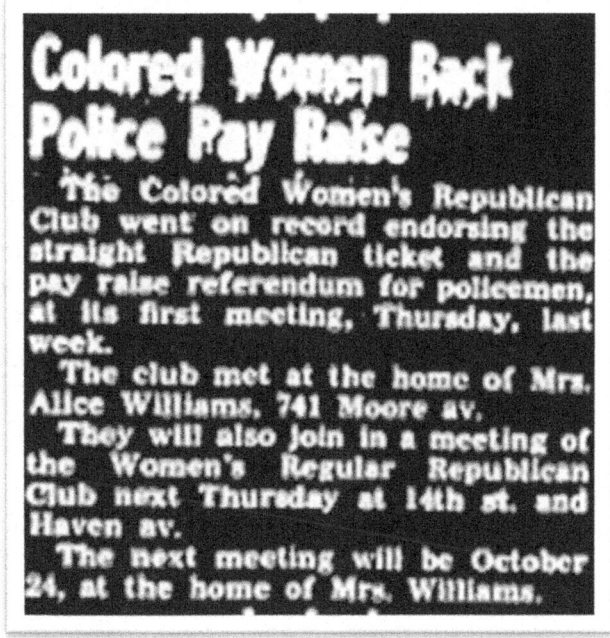

Colored Women Back Police Pay Raise

The Colored Women's Republican Club went on record endorsing the straight Republican ticket and the pay raise referendum for policemen, at its first meeting, Thursday, last week.

The club met at the home of Mrs. Alice Williams, 741 Moore av.

They will also join in a meeting of the Women's Regular Republican Club next Thursday at 14th st. and Haven av.

The next meeting will be October 24, at the home of Mrs. Williams.

In 1915, widow Ida Bush, age forty-one years, lived in a large rooming house on the northwest corner of 7th Street and Haven Avenue where she earned a living as a laundress before opening her corner ice cream store. Several years later, she remarried and opened the Bush Employment Agency. From the 1920s through the 1960s, several women including Tonchie Rodgers, Lillian Turner Johnson, and Cordelia Maddox owned West Avenue employment agencies arranging seasonal help for Ocean City's thriving tourist industry.

The Westside had its own taxi business, enough to support several privately owned neighborhood taxi cabs. Few Westside women drove cars in the 1920s. Women who did day's work walked to work, took taxis when necessary, or had employers pick them up from home. Families in the taxi business included the Morgans, Stevens, and Stewarts.

Originally from Dover, Delaware, (Isaac) Frank Morgan and wife Eliza arrived in Ocean City around 1920 and lived next to Willard Drain(e). Frank worked as a church janitor for two years before he and his wife moved to Bay Avenue and went into the taxi business on the corner of 8th Street and Asbury Avenue. George Morgan arrived around 1930 taking up residence near Frank. The two men worked the taxi business together as brothers buying premium advertising space on the back page of the local Polk's Directory. George Morgan was still a resident of Ocean City when he died in 1955. He is buried with Lenni Lenapes at Immanuel Union Methodist Church Cemetery (Manship) in Cheswold, Kent County, Delaware north of Dover.

John Sylvester Pye came to Ocean City around 1922. A barber by trade, he took up residence in Willard Drain(e)'s rooming house. Pye worked from that location for two years before moving to a new location several blocks west on 7th Street near Bay Avenue. By 1928, Pye's customers included White clientele in the 9th Street and Wesley Avenue shop of a fellow barber, twenty-eight-year-old Italian Jerry Pullo.

> *"Pop Pye was a 'Jack of All Trades' who worked as a cook, calciminer, and paperhanger. He laid sewer pipes in Ocean City and spiked railroad tracks at $0.35/day. Using lumber salvaged from the town dump at 20th Street, he along with family and friends built a house on the corner of 2nd Street and Simpson Avenue surrounded by award winning hydrangeas."*
> *Donovan Butler, 2022*

> *"I recall Mr. Pye driving a horse and buggy around town.*
> *Nathan Davis Jr., 2023*
> *OCHS Class of 1955*

Agnes Anderson Wright operated a catering business in Philadelphia in 1920. She continued the business upon arrival in Ocean City in 1924 opening the Southern Home Bakery at 424 West Avenue. Richard "Dick" Grimes delivered baked goods from the Wright's Bakery to customers in the Gardens Section of Ocean City.[29] Following in her mother's footsteps, Naomi Wright operated Naomi's Catering Service in Brooklyn, New York and at 433 West Avenue, Ocean City. Her specialty was edible bread baskets.[30]

The 1930s were devastating years for the Westside as the nation fell into the Great Depression despite citywide Black residency reaching a healthy 8.2%. At the height of the Depression in 1933, 25% of the nation's populace was out of work. Unemployment on the Westside skyrocketed.

When insolvency hit First National Bank (FNB) Ocean City and private financing dried up, Westside hoteliers and businesses felt the pinch. Sheriff sales increased across the island. Plans for housing associated with Shiloh Baptist Church withered on the vine. The Thomas Hotel constructed specifically for Colored failed. Rev. Comfort's sister-in-law, Louanna Shaw, became a key figure in the development of the north end, managing to hold on to several Comfort properties through the Depression.

As the economy plummeted, men and women thrust into unemployment found work with the Works Projects Administration (WPA). The government program put people to work on public infrastructure programs building roads, parks, schools, airports, and housing. Among those businesses that managed to survive through the Depression were a confectioner, grocer, baker, several restaurants, printer, ice salesman, garbage collector, and an occasional guest house. In the late 1930s as the Westside worked its way out of the Depression, Edna Mae Thomas operated a beauty salon at 208 6th Street.

The 1940s saw the birth of many new businesses. World War II veterans Edward and David Turner opened a service station on the corner of 7th Street and West Avenue in the heart of the Westside. John Motley assumed an ice delivery business from his ailing father. Sylvester Thompson went into the dock building business, later becoming Sylvester W. Thompson & Sons, Inc., a general contracting company, and this book's feature business. In 1948, Edna Mae Thomas relocated from a side street to 921 West Avenue in the heart of the business area where she operated a cottage and weekend beauty salon servicing Colored clientele. Hairdressing was always a major source of employment for Westside women.

The 1950s introduced a new era on the Westside with development of the sparsely settled north end setting the pace. The Comfort, Shaw, and Williams families owned most of the properties on the east side of the 200 block of Bay Avenue including several income-producing guest houses. Rev. Samuel J. Comfort made his first purchase in 1901 from Ocean City founding father James Lake. Comfort's sister-in-law, Louanna Shaw, became a key figure in the development of the north end, managing to hold on to several properties through the Great Depression.

In 1953, New York investor George Walker Williams and Annie Mae Hankerson Williams purchased several properties on the ocean side of Bay Avenue. Louanna Shaw, heir of Rev. Comfort, sold the Hotel Comfort at 2nd Street and Bay Avenue to Williams in 1957. Williams eventually amassed six properties in the same block. The Westside slowly expanded northward into the 100 block.

George Williams and friend Chris Montagna, owner of Chris' Seafood Restaurant, often went boating together.

Jane Williams Foster, granddaughter of George Williams
August 26, 2023 telephone conversation

Still Waters Stress Center. Partners Donna Machin and Irina Venecia with Ronald Rolls Pennington, 1999. Pennington operated parlors at Trump Plaza, Caesars, and Bally's for 18 years prior to opening Still Waters.

Partners watch as Mayor Bud Knight performs ribbon cutting for Still Waters, August 23, 2002.

50

> *"The Thompsons built most of this city."*
> *~Mayor Jay Gillian, 2018*
> *Black History Month Exhibit*
> *Ocean City Historical Museum*

FEATURE:
Sylvester W. Thompson & Sons, Inc.
624 and 625-629 Haven Avenue, Ocean City, New Jersey
General Contractors
Real Estate Acquisition, Foundations, Bulkheads, Docks, and Piers
1940 – 1996

Sylvester Willis Thompson, Sr.
(1914-1996)

Dorothy Gordon Thompson
(1917-1984)

Sylvester Willis Thompson, Jr. (1935-2006)

Wayne Armour Thompson, Sr. (1938-1998)

Sylvester Willis Thompson entered this world with a bang. Dr. Herchel Pettit delivered "Ocean City's New Year's Baby 1914!" at the family home at 738 West Avenue on Rose Court. Sylvester lived his entire life in several houses within a four-block area (6th Street to 7th Street, West Avenue to Haven Avenue). He attended local schools and St. James A.M.E. Church. He married Florida transplant Dorothy Gordon in 1935.

Before starting his own business, Sylvester, Sr. "Pete" Thompson worked as a dock builder for William Lake Gilbert, grandson of Civil Engineer and Surveyor William Lake who laid out the plan of lots for the City of Ocean City. Starting with jury-rigged equipment and lessons learned from the Civilian Conservation Corps and Gilbert Construction, Pete went into business hauling topsoil, gravel, and furniture. In time, he purchased a tractor. His first hoisting equipment was a crane he built himself. He soon owned his own construction company installing piling foundations. Topsoil and cedar trees for use as piling came from twenty-five heavily wooded acres he purchased offshore in Upper Township in a private and secretive deal with an owner who did not want it known he had sold land to a person of color. Today, homemaker Dorothy would be classified as an unpaid worker who performed all the domestic duties but also answered telephone calls and served as payroll clerk.

Sylvester incorporated in 1963 bringing oldest sons Sylvester Jr. and Wayne in as partners. Sylvester, Sr. maintained principal ownership with 80% of the stock with the two sons holding 10% each.

Wayne's graduation gift from his uncle, Alvin Thompson, was a pair of hip boots.
William Griffin, April 2024.

The general contracting company specialized in real estate investment and marine construction. Their Ocean City holdings included business related properties, residential homes, and income properties. They also financed the purchase of homes for area residents holding unrecorded, interest free mortgages and lease/purchase agreements.

They installed creosote and pressure treated piling foundations for many homes and large Ocean City projects well into the 1970s. Larger industrial projects required expansion into the installation of metal sheet piling. With the only large crane on the island, Thompson was hired for many jobs requiring a big rig, including the installation of beach bags at 17th Street in an experimental city project to stop beach erosion, erecting amusement rides and Ferris wheels at Wonderland Pier for Mayor Gillian, and pulling an occasional car out of the water after mishaps on the 9th Street bridge or Tennessee Avenue boat ramp. Sylvester, Sr. also served as a State of New Jersey Transportation Department Condemnation Commissioner.

Some of Thompson's regular clients included Howard Stainton, Walt Hostler, Charles Mumford, Fred Tarves, Bill Matheson, Jack Nixon, Frank Foglio, Dickenson, Bob Stahler, Ralph Clayton, Hump Pontiere, and Bob Gill.

Employees:

- Sylvester W. Thompson, Sr.
- Dorothy Gordon Thompson
- Sylvester W. Thompson, Jr.
- Wayne A. Thompson, Sr.
- Jerry E. Thompson, Sr.
- Kenneth H. Thompson
- Alva P. Thompson
- Alvin L. Thompson
- Mable Thompson Griffin
- William G. Griffin
- Carl "Mikey" Henry, Sr.
- Joseph Henry
- Tyrone Foxworth
- John I. Motley
- McKendree Casson "Mr. Mack"
- Simuel Woods
- Frank (Simuel Woods's friend)
- John Phillip Peterson
- Charlie Patton
- Tommy Adams
- Willie Thomas
- Jay Hannah
- Lemuel Brown
- Kent Granger
- John Brown
- Craig Brown
- Michael Manning
- Jerome McCrea
- Jerome McKiever
- Willie Dunmore

Merion Park housing project meeting, 625 Haven Avenue. Housing later renamed 1634 Association. L-R rear: McKendree "Mr. Mack" Casson, Sylvester Thompson, Jr., Alvin Thompson, Simuel Woods, Sylvester Thompson, Sr. In front, Stainton's Secretary/Treasurer Mary E. Oehlschlager and engineers review construction plans. Photo c. 1950s.

REPRESENTATIVE PROJECT LIST

Foundations:

Bob Gill's 34th Street bank	
Brigantine Castle & Amusement Pier	1976
Brigantine Hotel foundation	
Camden Skill Center	
Cape May Coast Guard	
Cape May County Municipal Utilities Authority –	
Wildwood/Lower Twp. Wastewater Treatment Plant	1985-86
Coastal Bank, 9th Street (now TD Bank)	
Crosswinds Motel, 34th Street near Wawa	
Egg Harbor Township Municipal Utilities Authority	
Most residential homes in Ocean City	pre 1970
Newark State Prison foundation and steelwork	
Ocean City Civic Center	
Ocean City Housing Authority Senior Citizen Project (Bayview Manor)	
Ocean City Intermediate School addition	
Ocean City Music Pier	
Ocean City Primary School	
Ocean City Recreation Center	
Ocean City Sentinel Ledger building	Jul 1960
Ocean Gardens, 16th Street opposite former Chevrolet dealership	
Pennsylvania Sewer & Water Company	
Pier 4, Somers Point	1972
Port-O-Call Hotel and Motor Inn	1964
Sea Isle City Public Safety Building	Feb 1977
Stoeco Homes Merion Park housing project (Howard S. Stainton)	1950s
Whitman Park Low Income Housing Project, Philadelphia	
Yesterday's Bar, Upper Township	

Thompson's completed the Whitman Park project under police protection from citizens opposed to low-income housing. We stayed in Camden with Uncle Morris and Aunt Sarah during the week and came home Friday night to be able to do jobs in Ocean City on the weekend.

William Griffin, April 2024

Bulkheads, Docks, and Piers:

All Seasons Marina, 34th Street	
Mahoney's Harbor House, 2nd Street & Bay Avenue	1983
Manayunk Canal bulkhead and bike path, Philadelphia	1978
Margate Fishing Pier	
Ocean City Fishing Club 14th Street Fishing Pier	1962
Snug Harbor bulkheads and docks	
Stainton's Stoeco Homes 8th Street Yacht Lagoon	1949
Strathmere Wood Jetties	1964

The Unusual

du Pont hazardous waste treatment project, Carneys Point
Gillian's 8th Street Arcade
Gillian's Wonderland, 6th & Boardwalk, erect Ferris wheel & runaway train
House moving
Jilly's 12th Street Arcade
Ocean 17 apartment complex rescue
Ocean City 17th Street experimental beach bag project   1967
Ocean City boardwalk construction
Ocean City Memorial Monument relocation   1947
Royal Turo Lee apartments rescue   1958
Submerged vehicles and boats raised   1968

On the Jilly's project, we hand carried piling to the boardwalk and installed them through the floor.

William Griffin, April 2024

Door panel.
Company logo
yellow on green.

Thompson license plate incl. fuel truck.

Thompson license tags. Transit. 1947.

55

Representative Project List Photo Gallery

Yacht Lagoon, O. C. Development Being Built With Private Capital

Work was begun Tuesday morning on constructing a bulkhead around the newly-dredged lagoon on the Ocean City bayfront, a project of Stoeco Homes Inc., it was announced by a member of the corporation last night. It's strictly a business enterprise, for profit, but goes to show what can be done in the way of creating an inland harbor with private financing.

Ewing T. Corson, prominent Ocean City realtor and vice president of the corporation, announced that the bulkhead contract recently was awarded in two parts, one to the Gilbert Constructing Co., the other to the Sylvester Thompson Co., in order to speed up construction.

The new lagoon, an addition to the original housing project (between Eighth and Ninth sts.) is located just south of Eighth st. and extends to Bay av. Dredging operations began around the middle of December and were completed shortly after Christmas.

Construction of the bulkhead is expected to be completed within six weeks, weather permitting, a corporation spokesman said. Working simultaneously, one construction company will build on the Ninth st. side and the other on the Eighth st. side of the 550 by 145 foot lagoon. When completed the project will comprise about 1100 feet of bulkheading.

No Two Alike

Plans call for 22 lots bordering the lagoon, with a minimum frontage on the lagoon of 40 feet. The buildings will vary in size and will average three to four bedrooms with two baths, he said, at a cost of $15,000 to $20,000.

The new lagoon is of particular interest to owners of large pleasure boats, who, Carson pointed out, have been by-passing Ocean City for other resorts because of inadequate dock facilities. With the anticipated removal of the old Shore Fast Line trolley rails between Ocean City and Somers Point, the lagoon will be open to the main channel and bay.

Extension of Eighth st. and Revere pl. (the latter being in a new street paralleling Ninth st), will be carried through to the bay as building progresses on the lagoon development. Some work already has been done on Eighth st. in this project.

Howard Stainton, leading Ocean City businessman, is president of Stoeco, and Mrs. Mary E. Oehlschlager is secretary-treasurer.

Yacht Lagoon, O.C. Development Being Built with Private Capital.
Atlantic City Press, February 18, 1949. Courtesy Margate Historical Society.

Long time business associates Gilbert Constructing Co. and Thompson Construction collaborated on the installation of bulkheads for Howard Stainton's Stoeco Homes yacht lagoon on the bay between 8th and 9th Streets.

Merion Park newspaper advertisement
Ocean City Sentinel Ledger 1953.

Thompson beachfront rescue. Sentinel Ledger, 1962

Thompson work crew installing beachfront bulkhead.

Thompson & Sons rescue Royal Turo, 14th Street and beach, Ocean City. April 1958.[31]

THURSDAY, APRIL 10, 1958   Publication Office
Sentinel-Ledger Building, 8th st. and Haven av.

Extra $125,000 Ple
By State For Beach

What All the Excitement Was About

FOCAL POINT for thousands of interested sightseers last week was the Royal Turo Lee apartment building shown here at 14th st. Hastily-erected bulkhead and many tons of dirt filled in behind it saved $100,000 property from probable destruction by abnormal tides. Work started after water had advanced to beneath edge of the bath house, small building in foreground.—Senior Studio photo.

Determined Men Win Rugged Day-and-Night Battle to Snatch Apartment House From Sea

By V. T. MICHELETTE

Determined man tangled with a relentless sea in a titanic struggle for three suspenseful days last week before human ingenuity prevailed and warded off the bid of the ocean to claim the $85,000 Royal Turo-Lee Apartments on the beachfront at 14th st.

A man-made bastion of gravel and wood hastily constructed under precarious and often dangerous conditions protected the five-unit house through the most murderous buffeting that a storm-tossed sea could throw against it on the flood tides of the full moon.

The vicious sea raged to within 10 feet of the rear wall of the building on the high tide last Wednesday morning when men and equipment were rushed to the area by the Monihan and Sagerholm Construction Co. to begin the seemingly hopeless job of turning it back.

The struggle was touch-and-go throughout Wednesday when ton upon ton of dirt was sacrificed to purchase time needed by bulkhead builders to jet in pilings across the battleline and throw up the wave-breaking cross planking of the temporary barrier against the roaring surf.

A fleet of five eight-ton dump trucks operated by Fred Field, John Carroll, Louis Fiorentino, Marshall Wallace and John Signorile raced the 15 miles to the Upper Township gravel pit where Bill Field supervised the loading. Back they came to dump their loads in front of the bulldozer blade with which Norman Johnson pushed the gravel over the brink behind the newly installed piling.

For every load of gravel dumped on the site, it seemed that the waves carried away two. F. N. Sagerholm,

who directed the operation, estimated that 200 of the 375 truck loads of material were washed out to sea. The waste was necessary to buy time for construction of the wooden barrier.

The battle between gravel and waves was deadlocked by late afternoon, so another fleet of seven trucks joined the five that had been hauling all day. Bill Brown brought in four extra trucks, and Pat Smith rolled in with the Stoeco rig. Jerry Camp, George Mason, Joe Brown, Fred Walker and Clarence Reynolds helped as drivers of the added fleet.

Meanwhile, the work crew directed by Sylvester "Pete" Thompson was exposed to the dangers of pile driving with heavy seas breaking around them up to their thighs. On the ebb tide about 9 a. m. Tuesday Thompson's gang moved in and started driving piling on the north

See Page 3, column 1 Please

Royal Turo Apartments Rescue[32]

Progressives To Bide Their Time Until Next Fall

Busy Season Not Time For Civic Controversy

David L. Simpson, president of the Ocean City Progressive Association, last night announced that his group would take no action on this city's controversial Sunday closing ordinance until "after the summer season."

"We believe that our interest in Ocean City is every bit as great as that of the city commissioners and the Tabernacle Association," he declared. "We do not intend to do anything to injure Ocean City now or later or to lower its tone when we do take action — but the busy summer season is simply not the time to initiate any legal proceedings whatever. Our plans are complete. We are just awaiting the proper time."

SPINDLY FOREST? These creosoted piling resemble a grove of bare trees, but they are the pilings on which will rest the new Sentinel-Ledger plant at 8th st. and Haven av. Sylvester Thompson's crew this week started driving the piling for the foundation of the building being constructed by H. C. Pontiere and Robert Gill. The construction is expected to be completed by mid-September. In the background rises the current quarters of the Sentinel-Ledger. —Senior Studio photo.

Sylvester Thompson & Sons installing piling foundation for Ocean City Sentinel Ledger's new building at 8th Street and Haven Avenue. The Sentinel Ledger operated from a location in Redmen's Hall (in background) before moving to the new location.[33]

The Ocean City Fishing Club is the oldest continuously operating fishing club in the United States. It is a membership only club; therefore, most Ocean City residents and visitors have never been inside the clubhouse. The fishing pier at 14th Street and the boardwalk, originally constructed in 1916, was damaged by strong east coast storms in 1916, 1945 and 1949. The storm of March 1962 completely destroyed the fishing pier, leaving only the remains of support piling.

NEW FISHING PIER—Officials of the Ocean City Fishing Club gather with city commissioners Wednesday afternoon at the start of construction of a $35,000 fishing pier at 14th. St. The old pier was washed away by the March storm. The 420 foot long pier will service the club's 151 members and is expected to be completed by Nov. 15. Shown above, left to right, are: Commissioner D. Allen Stretch; Alva Scherneck, building chairman of the club; Harry Stelwagon, club president, and Mayor Nathaniel C. Smith.   (Senior Studio Photo)

Ocean City Fishing Club Officials
Ocean City Sentinel Ledger,
September 20, 1962

Club members hired local marine contractor, Sylvester Thompson, Sr., to design and construct a new pier. The new pier extending 420 feet into the Atlantic was finished in summer 1963 with the clubhouse finished in 1964. Subsequent sand dredging projects to replenish storm battered beaches and recurring storm damage periodically require work to repair and extend the pier further into the ocean. The Fishing Club completed the most recent extension in January 2021.

Remains of Ocean City Fishing Club's 14th Street fishing pier following the storm of March 1962. Photo originally submitted by Jeff Morris, Facebook 2020.

Thompson crane on 14th Street fishing pier during construction. c. 1963

Sunrise postcard. 14th Street fishing pier Sylvester Thompson & Sons designed and constructed for Ocean City Fishing Club following the 1962 storm.

14th Street pier extended 2021.[34]

Thompson & Sons, Inc. work crew during construction of the Port-O-Call Hotel,
Ocean City's first high rise building at eight stories tall. Photo c. 1964.
Photographic Collection. Hotels Book 8. Courtesy Ocean City Historical Museum

Port-O-Call Hotel, east side. Foundation by S. W. Thompson & Sons.[35]

Port-O-Call Hotel, 1510 Boardwalk. Aerial view of west side. Opened 1966.[36]

Sylvester Thompson & Sons   Aug 8, 1967

SOUTH JERSEY   Atlanti

SECOND SECTION   ATLANTIC CITY, N.

(Andrea Libbi Photo)

BEACHFRONT PROTECTION — Youthful strollers on Ocean City Boardwalk Monday pause to watch workmen installing a bulkhead at 17th Street, one of several efforts being taken to halt constant inroads of sea which have wiped out much of bathing beach and now threaten beachfront properties.

O. C. to Try Nylon Bags To Slow Beach Erosion

OCEAN CITY — A comprehensive program to combat beach erosion on center city beaches here by filling nylon bags with sand and placing them at strategic places along the beachfront will be undertaken by City Commission early this fall, if permission is granted by the State Department of Conservation and Economic Development.

Mayor Robert L. Sharp said at a meeting of city officials, local beach erosion Advisory Board members and a representative of the Allied Chemical Corp. that the city was definitely interested in any program to preserve bathing beaches here.

Allied Chemical representative Paul Barber said the city could purchase as many bags as it wanted, for $8 a bag.

"The bags are made of high tenacity nylon, woven together at the top and bottom," Barker said. "They can withstand the beating of the ocean for years."

Barker pointed out that bags could be filled and place by

Nylon bag beach erosion project, 17th Street and beach.[37]

near the zone dividing Vietnam. | Cong gunners hurled 17 rounds | enemy opened up on the 3[a] | attacked th

(Press Photo)

BRIDGE FATALITY — This panel truck driven by James Bush, 56, of Pleasantville, plunged through the railing of the Beach Thoroughfare bridge on the causeway into Ocean City. The truck crossed into two lanes of eastbound traffic before toppling into Great Egg Harbor Bay where Bush's body was removed from 30 feet of water by a county skin-diver.

The truck was pulled from the bay after several attempts by a crane from the Sylvester Thompson Construction Co., which was working in the area.

Traffic was reduced to one lane each way on the four lane bridge after the accident. More than 30 boats surrounded the rescue area picking up bundles of laundry floating up the bay with the tide.

Bridge Fatality. Atlantic City Press, July 9, 1968
Courtesy Margate Historical Society

Pier 4 Hotel, 6 Broadway, Somers Point overlooking Great Egg Harbor Bay.
Foundation and bulkheading by S. W. Thompson & Sons. c. 1972.

Original Ocean City Housing Authority Senior Housing, 6th Street and West Avenue.

Mahoney's Harbor House docks, piers and boat slips, 2nd Street and Bay Avenue, Ocean City. 9th Street bridge in background. Photo c. 1983.

Ferris wheel at Gillian's Fun Deck erected by S. Thompson & Sons. Photo credit Gillian family.

Local architect Jack Snyder documented Thompson's construction techniques in the series of undated photographs below showing work along the beachfront.

Photos courtesy Ocean City Historical Museum.

Damaged bulkhead prior to replacement.

Wayne Thompson standing left, Pete Thompson crane operator.

Simuel Woods hatchet man,
Kent Granger helper.

Wayne Thompson on tractor backfilling bulkhead.

Brigantine Castle & Amusement Pier. Al Faulkner and Sylvester Thompson teamed up to install the foundation piling and pier for the amusement pier project. Photo c. 1976.[38]

The Brigantine Castle featured restaurants, miniature golf, arcade games, gift shops, and a fishing pier. Live spooks haunted five levels of twisting walkways and scary artwork.

When fire trapped and killed eight teenagers inside a haunted house at Six Flags Great Adventure in 1984, Brigantine officials required an engineering study to determine the safety of Brigantine Castle. The study revealed that the structure was unsafe and in need of significant repairs. The renovated castle was ready to reopen for the 1985 season, but tensions continued between the owner and City officials. Owners decided to close for good and sold it to a developer who planned a condominium complex.

A few months later, a fire broke out destroying the Castle and pier. All that remained were some of the foundation pilings. In January 1988, two Atlantic City men were arrested and charged with arson.

Schuylkill River Navigation System and Manayunk Canal

The 106-mile-long Schuylkill River navigation system was once the country's largest coal-carrying waterway. It was one of the first anthracite canals built to bring coal down from coal rich regions above Reading, Pennsylvania to ports along the Delaware River. The waterway stretched from the anthracite region of Schuylkill County down the Schuylkill River into Philadelphia. Several dams were built to control slackwater. Digging started in 1819 and was completed in 1823 spurring Philadelphia's Industrial Revolution while also shaping the growth of adjacent communities.

Manayunk Canal bike path map.[39]

Schuylkill River, Manayunk Canal, and towpath as they pass through Manayunk, a community of mills and factories on hilly, cobblestone streets on the banks of the Schuylkill River in Northwest Philadelphia.[40]

Sylvester Thompson & Sons, Inc. clearing the Manayunk Canal and towpath. Photo c. 1978.[41]

Sylvester Thompson & Sons, Inc. of Ocean City, New Jersey played a vital role in saving the historic Manayunk Canal and towpath. Pictured above are members of Thompson's crew clearing debris from the canal bed in preparation for the installation of bulkheading to stabilize the walls of the canal. The three-year project included the construction of a bike path alongside the canal to link Center City and Valley Forge.

Antique bottles recovered from the Manayunk Canal during construction of bulkheading and bike path.
Kenneth Thompson collection

74

Manayunk Canal bulkhead and bike path, Philadelphia. Photo c. 2019.
Loretta Thompson Harris collection.

The canal and path are part of the Manayunk Main Street Historic District and are listed on the National Register of Historic Places. The canal itself is listed on the Philadelphia Register of Historic Places. The towpath has been redeveloped several times since it was first installed in 1978, adding lighting, murals, and greenery. The Manayunk Development Corporation is currently organizing a full restoration of the Manayunk Canal.

Manayunk Canal and bike path (towpath). Buildings along the canal are
reflected in the newly reopened waterway.[42]

The Manayunk Canal section of the waterway was built in segments with inlet and
outlet locks around difficult sections of the river. Active mills along the canal began
closing in the 1960s sending Main Street into a deep decline. Manayunk Canal
became nothing more than a ditch filled with tires, trash, and discards from adjacent
textile mills, breweries, and bottlers. Local officials considered filling the ditch and
building an expressway to relieve Main Street traffic congestion. They also
considered filling in the canal to create parking.[43]

Originally, mules towed barges up and down the Manayunk Canal from a towpath
alongside the Manayunk Canal. Old rail lines, canal locks, ruins of the lock tender's
house, and old textile mills are visible along the towpath. In 1969, area residents and
Boy Scouts started cleaning up the canal. The Manayunk Canal was the only intact
canal section within Philadelphia City limits. Volunteers continued the clean-up
work until 1977 when the City of Philadelphia took over the effort bringing city and
federal resources to bear. The revitalized area attracts a mix of upscale businesses, a
performing arts center, and chic lofts and condominiums, some of which are housed
in the original mill buildings.[44,45,46]

Newly restored waterway.[47]

Today, the former towpath is a favorite path for biking enthusiasts.[48]

Local firm receives $4 million contract

A local pile-driving firm has been awarded a $4.3 million subcontract for the construction of the Cape May County Municipal Utilities Authority's Wildwood / Lower region wastewater treatment plant, the largest award in the company's 40-year history.

But big projects are no small potatoes to Sylvester Thompson and Sons of 625 Haven Av. whose past endeavors include work on the Newark State Prison, the Manayunk Canal and Whitman Park housing project in Philadelphia, the Ocean City Fishing Pier which the firm also designed, addition to the intermediate school and the Housing Authority's senior citizen complex on West Avenue.

"We've saved numerous buildings after storms like Ocean 17 and the Touralee Apartments," noted Sylvester Thompson Sr. "We even made national TV on that one."

According to Thompson, the contract will put 20 employees to work for the duration of the job he expects to take about eight months.

The local firm was awarded the subcontract following an invitation for minority and women-owned businesses to bid on the project by Fluor Constructors Inc. of Irvine Calif., general contractor for the wastewater facility, according to the MUA.

Gov. Thomas Kean and outgoing state Department of Environmental Protection Commissioner Robert E. Hughey were present at recent ceremonies congratulating the Thompson firm.

"I am extremely impressed with both (MUA and Fluor) performances," Hughey said. "The Authority clearly delineated minority business enterprise and women business enterprise requirements in their instructions to bidders and the prime contractor has demonstrated an ability to comply with these requirements with immediate results."

Minorities will comprise 11.2 percent of the project

with women-owned businesses comprising 2 percent.

Fluor initially made contacts with Sylvester Thompson and Sons and other firms during a one-day conference for minority and women-owned businesses sponsored by the NJDEP in October 1985.

The prime contractor then followed this initial outreach, the officials said, with letters to minority and women-owned firms to submit quotes for subcontract work.

The selection of firms receiving subcontracting awards was based upon the lowest bids submitted.

Accompanying the Thompsons in Trenton were state Sen. James R. Hurley of Millville, whose public relations firm handles the MUA account; Gary Jernigan, project engineer for Fluor Constructors, and MUA officials William F.X. Band, chairman, and George Marinakis, executive director.

Sylvester Thompson, Sr. far left. Sylvester, Jr. and Wayne Thompson 5th and 6th from left. Fluor Constructors of California awarded the subcontract for foundation work on the new Cape May County Municipal Utilities Authority Wildwood/Lower region wastewater treatment plant to Sylvester Thompson & Sons of Ocean City.[49]

Thompson employed a crew of twenty men and two cranes to install steel poles at the Cape May County Municipal Utilities Authority wastewater project. c. 1986.

Sylvester Thompson & Sons, Inc. using a tripod to construct Margate fishing pier.

The Vehicle Graveyard

Old cars, trucks, cranes, Ferris wheels, and piling went to Thompson's vehicle graveyard in Palermo to die. Once stripped of all usable parts, they were hauled away and sold as scrap metal.

Abandoned Wayne crane (coincidentally same name as Thompson's son).

Abandoned vehicle chassis stripped of reusable parts.

Old cars, trucks, and Gillian's Ferris wheel carts end up in the graveyard.

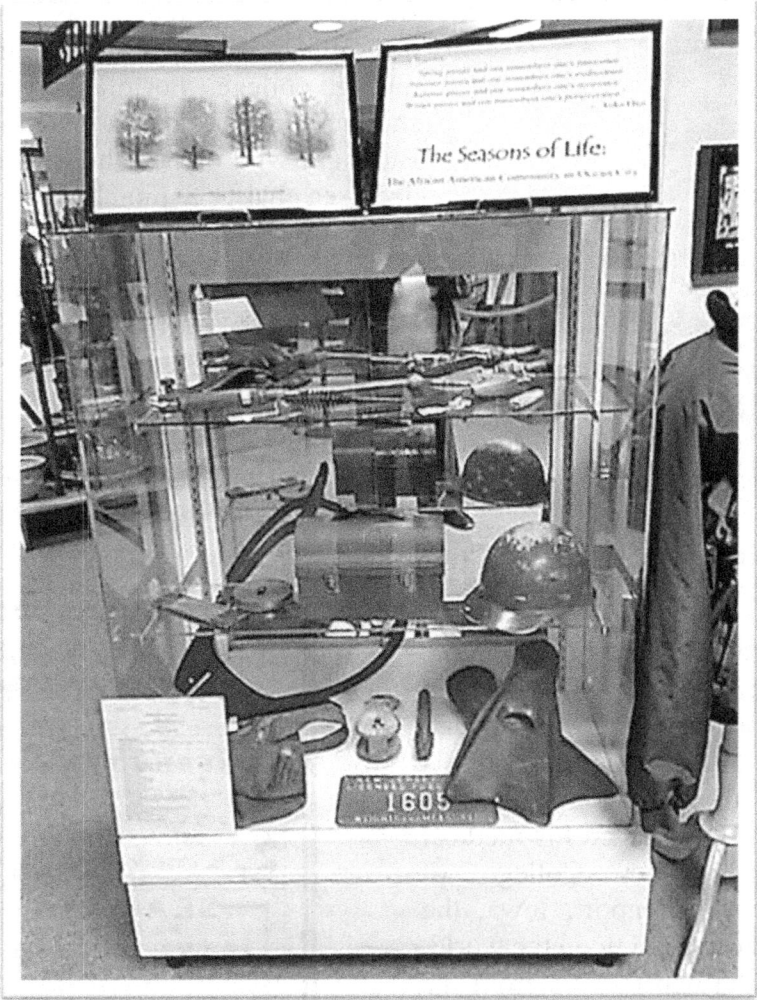

Sylvester W. Thompson & Sons, Inc. Small tools exhibit.
Ocean City Historical Museum, Black History Month, 2018.

Doctors, Lawyers, and Indian Chiefs

Doctors

Ocean City is home to several people of color who have earned distinctions with doctoral degrees in various fields.

Jerry Evans Thompson, Sr., D.C. (1942-2016)
OCHS Class of 1960.

Jerry Thompson was a native of Ocean City who was born at Shore Memorial Hospital in Somers Point. He graduated from Ocean City High where he focused his study on Biology in anticipation of a career in the medical field.

Being number three of six children, Jerry determined he would work his own way through college. For many years during the summer, he worked as a mate for Captain Al Burchard who owned the Silver Spray II, a deep-sea charter fishing boat.

Not only was Jerry mate on the boat, but he also dug and sold clams to patrons for bait. He ran the pool for the largest fish of the day which added tips to his earnings. Jerry sold the fresh fish he caught to fish markets and restaurants in South Jersey and Philadelphia, including Bob's in Northfield and Absecon and Woodburn's in Somers Point.

Jerry received his bachelor's degree from historic Lincoln University in Oxford, Pennsylvania, the United States' first degree granting HBCU (historically Black colleges and universities). He received his medical degree from Palmer College of Chiropractic in Davenport, Iowa, the first school of chiropractic in the world. "Doc" practiced chiropractic from his Spruce Street office in Philadelphia.

Silver Spray II deep sea charter fishing boat.
Ocean City Sentinel Ledger.

GOOD NEWS
from
THOMPSON
Chiropractic Clinic

5904 Spruce Street
Philadelphia, Pa. 19139

SH 8 - 0500

Dr. J. Thompson . Sr.

Jerry refused to allow his small stature to preclude his participation in sports. In his youth, he played baseball and was third baseman on Dick Grimes' winning team in their first year in the Babe Ruth baseball league. An avid fisherman, Jerry spent his retirement years trailering his boat for daily fishing trips in area waters. He was a volunteer cook for the Elks Lodge at Brotmanville in Cumberland County where he supplied the lodge with fresh fish for their fundraisers.

Bishop Charles Rayfield Lyles, honorary Doctor of Music. OCHS Class of 1969.
New Victory First Presbyterian Deliverance Church.

Dr. Roland Arlington Wiggins (1932-2019). Senior photo, OCHS Class of 1949
Photos courtesy Ocean City Historical Museum.

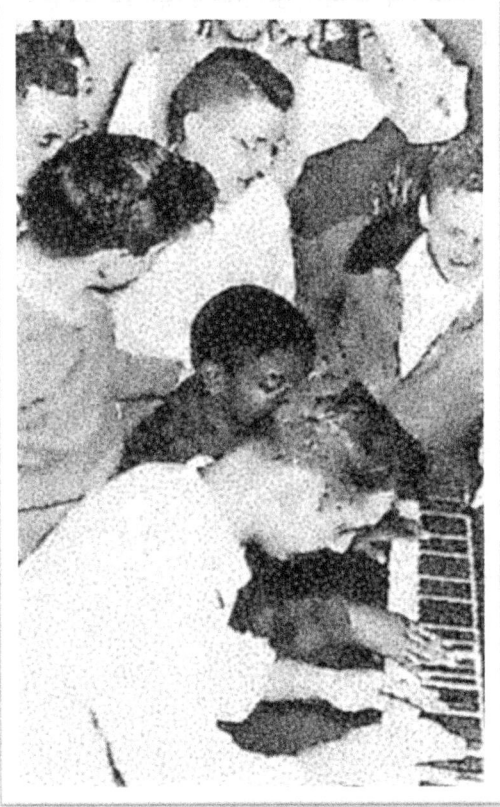

Roland Wiggins,
Ocean City Youth Center duet.

Roland Wiggins was an American music theorist and educator born and reared in Ocean City. A recognized musical prodigy, Roland began formal lessons at age eight and was a featured performer on Atlantic City's Steel Pier at age fifteen.

While still in high school, he studied classical piano with several great theorists and composers at the Philadelphia Conservatory of Music. He continued his studies following a term in the Air Force during World War II, ultimately leading to a position teaching the Schillinger System of Musical Composition.

A consummate musician, Roland enrolled at Combs College & Ornstein School of Music at the University of Pennsylvania where he earned his undergraduate, master's, and doctorate degrees. Among his many students at various schools where he taught were John Coltrane, Thelonious Monk, Yusef Lateef, Sonny Fortune, Barry Harris, Archie Shepp, Buster Williams, Jimmy Owens, and Billy Taylor.[50,51]

Roland had a Saturday morning radio show. Neighborhood residents turned up the volume on radios and opened house windows so all could hear him play. Although Roland served as a lifeguard, he was excluded from the annual beach patrol ball. Instead, he was asked to play the piano and entertain attendees at the event. [52,53]

Front Row: Roland Wiggins center. Back Row L-R: Father Leonard Leondis Wiggins (superimposed), sister Rozelia Wiggins, mother Rozelia A. Shaw Wiggins, brother Leonard Wiggins, Jr.[54]

Resort Boy, Who Discovered Music With Boogie Woogie, Faces Bright Future

Wiggins May Go To Hollywood

A totally untrained high school freshman, who created a local sensation when he began pounding out boogie woogie on a high school piano several years ago, is now on a broad musical highway that promises to lead him to fame.

Roland Wiggins, unassuming son of Mr. and Mrs. Leonard Wiggins, 302 West av., is now in the U. S. Air Force, where he has seized every possible opportunity—with plenty of encouragement from his officers—to advance his musical education.

Unable to read a note of music, Roland began picking out tunes on a high school piano, back in his Freshman days, and soon was producing boogie woogie with a zest that proved he had a natural talent for music.

Fired with enthusiasm, he saved his money and bought a second-hand piano. Then he took some lessons from Miss Helen Derrick, public school vocal music supervisor. Miss Derrick, quickly recognizing his latent talent, gradually directed him into an appreciation for the best in music.

Roland, who spent the past week end visiting his parents, brought The Sentinel-Ledger up to date on his subsequent career.

After leaving high school, he studied for two years at the Philadelphia Conservatory of Music, where he was awarded a bachelor's degree in music. He majored in piano.

Enlisting in the Air Force in January, 1951, he was assigned to Selfridge Field, Mt. Clemens, Michigan. In his spare time he studied under a touch specialist for piano, in Detroit.

Later he was transferred to the Stewart Air Force base, New York. In New York City, he has been studying piano and the Shillinger System of Musical Composition. He also has been studying the Hammond organ.

His ambition, when his hitch with the Air Force ends, a year and a half from now, is to go to Hollywood, where he hopes to write background music for mo-

Hopes to Compose Film 'Background'

tion pictures.

By way of versatility, he is now playing a tuba and percussion instruments with the Air Force Dance Band at Eads Headquarters. Stewart field, and piano with the Air Force orchestra, which appears once a month on the DuMont television network, broadcasting from New York City.

He also is conducting the Air Force Glee Club, recently organized.

In reporting his rapid progress, he expressed his appreciation to Chief Warrant Officer Elmer Reade, squadron commander, whose interest in him has made it possible to pursue so diversified a musical role, and to Miss Derrick and others in Ocean City who encouraged him in his fledgling days.

His brief visit home was occasioned by the illness of his mother.

Four Fined On Motor Charges

2 Speeding, One For Noisy Muffler

Four persons were arrested Sunday on motor vehicle violations, and paid the mandatory fines to the court clerk, Joseph Guarracino, at city hall.

Timothy Fitzgerald, Jr., 26, of 1045 Asbury av., was fined $17 and $3 costs on a charge of speeding on Somers Point blvd. Police reported that he was going 70 miles hour, exceeding the 50-mile limit on the highway.

Bill Hasharva, 50, of 1146 Asbury

Sentinel-Ledger, June 11, 1953

Charlottesville web article: Hitting the Right Note –
Jazz Legend Roland Wiggins Reflects on a Lifetime of Musical Expression[55]

Charlottesville News and Arts Weekly, 2019. Courtesy Barbara Potts Bonaparte.

Dr. Roland A. Wiggins at piano. Jefferson School.[56]

2020 SESSION

ENROLLED

HOUSE JOINT RESOLUTION NO. 419

Celebrating the life of Roland Arlington Wiggins.

Agreed to by the House of Delegates, March 3, 2020
Agreed to by the Senate, March 5, 2020

WHEREAS, Roland Arlington Wiggins of Charlottesville, a distinguished music educator known for his innovative applications of advanced musical theory, died on November 20, 2019; and

WHEREAS, a native of Ocean City, New Jersey, Roland Wiggins was recognized as a musical prodigy at a young age and began formal study of the piano when he was eight years old; by 15, he was a star performer at Atlantic City's Steel Pier amusement park; and

WHEREAS, Roland Wiggins continued to study the piano at the Philadelphia Conservatory of Music, then served his country as a member of the United States Air Force, during which time he played with the renowned jazz trumpeter Donald Byrd and studied composition with one of the most innovative composers of the 20th century, Henry Cowell; and

WHEREAS, Roland Wiggins subsequently became an authorized instructor of the Schillinger System of Musical Composition, a comprehensive, mathematical approach to musical analysis and composition, and pursued a career in education after graduating from Combs College with bachelor's, master's, and doctoral degrees; and

WHEREAS, Roland Wiggins' joyful approach to composition focused on individual expression and truthful communication through music, and he provided guidance to many well-known artists, including John Coltrane, Yusef Lateef, and Thelonious Monk; he conducted groundbreaking research into the production of electronic music and used computerized analyses of famous musicians to teach key concepts; and

WHEREAS, in addition to teaching at Combs College, Roland Wiggins worked at several high schools and junior high schools, the University of Massachusetts Amherst, Williams College, Amherst College, Hampshire College, and the University of Virginia; and

WHEREAS, Roland Wiggins relocated to Charlottesville in 1989 and quickly became a cherished member of the community; and

WHEREAS, Roland Wiggins will be fondly remembered and greatly missed by his wife, Muriel, and his daughters, Rosalyn, Suzan, and Carol; now, therefore, be it

RESOLVED by the House of Delegates, the Senate concurring, That the General Assembly hereby note with great sadness the loss of Roland Arlington Wiggins, a luminary of jazz music who inspired countless students as an instructor; and, be it

RESOLVED FURTHER, That the Clerk of the House of Delegates prepare a copy of this resolution for presentation to the family of Roland Arlington Wiggins as an expression of the General Assembly's respect for his memory.

ENROLLED

HJ419ER

Resolution Celebrating the Life of Roland Arlington Wiggins[57]

Lawyers

Nathan Davis, Jr. Esq., OCHS Class of 1955
Photos courtesy Nathan Davis, Jr.

Nathan "Nate" Davis is a native of Ocean City born at home at 208 7th Street. He is one of four children (Noel, Nathan, Jr., Louis, and Carlton) of Nathan, Sr. and Louisa Waters Davis.

The family moved to a large house on the corner of 5th Street and West Avenue where his parents closely monitored and guided the children's education. Nate graduated from Ocean City High where he was an honor roll student and participated in basketball, football, track, band, and glee club.

Nathan received his bachelor's degree in political science from Rutgers University and his Juris Doctorate from Howard University. He practiced law for the firm of Charles W. Sandman who represented Cape May County in the New Jersey Senate and Southern New Jersey in the United States House of Representatives.

Nate opened his own law office in Atlantic City in 1972 where he remained until 1985 when he became a public defender for the State of New Jersey. Five years later, he was appointed Deputy Public Defender of Salem County.

Nathan served on the Board of Trustees of Shore Memorial Hospital, as President of the Egg Harbor Township Board of Education, and as President of the Egg Harbor Township Municipal Utilities Authority. A long-time member of Macedonia United Methodist Church, Nate served as lay leader and President of the Administrative Board. He also served as President of the Ocean City Ecumenical Council.

Sandman Names Davis Area Representative

Nathan W. Davis, Jr., of Ocean City, the first Negro attorney to practice law in Cape May County, will be Congressman-elect Charles W. Sandman's county contact man when Sandman goes to Washington next week. Davis is associated with Sandman in his law office at Cape May City.

Sandman made the announcement at a press conference Tuesday. He said he will maintain offices in all four counties of the second Congressional district and will visit each of them one Saturday morning a month.

Sandman said he has appointed Joseph T. Sullivan, former executive assistant to Senator Harrison "Pete" Williams, as his administrative assistant. Sullivan left Williams some time ago.

As his press secretary Sandman has appointed Joseph Cardamone, a former teacher and an editor of the Cape May Star and Wave, a weekly newspaper. Mrs. Franklin Woodruff will be Sandman's head office secretary in Washington. She has been Sandman's secretary in his law office.

Sullivan, a former newspaperman, is regarded as a "pro" in handling affairs for legislators. Prior to working for Williams, a Democrat, he was employed by two Republican congressmen.

James Sanford, a Wildwood builder of amusement devises and a licensed

Congressman's Aide

Nathaniel Davis, Jr.

airplane pilot, will be Sandman's liaison officer between Sandman's Washington office and the four counties in the district, Sandman said.

Actually, according to friends of Sandman, Sanford will be Sandman's personal pilot. Friends have raised a fund to charter a plane so Sandman may commute from Cape May County to Washington.

Christopher D. Robertson, Esq., OCHS Class of 1978. Pictured in Navy uniform. Photo courtesy Christopher D. Robertson

Christopher Robertson is a former Judge of the New Jersey Municipal Court, Assistant County Prosecutor, and Managing Partner with the Law Firm of Robertson & Fendt. He is a litigation attorney with trial experience in both civil practice and the criminal justice system.

Christopher attended the University of Southern California and Stockton University where he was a founder of Alpha Phi Alpha Fraternity, Pi Xi Chapter and received a Bachelor of Arts degree in Public Administration. He received his Juris Doctorate from Temple University School of Law, Philadelphia, Pennsylvania.

Attorney Robertson is a member of the New Jersey State Bar, New Jersey Association for Justice, Garden State Bar Association, and the American Legion. He has served as an Adjunct Professor of Law at Atlantic Cape Community College; Former Finance Chair, City of Pleasantville Urban Enterprise Zone; Assistant Solicitor, City of Atlantic City; Assistant Prosecutor, Cape May County, and First Black Municipal Court Judge in Cape May County.

He is the recipient of numerous awards and honors. Among them are the Cape May County Prosecutor's Award for Outstanding Service; the Atlantic City Business and Professional Women's Club Community Service Award; Macedonia United Methodist Church Outstanding Accomplishment in The Practice of Law Award and Cape May County Certificate of Appreciation for Outstanding Legal Service.

Indian Chiefs

Charles Cullen Clark
"Chief Little Owl"
(1894-1971)[58]

Nanticoke chief Charles Cullen Clark entered the military from Ocean City in February 1919. He enlisted at the Naval Recruiting Station in Philadelphia as a Mess Attendant 3 assigned to the U.S.S. Glacier. He was discharged in 1919 as a Mess Attendant 1 in Brooklyn, New York.

His war service was credited to Delaware. Clark was part of a family of Indian chiefs in the Millsboro area of Sussex County, Delaware. He is buried in Millsboro, Delaware.

WW I	WW II	KOREA			ORIGINAL

14. NAME AND LOCATION OF CEMETERY (City and State)
Clark Family Cem. @ Millsboro, Delaware

Suspended MAY 26 1971

1. NAME OF DECEASED - LAST - FIRST - MIDDLE (Print or Type)
Clark, Charles Cullen

IMPORTANT - Item 18 on reverse side must be completed. See attached instructions and complete and submit both copies.

2. SERVICE NUMBER 434422
War Ser. Cert. No.

3. PENSION OR VA CLAIM NUMBER

15. This application is submitted for a stone or marker for the unmarked grave of a deceased member or former member of the Armed Forces of the U.S., soldier of the Union or Confederate Armies of the Civil War or for an unmarked memorial plot for a non-recoverable deceased member.
I hereby agree to accept responsibility for proper placement at the grave or memorial plot at no expense to the Government.

4. ENLISTMENT DATE (Month, day, year)
Aug. 30, 1917

5. DISCHARGE DATE (Month, day, year)
Feb. 8, 1919

6. STATE
Delaware

7. DECORATIONS

NAME OF APPLICANT (Print or Type)
Kenneth S. Clark

RELATIONSHIP
son

8. GRADE OR RANK
MAH1C

9. BRANCH OF SERVICE, COMPANY, REGIMENT, DIVISION
Navy - served R.S. at Norfolk, Va. - U.S.S. Glacier

ADDRESS OF APPLICANT (Street address, City and State)
Oak Orchard
Millsboro, Delaware

10. DATE OF BIRTH (Month, day, year)
Oct. 29, 1894

11. DATE OF DEATH (Month, day, year)
April 13, 1971

SIGNATURE OF APPLICANT
Kenneth S Clark

DATE
4/16/71

12. RELIGIOUS EMBLEM (Check one)

13. CHECK TYPE REQUIRED

16. FREIGHT STATION
Millsboro, Delaware

XX **LATIN CROSS** (Christian) — **UPRIGHT MARBLE HEADSTONE**
STAR OF DAVID (Hebrew) — **FLAT MARBLE MARKER**
NO EMBLEM — **FLAT GRANITE MARKER**
X **FLAT BRONZE MARKER**

17. NAME OF CONSIGNEE WHO WILL TRANSPORT STONE OR MARKER
James & Watson Funeral Home

DO NOT WRITE HERE

ADDRESS OF CONSIGNEE (Street address, City and State)
Main St., Millsboro, Delaware 19966

FOR VERIFICATION

ORDERED
1 0 JUN 1971

I HAVE AGREED TO TAKE THE STONE OR MARKER TO THE CEMETERY.

B/L *72420*

CONTRACTOR
Sheldon Bronze
Ringwood, West

SIGNATURE OF CONSIGNEE
James & Watson F.H. per Richard T. Watson

MAH1 US NAVY / WW I

DD FORM 1330, 1 NOV 62
EDITION OF 1 DEC 61 MAY BE USED.

APPLICATION FOR HEADSTONE OR MARKER

Charles Cullen Clark application for headstone.

Loretta's Historic Westside Business Directory

Loretta's Historic Westside Business Directory captures data from local directories, census records, newspapers, and personal interviews. It includes data from 1884 when the Still family arrived to current day 2024.

Loretta's Historic (1884-2024)

OCEAN CITY

CAPE MAY COUNTY, NEW JERSEY

WESTSIDE BUSINESS DIRECTORY

Containing an alphabetical Business Directory,
Classified Advertisers Guide, and
Churches and Organizations Listing

This book is the property of
INDELIBLE INK, LLC, Publisher
P. O. Box 655, Marmora, New Jersey 08223

Alphabetical Business Directory
(White Pages)

Bakeries	Proprietor	Ref.*
Bush's Bakery, 701 Haven Ave.	Ida J. Bush	1999
Dorsey's Bakery and Cooking		1933
Southern Home Bakery, 424 West Ave. rear.	Agnes Wright	1928
Southern Home Bakery, 432 West Ave.		
Wright's Bakery, 433 West Ave.	Edward Wright, father Lawrence	1999

Barbers and Beauticians	Proprietor	Ref.*
Archie's Barber Shop, 736 West Ave.	Archie Alston	1948
Archie's Barber Shop, 626 Haven Ave.	Archie Alston	1950
Archie's Barber Shop, 626 Haven Ave.	Rachel Alston	1960
Bertha's Hairdressing Shop, 710 West Ave.	Bertha Quinton	1930
Boyer's Barber Shop, 724 West Ave.	Francis Boyer	1915
Bryant's Hairdressing, 3rd St. east of West Ave.	Juanita Bryant	
Carlos' Barber Shop, 719 Haven Ave.	Carlton Davis	1969
Drain(e)'s Barber Shop, 660 West Ave.	Willard Drain(e)	1915
Edward Turner, Loretta's Beauty Salon, 210 West Ave. Hairdresser.	Loretta	1963
Edna Mae's Beauty Salon, 208 E. 6th St. Beautician.	Edna Mae Thomas	1937
Edna Mae's Beauty Salon, 921 West Ave. Hairdresser.	Edna Mae Thomas	1954
Frazier's Beauty Shop, 316 West Ave.	Laura M. Frazier	1928
Gillett's Barber Shop, 740 West Ave.	Charles C. Gillett	1914
Glenn's Barber Shop, 636 Simpson Ave.	Marcellus Glenn	1950
Green's Hairdressing Shop, 721 West Ave.	Emma E. Green	1930
LaFrank's Beauty Salon, 622 Haven Ave.	Addie LaFrank	1937
Larkins' Barber Shop, 740 West Ave.	Elijah Helbert Larkins	1909
Madam Rachel A. Bryan, 115 7th St. Beauty culture.	Rachel A. Bryan	1928
Mamie's Hairdressing, 710 West Ave.	Mamie Battle	1948
Miss Singletary's, 207 7th St. Beautician.	Lottie Brown Ballard Manning Singletary Collins	1930
Nichols' Hairdressing, 712 West Ave.	Thelma Nichols	1937
Pye's Barbering, 660 West Ave.	John S. Pye	1922
Sarah E. Thompson, 732 West Ave. Ladies' Hairdresser.	Sarah E. Thompson	1916

Building Contractors	Proprietor	Ref.*
Buston's, 745 West Ave. rear. Paperhanging.	Enoch K. Buston	1930
Davis, 644 West Ave. Roofer.	George Davis	1937
Davis, 315 4th St. General contractor.	William D. Davis	1922
Driscoll. Pile driver		
Hannah's Masonry, West Ave. Mason.	Joseph Hannah	1957
Peters' Cabinets. Cabinetmaker.	Lewellyn Peters	1915
Pye Paperhanging, 6 2nd St. Paperhanger.	John S. Pye	1948
Rowell's, 223 Haven Ave. House painting.	Earl Rowell	

S. Pye, 660 West Ave. Wall scraping and calcimining.	S. Pye	1922
Streeter Painting. House painting.	John Streeter	1930
Sylvester Thompson, 624 Haven Ave. Dock builder.	Sylvester Thompson, Sr.	1940
Sylvester Thompson & Sons, Inc., 625 Haven Ave. General Contractor.		1963
William Brown Hauling, Inc. 7th & Simpson Ave. Hauling.	William R. Brown	1953
Wood Doctor, 434 West Ave. Carpenter.	Kenneth Wright	

Caterers	**Proprietor**	**Ref.***
Baker & Livingston Caterers		1975
Naomi's Catering Service, 433 West Ave.		1971
Palace Restaurant, 800 block Asbury Ave.	John Sheppard Trower	1896

Employment Agencies	**Proprietor**	**Ref.***
Bush Employment Agency, NE Cor. 7th St. & Haven Ave.	Ida Bush	
Domestic Employment Agency, 400 West Ave.	Lillian R. Turner	1928
Employment Agency, 444 West Ave. rear.	Lillian R. Turner Johnson	1930
Ida J. Dossar Employment Agency, 658 Haven Ave.	Ida J. Dossar	1928
Ocean City Employment Agency, 921 ½ West Ave.	Cordelia Maddox	
Ocean City Employment Agency, 3rd St.	Cordelia Maddox	
Tonchie Rogers Employment Office, 730 West Ave.	Tonchie Rogers	1902

Entertainment and Leisure	**Proprietor**	**Ref.***
Blue Circle Pool Room, 720 West Ave. Pool room.	William Reynolds, Sr.	1931
Neal's Pool Room, 719 Haven Ave. Pool room.	Charles Neal	
Reynold's, 712 West Ave. Billiard hall.	William Reynolds, Sr.	1930
Silver Slipper, 722 West Ave. Dance hall.	E. C. Williams	1922
Thompson Bros., 625 Haven Ave. Thoroughbred horse racing.	S. & W. Thompson	
Turner's Pool Hall, 719 Haven Ave. Billiard hall.	David R. Turner, Jr.	
Turner's Pool Hall, 719 Haven Ave. Billiard hall.	David R. Turner, Sr.	
Turner's Pool Hall, 722 West Ave. Billiard room.	David R. Turner, Sr.	
William H. Thomas, 636 West Ave. Pool room.	William H. Thomas	
William H. Thomas. Pocket Billiards & Restaurant.	William H. & Ida Thomas	
Williams' Auditorium, 722 West Ave. Pool hall, Elks Lodge.	Edward C. Williams	1922 & 1948

Financiers	**Proprietor**	**Ref.***
Thompson, 625 Haven Ave. Financier.	Sylvester W. Thompson. Sr.	
Thompson Brothers, 625 Haven Ave. Real Estate Investment.	S. & W. Thompson	
Trower Financial. Real Estate Investment, Finance.	John Sheppard Trower	1896

Grocers	**Proprietor**	**Ref.***
Anna May Davis	Anna May Davis	1937
Joseph Noel, 442 West Ave.	Joseph Noel	1948
Thomas H. Gunby, 201 Bay Ave.	Thomas H. Gunby	1950

Hoteliers and Guest House Owners	Proprietor	Ref.*
Al-May Inn. Inn and Limousine Service.	Algernon & Mary Carpenter	1937
Berlyn Cottage, 626 Haven Ave.	Catherine Simon	1921
Berlyn Cottage, 624 Haven Ave.	Catherine Simon	1928
Bolden's, 742 & 744 Moore Ave. Rooming house.		1937
Buck's Rooming House, 951 West Ave.	Rose Buck	1940
Davis Hotel, 315 4th St. Hotel.	William & Joanna Davis	1922
Edna Mae's Cottage, 921 West Ave. Furnished Rooms.	Edna Mae	1948
Egg Harbor Inn, 921 West Ave. Inn.	Cora Cooper	1937
Franklin Cottage, 730 West Ave. Boarding house.	Tonchie Rogers	1908
Hotel Comfort, 201 Bay Ave. Hotel & Café.	Samuel & Maggie Comfort	1925
Hotel Comfort, 201 Bay Ave. Hotel.	George Walker Williams	1957
John H. Carroll, 658 Haven Ave. Rooming house.	John H. Carroll	1948
Motley's, 913-915 West Ave. Furnished Rooms.	Isaac & Annie Motley	1928
Patrick Hotel, 4th St. & West Ave. (preceded Wawa). Rooming House		
Randolph Hotel, 7th St. & Simpson Ave. Hotel & Magistrate's Court for Blacks[59]		1999
Southern Inn, 656 West Ave. Inn.	Alford Bryant	1937
Thomas Hotel, 12 6th Street. Hotel.	William & Ida Thomas	1925
Washington Hotel (Pink Hotel), 12 6th Street. Hotel	Charles & Sarah Brydson	1945
Williams Bay View Guest House, 217 Bay Ave. Guest House	Annie M. Williams	1955
Williams Guest House, 221 Bay Ave. (former Hotel Comfort out building)	George Walker Williams	1972
Williams Guest House, 225 Bay Ave. Guest House.	George Walker Williams	1972

Landscape Gardeners	Proprietor	Ref.*
Alves's, 225 Bay Ave. Gardener, Florist.	William & Viola Alves, Lillian Cuff	1930
Brown's Landscaping, 11 W. 7th Street. Gardening.	William R. Brown	
Decker Gardening, 119 7th St. Gardening.	Rev. William H. Decker	1914
Decker Gardening, 656 Central Ave. Gardening.	Rev. William H. Decker	
Flowers Gardening, 636 West Ave. Gardening.	Monterey Flowers	1921
Money's Landscaping, 201 Simpson Ave. Gardening.	Elmer O. Money	
Pye Landscaping, 6 2nd St. Gardening.	John S. Pye	

Launderers	Proprietor	Ref.*
Baltimore Laundry, 326 West Ave. Laundry.	Mary Jackson	1893
Bay Villa Laundry, 217 Bay Ave. Laundry.	Nathan & Frances Freeman	1916
Draper's, Asbury Ave. below 4th St. Laundry.	Elizabeth Draper	1914
Freeman's Laundry, 231 Bay Ave. Laundry.	Nathan & Frances Freeman	1930
King's American Laundry, Asbury Ave. below 4th St. Laundry.	Anna King	1892
Spick and Span Laundry, 420 West Ave. Laundry.	Mary Patterson	1925

Restaurateurs	Proprietor	Ref.*
701 Mosaic, 701 4th St. Jamaican Restaurant.	Herb Allwood & Pamela Womble	2021
Aunt Gert's Light Lunch, 706 West Ave.	Gertrude Pennington	1937
Bean House, 7th St. west of Haven Ave.	Tommy Miles	
Blue Circle Café, 113 7th St.	Richard & Mary Murrel	1928
Chinese Restaurant, 712 West Ave.	Roger & Beatrice Williams	1950
Dick's, 717 West Ave.	Richard Warren	
Dick's, 730 West Ave.	Richard Warren	
Dirty Slim's, 712 West Ave.	Slim Jordan	
Emma Smith's, 644 West Ave.		1911
Ernest Lee, 727 West Ave.	Ernest S. Lee	1937
Green Pea Café, 113 7th St.	Ernest & Edmonia Casson	1937
Hughes', 654 West Ave.	Pauline Hughes	1930
Ida's, 658-660 Haven Ave. Ice Cream Store.	Ida J. Bush	1922
Isaac Motley & Sons, 915 West Ave. Light Lunch & Sandwiches.	Isaac Motley	1937
Johnson's, 442 West Ave.	John & Minerva Johnson	1937
June Bug's Fish Market, 744 West Ave. Fresh or Fried Fish.	June Bug	1974
Mom Pat's, 733 West Ave.	Mary Patterson	
Mr. Eddie's, 733 West Ave.	Eddie Williams	
Pop Sample's, 101 7th St.	Edward C. Sample	1948
Pop's, 735 West Ave.	Edward C. Williams	1911
Rickett's, 418 West Ave.	Joseph & Estelle Ricketts	1928
Sample's, 101 7th St.	Edward C. Sample & Wilbert Gerald	1960
Steven's, 100 6th St. Restaurant & Soda Fountain.	Melvin & Catherine Stevens	
Tasty Luncheonette, 101 7th St.	Charles Wright	1948
Thomas, 727 West Ave.	William H. Thomas	
Washington Tea Room, 210 7th St.	Marion & Hattie Rutter	1937
Watson's Coffee Shop, 717 Simpson Ave.	Eliza Spruill	1948
Westside Luncheonette, 7th St. west of Haven.	Lawrence & Mrs. Elliott	1976
Whitby's, 406 West Ave.	Timothy Whitby	1928
Williams & Hawkins. Café.	E. C. Williams & A. B. Hawkins	1918

Retailers	Proprietor	Ref.*
Alice's, 442 West Ave. Variety Store.	Alice Barnes	
Bryant's, 442 West Ave. Variety Store.	Minerva Bryant	
Ida J. Bush, 658-660 Haven Ave. Ice Cream Store.	Ida Bush	1922
Money's, 626 West Ave. Variety Store.	Elmer & Elizabeth Money	1937
Mosley/Collins, 424 West Ave. Confectioner.	Fred Mosley, Letha Collins	1948
Still's, 8th St. & Boardwalk. Confectioner.	Jacob Still	1893
Tia's Beauty Supply, 626 Haven Ave. Beauty Supply.	Tia D. Money	
Trower's Ice Cream Parlors, 8th St. & Asbury Ave.	John Sheppard Trower	1897

Sales & Service	Proprietor	Ref.*
Ace Photography, 424 West Ave. Photographer.		
Archie Harris, 636 Simpson Ave. Jobber.	Archie Harris	1922
Brady's Shoe shop. Shoe Repair.	One leg Brady	
Carroll's Sinclair Service Station, 6th St. & West Ave.	John Carroll	
Carter's Chemical Co., 106 6th St. Bleach Bottling.	Irving & Esther Carter	1948
Cooper's, 312 Oxford Ct. Garbage Contractor.	Webster Cooper	1937
Daniel L. Money, 609 Bay Avenue. Dog Trainer		1970
Diamond Tailor Shop, 104 6th St. rear.	Joel Brown Still	
Florida D. Jones, 632 Simpson Ave. Job Printer.	Florida D. Jones	1922
Freeman Junk. Junk Dealer.	Nathan Freeman	1915
Gerald's Janitorial Service, 448 Asbury Ave. General Maintenance	Wilbert Gerald	1976
Glenn's. Fish Monger.	J. C. Glenn	
Granger's Janitorial Service, 740 West Ave.	Peter Granger	
Green's Coal. Coal Retailer.	Oakford Green	1930
Harrison Martin Miller Florists, 217 4th St.	Harrison Martin Miller	1915
Harrison Shaw, 201 Bay Ave. Blacksmith		1915
Hawkins Dressmaker, 721 West Ave.	Mary B. Hawkins	1914
Henry's Ice. Ice Sales & Delivery.	Daniel Robinson Henry	
Hogan's Tailors, 721 West Ave.	John Hogan	1921
Hutchens' Rags, 450 West Ave. Rag picking.	Gilbert Hutchens	
Isaac Motley & Son, 915 West Ave. Ice Sales & Delivery	Isaac Motley	1937
Mallory Druggist. Druggist.	Emmett Mallory	1930
Motley's, 706 West Ave. Ice Sales & Delivery.	John Motley	
Motley's Press, 444 West Ave. Printer, Newspaper Columnist.	Clarence Motley	1937
Pennington Day Spa, 636 Asbury Ave.	Ronald Rolls Pennington	
Polk's Tailor Shop, 724 West Ave. Clothes Maker.	Earl Martin Polk	1930
Pote's Tailor Shop, West Ave.	Benjamin Pote	
Quinton's, 710 West Ave. Junk Dealer.	Samuel Quinton	1930
Raglin's, 708 West Ave. Junk Dealer.	Alphonso Raglin	1930
Still Waters, 8th St. & Wesley Ave. Massage Parlor.	Ronald Rolls Pennington	1999
Still's, 609 Asbury Ave. Tailor Shop.	Joel Brown Still	1937
Turner Bros. Service Station, 7th St. & West Ave.	Edward & David Turner	1937
Turner's Mobil Station, Cor. 7th St. & West Ave.	Edward Turner	1948
Washington Pianos, 630 Haven Ave. Piano Tuner.	John E. Washington	1922
William Mitchell, Sr. & Son. Photographer.	William S. Mitchell	1930
Mary Jane's Nursery, 439 West Ave.	Mary Jane Granger	1996
Miles Window Washing, 220 Haven Ave. Window Cleaning.	Tommie Miles	
Williams Windows, 708 West Ave. Window Cleaning.	George A. Williams	

Transportation Expresses	Proprietor	Ref.*
Carroll's Hauling, 658 Haven Ave. Truck Hauling.	John H. Carroll	1948
George Fleming, 613 West Avenue. Teamster.		1910
George H. Fleming, 225 Simpson Ave. General Hauling.		1930
Griffin's Towing Service, 632 Haven Ave.	William Griffin	1978
Hughes, 654 West Ave. Drayman.	Benjamin K. Hughes	1930
John B. Thompson & Son, 732 West Ave. Bakery Delivery.	J. Thompson	

Johnson's. Trucking & Teaming.	George A. Johnson	1948
Morgan Brothers, 629 Bay Ave. Taxi service.	George & Frank Morgan	1928
Morris'. Trucking & Teaming.	Sye Morris	1948
Ocean City Taxi Company, 302 8th St. Taxi Service.	George W. Morgan	
Rowell's Moving & Hauling Co., 437 Simpson Ave. Moving.	Sam Rowell	
Royal Taxi, 8th St. & Asbury Ave. Taxi Service.	George W. Morgan	1922
Steven's Taxi Service, 100 6th St. Taxi Service.	Melvin Stevens	1930
Stewart's Taxi Service. Taxi Service.	Johnnie Stewart	
Union Transfer Company, 8th St. & West Ave. Baggage Handling	John B. Thompson	1901

Churches	Leader	Ref.*
Church of God in Christ (COGIC), 900 block Simpson Ave.	Willie Parrish	
Divine Spiritualist, 410 West Ave.	Frances Stephenson	1937
First Spiritualist, 301 West Ave.	Mozelle Neal	1937
Hopewell Baptist, 207 3rd St.	Archie H. Harris, Sr.	c. 1928
House of Prayer, 205 3rd St.	H. H. Harris, Conductor	1924
Macedonia United Methodist, 10th St. & Simpson Ave.		1899
Shiloh Baptist, 7 E. 7th St.	Israel Grant Harris	1912
St. James African Methodist Episcopal, 7th St. & Haven Ave		1906
(Union) Tabernacle Baptist, 760 West Ave.	William T. Amiger	1901

Organizations	Leader	Ref.*
Choraleers Combined Choir		
Economic, Civic & Community League	Samuel J. Comfort	
Eastern Star, Ladies' auxiliary		
Geranium Temple of Lady Elks Lodge 767.	Anna M. Taylor	
Girl Reserves.	Martha Brown, Advisor	
Knights of Pythias, 722 West Ave. Fraternal organization		
Knights of Pythias, 707 Asbury Ave. Fraternal organization		
Maiden Dukes Athletic Club (Duchesses).	Anna Mae Cooper, Advisor	
Neighborhood Preservation Committee	Loretta Harris, Chairperson	2008
Ocean City Old Timers. Social club		
Pride of Ocean City Elks Lodge 767, 618 Bay Ave.		
Prince Hall Lodge No. 27 Free and Accepted Masons		
Progressive Four		
Queen Esther Court. Ladies' auxiliary		
Sabre Gents, 625 Haven Ave. Boys' club and basketball team		
West Side Independent Club		
Westside Hunting Club, 625 Haven Ave.		

Ref. denotes the year the business or entity was first identified and not the year it was established.

Classified Advertisers Guide
(Yellow Pages)

Bakeries

Southern Home Bakery 432 West av

Barbers and Beauticians

Barbers
Alston Archie 736 West av

Polk's Ocean City Directory and Guide, 1948

COMPLIMENTS of

CARLOS BARBER SHOP

719 Haven Avenue, Ocean City, N. J.

Carlos Davis, Prop.

Carlos Barber Shop, St. James A.M.E. Church Men's Day program booklet, 1969

BARBERS
DeFranco Geramo Boardwalk cor
Gillett Charles C 740 West ave
Murray Daniel J 754 Asbury ave

Charles C. Gillett, 740 West Ave.
Polk's Ocean City Directory and Guide, 1913

Barbers
Adelizzi Anthony 950 Asbury av
Annarelli Michl 1014 Asbury av
Cangelliero Angelo 119 10th
Cerruti Peter 711 Asbury av
Corona Alexander 518 9th
Draine Willard C 660 West av
Gerbasio Domenic 615 8th
Haller Clarissa J 740 West av
Nocito Fred 311 4th
Pye John S 15 7th

Willard C. Drain(e)e, Clarissa Haller, and John S. Pye. Polk's Ocean City Directory and Guide, 1924

Barbers—Contd
DeLuca Benj 955 Asbury av
D'Imperio Fred 617 8th
Draine Willard C 660 West av
Graham Jas W 407 8th
Haller Clarissa J 738 West av
Ideal Shaving Parlor 420 8th
McCusker Patk 311 4th
Ouerques Gaetano 1136 Asbury av
Pullo Jerry 518 9th
Pye John S 518 9th

Willard C Draine; John S. Pye and Jerry Pullo were barbers at the same shop on 9th Street.
Polk's Ocean City Directory and Guide, 1928

Beauty Culture   First Class Service

Madam Rachel A. Bryan
Hair Dresser

115 7th St.   Ocean City, N. J.

Madam Rachel A. Bryan, hairdresser
Polk's Ocean City Directory and Guide, 1928

EDNA MAE'S
BEAUTY SALON

921 West Ave.   Phone 0929

Styling · Hair Tinting · Manicuring

Specialty: Children's Clinic · Friday and Saturday · Special Rates
Colored Clientele

Edna Mae's Beauty Salon, 921 West Avenue.
Ocean City Sentinel Ledger, July 3, 1954

LADIES' HAIR DRESSERS

Allen Margaret 910 Boardwalk
Jarvis Mrs Boardwalk nr 8th
Thompson Sarah E 732 West ave

Sarah E. Thompson, 732 West Ave.
Ocean City Business Directory, 1916-1917

Building Contractors

PAUL S. DAVIS
General Contractor
HAULING and TRUCKING
Dealer in
SAND, GRAVEL and TOP SOIL

421 West Ave.   Phone Connection

Paul S. Davis, General Contractor
Polk's Ocean City Directory and Guide, 1928

JOSEPH HANNAH
Brick Mason
Concrete - Brick & Stone Work
213 Simpson Avenue
Ocean City, N. J.
Phone 399-1873

BRICK, BLOCK, STONE, STUCCO AND CONCRETE WORK

JOE HANNAH

213 SIMPSON AVENUE
P.O. BOX 291   398-2816
OCEAN CITY, NEW JERSEY 08226   399-1873

Joseph Hannah, Mason. St. James A.M.E. Church Annual Men's Day Program, 1969 & I.B.P.O.E. of W Geranium Temple No. 469 Appreciation Dinner, 1975

WILLIAM DAVIS
GENERAL
CONTRACTOR

DAVIS HOTEL

Cementing   Pile-Driving
Lawn-Work

315 Fourth Street and 346 West Ave.
OCEAN CITY, N. J.

PHONE 169-J

William Davis, General Contractor, 315 4th St. and 346 West Ave. Boyd's Directory, 1929

Archie Harris, 636 Simpson Ave. Jobber.
Ocean City Sentinel, July 13, 1922

S. PYE

Expert Wall Scraping and Calcimining

WHITE WASHING

660 West Avenue
OCEAN CITY, N. J.

S. Pye, Scraping and Calcimining, 660 West Avenue
(Drain's Rooming House).
Polk's Ocean City Directory and Guide, 1922

Paper Hangers

Fischer Fredk E 7 Walton pl
Fisher Calvin L 808 Wesley av
Hutchins E Thos 334 Central av
MAXWELL ELLWOOD H, 343 Asbury av, Tel 0161
Pye John S 6 2d

Paper Hangers.
Ocean City Directory and Guide Book, 1948

Pullen Robt (Esther; Ferguson's Coal) r Palermo
—Wm T (Mary A) clk A&P h1130 Haven av
Pullins Jas J (Emma) h609 Ocean
Pullo Jerry (Marie) barber 406 7th h432 Asbury av
—Paul V (Jewel) barber Jerry Pullo h137 Asbury av
Pursell E Henrietta r1209 Asbury av
Putnam Anna G Mrs r1326 Wesley av
Putney Chas M (Mabel M) metallurgist h102 E 13th
—Geo N student h102 E 13th
Pye John S (Fannie) paper hngr 6 2d h do

John S. Pye, Paper Hanger.
Ocean City Directory

Painting, Powerwashing, & Tree Trimming

Earl Rowell
223 Haven Ave., Ocean City, NJ
(609)225-3040
(609)399-7531

Earl Rowell, painter
Business card.

Earl Rowell
Painting · Powerwashing · Tree Trimming

223 Haven Avenue · Ocean City, NJ 08226
Phone (609) 399-7531 · Cell (609) 231-6015

Earl Rowell, painter
Business card.

Phones: 399-0207
399-8270

SYLVESTER THOMPSON & SONS, Inc.
BULKHEADS and FOUNDATIONS
Grading and Graveling -- Tractor Service

625 Haven Avenue   Ocean City, N.J.

Sylvester Thomphson & Sons, Inc.
Business card.

Ocean City (609) 399-0059   KENNETH WRIGHT
THE WOOD DOCTOR
Carpentry Specialty

Improvements   Alterations
Doors   Windows
Kitchens   Bath
Decks   Additions

443 N. Tennessee Ave.   Phone/Fax (609) 344-8904
Atlantic City, NJ 08401   Digital Beeper 525-4924

Kenneth Wright, The Wood Doctor, Business card.
Operated his carpentry business from Atlantic City
and later from 434 West Avenue, Ocean City.

S. W. Thompson, Pilings and Bulkheads. See feature business.

Caterers

Naomi's Catering Service
Ocean City Old Timers program booklet, 1969

Ann Battle Baker and Anna Bowen Edwards
Livingston caterers, I.B.P.O.E. of W Geranium
Temple No. 469, Appreciation Dinner, 1975

BASKET MADE OUT OF BREAD DOUGH

NAOMI CATERING SERVICE

Specializing in
Decorative Center Pieces,
Hors d'Oeuvres, Cocktail
Sandwiches, Bon Voyage
Parties
63 Kosciusko Street

Brooklyn, N. Y.
and Ocean City, N. J.

Naomi's Catering Service, Brooklyn and Ocean City. Naomi Wright operated a catering business in Brooklyn, New York and at 433 West Avenue, Ocean City. Her specialty was edible bread baskets.
Ocean City Old Timers program booklet, 1971

Employment Agencies

DOMESTIC EMPLOYMENT AGENCY
LILLIAN R. TURNER, Mgr.
First Class Help Furnished

400 West Avenue   Ocean City, N. J.   Phone 770

Domestic Employment Agency, 400 West Avenue
Polk's Ocean City Directory

IDA J. DOSSAR
EMPLOYMENT AGENCY
Reliable Help Furnished

658 Haven Ave.   Tel. 221

Ida J. Dossar Employment Agency,
658 Haven Avenue.
Polk's Ocean City Directory and Guide, 1928

OCEAN CITY EMPLOYMENT AGENCY
915 WEST AVENUE

MISS CORDELIA MADDOX, Proprietor

Phone 399-1986

OCEAN CITY
Employment Agency

915 West Avenue
Phone 399-1986

MISS CORDELIA MADDOX, Prop.
Res.: 242 Bodine Avenue
Res. Ph.: KI 3-1427 - Swarthmore, Pa.

Ocean City Employment Agency, Cordelia Maddox proprietor.
Ocean City Old Timers program booklet, 1969

Entertainment and Leisure

BILLLIARD AND POOL ROOMS AND BOWLING ALLEYS

Barnett Bros 916 Boardwalk
Bowling Casino Boardwalk cor Moorlyn ter
Chapman R Boardwalk nr 10th
Flemming George H 722 West ave
Seno M Boardwalk nr 7th

George Fleming, 722 West Avenue. Billiards, 1913

Hoteliers and Guest House Owners

A BEAUTIFUL LOCATION—

for a cool, quiet, restful, healthful vacation, go to

HOTEL COMFORT
Ocean City, N. J.

Situated at edge of the beautiful bay, and five minutes walk to the Ocean and boardwalk.

For reservations, write

C. A. GRAINE
HOTEL COMFORT
210 Bay Avenue, Ocean City, N. J.
C. A. Graine, Manager

Hotel Comfort, 210 (sic 201) Bay Avenue, C. A. Graine Manager   Cone's Smoke Shop postcard.

Mrs. M. B. Comfort proprietress of Hotel Comfort and Cafe in 1922.
Ocean City Ledger, June 14, 1922

Hotel Comfort matchbook (exterior).   *Hotel Comfort rates on matchbook (interior).*
George W. Williams proprietor. c. 1957.   *Reservations taken at Bay View guest house.*
Photos courtesy Carol Williams-Pullins.

Landscape Gardeners

WM. BROWN HAULING, Inc.
— Landscape Gardening —
"Your Dirt," Is Our Business
GRAVEL - TOPSOIL - FILL - STONES
7th and SIMPSON AVENUE
Phone 399-4575   Ocean City, N

Wm. Brown Hauling, Inc.
Ocean City Old Timers booklet, 1969

105

Phone 399-4575   Landscape Gardening

WM. BROWN HAULING, Inc.

"Your Dirt" Is Our Business

GRAVEL - TOPSOIL - FILL - STONES

7th and Simpson Avenue   Ocean City, N. J.

Wm. Brown Hauling, Inc.
Business Card.

Landscape Gardeners
Cairns John 347 West av
Davis Leon G 1500 West av
DAVIS WILLIAM, 215 4th, Phone 169-J
Flowers Montra 406 West av
Johnson Walter C 148 Asbury av
Martin John D 646 Haven av

William Davis, Montra Flowers, and John D. Martin.
Ocean City Directory, 1924

Launderers

BALTIMORE LAUNDRY,
326 WEST AVENUE,

All work done in First Class Style.

SATISFACTION GUARANTEED.

MRS. MARY JACKSON, Proprietress.

Baltimore Laundry
Polk's Ocean City Guide Book and Directory, 1892

King's American Laundry,
Asbury Ave., below Fourth St.,
OCEAN CITY, N. J.
All work done in first-class style.

MRS. ANNA KING, Proprietress.

King's American Laundry
Polk's Ocean City Guide Book and Directory, 1892

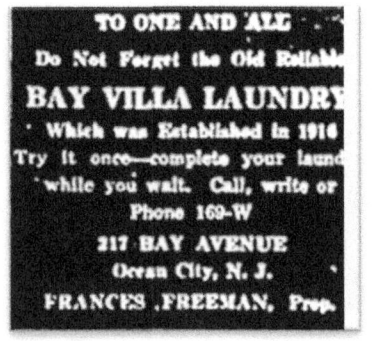

TO ONE AND ALL
Do Not Forget the Old Reliable
BAY VILLA LAUNDRY
Which was Established in 1916
Try it once—complete your laundry
while you wait. Call, write or
Phone 169-W
217 BAY AVENUE
Ocean City, N. J.
FRANCES FREEMAN, Prop.

Bay Villa Laundry. Frances Freeman, proprietor.
Established 1916. Ocean City Sentinel, June 1922

Spick and Span
LAUNDRY
SANITARY METHODS
FREE DELIVERY
We Guard Against Loss
420 West Avenue
OCEAN CITY, N. J.
MRS. MARY PATTERSON
Phone 144-W   Prop.

Spick and Span Laundry. Mary Patterson proprietor.
Ocean City Sentinel Ledger, July 1925

Restaurateurs

Restaurants
Blue Circle Cafe 113 7th
Carl's Restaurant 802-04-06 Boardwalk
Cheeseman John W 938 Asbury av

Blue Circle Cafe, Richard and Mary Murrel
Polk's Ocean City Directory and Guide, 1928

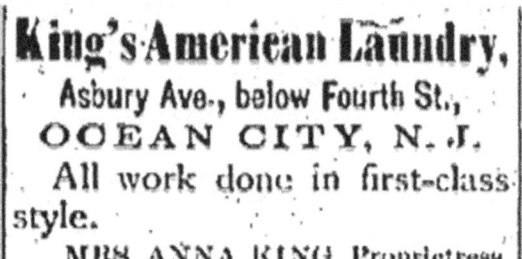

WEST'S RESTAURANT, 760
Guide and left top lines
Williams Edw 716 West av
Windsor Restaurant 396 Boa

Edward Williams, 716 West Avenue. Restaurant
Polk's Ocean City Directory, 1948

Williams & Hawkins (Edward C Williams and M B Hawkins) restaurant 735 West ave

Williams & Hawkins, 735 West Avenue. Restaurant.
Polk's Ocean City Directory, 1921

WESTSIDE
LUNCHEONETTE
Cor. 7th St. and Moore Ave
Ocean City, N. J.

Westside Luncheonette
Ocean City Old Timers program booklet, 1969

Mr. & Mrs. Elliot Lawrence
WEST SIDE LUNCHEONETTE
7TH STREET
OCEAN CITY, N.J. 08226

Elliot's Westside Luncheonette, St. James A.M.E.
Church Annual Women's Day program, 1976

Come Eat At "PETE'S"
740 West Avenue
Ocean City, N. J.
Soul Food All The Way
Lima Beans and Ham Hocks
Every Day
Take Out Service
PETE and MARY, Owners

Pete's, 740 West Avenue
Ocean City Old Timers program booklet, 1969

Tasty Luncheonette
Charles Wright owner, 1947

Retailers

BRYANT'S STORE
442 West Avenue
Ocean City, N. J.

Bryant's
Ocean City Old Timers program booklet, 1969

GERALD'S IMPORTS
WIGS - CLOTHES - PANTYHOSE - PARFUM - WOOD CARVIN(
P.O. BOX 583
— WE DELIVER —
PHONE 399-7425   OCEAN CITY, N. J. 08(

Gerald's Imports
Ocean City Old Timers program booklet, 1971

Still's, 8th St. and the Boardwalk.
Polk's Ocean City Directory, 1893

Sales & Service

1364 OCEAN CITY BUSINESS DIRECTORY, 1915-'16.

JUNK DEALER

Freeman Nathan 222 Simpson ave

Nathan Freeman, junk dealer
Ocean City Business Directory, 1915-16

WILBERT GERALD

Complete Janitor Service

Office - Home - Stores

717 West Avenue, Ocean City, N. J.

Phone 399-7425 or 399-9826

Wilbert Gerald Complete Janitor Service, St. James
A.M.E. Church Annual Men's Day program, 1969

WILBERT GERALD

COMPLETE JANITOR SERVICE

Floors - Windows - Etc. — Rug Shampoo

OFFICE - HOME - STORES - HOUSE CLEANING

717 WEST AVENUE

Phones: 399-7425 or 399-9826   Ocean City, N. J.

Wilbert Gerald Complete Janitor Service,
Ocean City Old Timers booklet, 1969

WILBERT GERALD'S
JANITORIAL SERVICE & WINDOW CLEANING
Commercial - Residential
Specializing in
High Rise Building Maintenance
Scaffold Window Cleaning
General Maintenance   Hourly House Cleaning
Floors - Rug Shampooing

448 Asbury Avenue   Ocean City, N.J. 0822

Wilbert Geralds's Janitorial. St. James A.M.E.
Church Women's Day program, 1976

GERALD'S
JANITORIAL SERVICE

448 Asbury Avenue
Ocean City, N. J. 08226

Phone: 399-7452

Gerald's Janitorial Service.

JONES FLORIDA D 632 Simpson ave Phone 427

CARDS   **BILL HEADS**
ENVELOPES   **LETTER HEADS**

FLORIDA D. JONES
Job Printer

632 SIMPSON AVE.
Phone 427

Florida David Jones, printer.
Polk's Ocean City Directory and Guide, 1922

EDWARD C. WILLIAMS

REAL ESTATE, INSURANCE
AND
NOTARY PUBLIC

923 West Ave.   Ocean City, N. J.   Phone 357

Edward C. Williams
Real Estate, Insurance and Notary Public,
Polk's Ocean City Directory and Guide, 1948

Williams Edward C (Williams & Hawkins) and tailor
737 and h 721 West ave

Williams & Hawkins. Tailors.
Polk's Ocean City Directory, 1921

WILLIAMS EDWARD C (Florence), Real Estate, Insurance and Notary 923 West av, Tel 357-J, Tailor 722 West av, h737 do, Tel 963 (See adv In Real Estate Dept)

Edward C. & Florence Williams, 923 West Ave. Real estate, insurance, and notary services. Telephone: Tailor shop at 722 West Ave. Residence 737 West Ave. with telephone. Polk's Ocean City Directory, 1928

Greetings From A Grand
Old Timer
WILLIAM MITCHELL, SR. and SON, BILL
Ocean City, N. J.

William Mitchell, Sr. and Son, Bill, photographers Ocean City Old Timers program booklet, 1971

TURNERS MOBILE STATION

7th 7 West Ave.

Ocean City, N. J.

Turner's Mobil Station, St. James A.M.E. Church Annual Men's Day Program, 1969

Ice—Dealers
American Ice Co 208 12th
Fitzgerald Jos F 301 10th
Motley John I 706 West av

Motley's ICE Service
706 West Avenue ◇ Ocean City, N. J.
Phone 9045

John Motley Ice. Ice Dealer. Joan Motley, firstborn of John Motley, on advertising piece. c. early 1940s. Photo courtesy John Motley, brother of Joan Motley.

COMPLIMENTS and BEST WISHES
DANIEL L. MONEY
DOG TRAINING CLASSES and INDIVIDUAL INSTRUCTIO
★ Obedience ★ Advanced Obedience ★ Specialized Tra
609 BAY AVENUE
Phone 399-2054   Ocean City, N. J.

Daniel L. Money. Dog Training. Ocean City Old Timers program booklet, 1970

PETER GRANGER MAINTENANCE CO.
740 WEST AVENUE
Phone 399-4748   Ocean City, N. J.
COMPLETE JANITORIAL SERVICE
Floor Cleaning and Waxing - Window Cleaning -
Gardening - Maid Service - Light Hauling
— We Serve Cape May County —

Peter Granger Maintenance Co. Ocean City Old Timers program booklet, 1969

Tommy Miles Window Cleaning was a home-based operation. Miles worked at Bob's Seafood, City of Ocean City Recreation Department, and Peter Granger Cleaning Services before branching out on his own. Photo c. 2022.

Transportation Expresses

Griffin's Towing Service
632 HAVEN AVENUE
OCEAN CITY, NEW JERSEY 08226
PHONE 399-0914

Griffin's Towing Service.

TEAMSTERS
Fleming George H, 613 West ave

George Fleming, Teamster.

Trucking and Teaming
Berger John H 3160 Asbury av
Johnson Geo 302 West av

George Johnson. Trucking and Teaming.
Polk's Ocean City Directory and Guide, 1928

TAXI SERVICE Tel. 611 Never Closed
CALL MORGAN BROS. Ocean City, N. J.

Morgan Bros. Taxi Service.
Polk's Ocean City Directory, 1924

Sam Rowell's Moving & Hauling.
Ocean City Sentinel Ledger

Samuel Rowell & Sons. Moving company.
Photo courtesy Ocean City Historical Museum.

SEVEN PASSENGER SEDAN — BY THE TRIP OR HOUR DAY OR NIGHT
Royal Taxi Service
(GEORGE W. MORGAN)
AUTOMOBILE SERVICE
Res. Phone 1095 — Ask for Morgan
Taxi Stand — Ocean City, N. J.
Eighth and Asbury Ave. — Phone 717

Royal Taxi Service. George W. Morgan
Polk's Ocean City directory, 1928

Baggage Called For and Delivered
Local and Long Distance Truck Service
Phone 236-W
J. B THOMPSON & SON EXPRESS
722 WEST AVENUE. OCEAN CITY, N. J.

John B. Thompson & Son Express Company

110

Ocean City's African American Neighborhood plaque. Dedicated 2010.

The Westside memorial plaque at 7th Street and West Avenue pays tribute to community founders and inspires future generations to be all that they can be.

> *"This small industrious community has produced policemen, firemen, military men and women, doctors, attorneys, educators, musicians, ministers, beauty queens, athletes, city laborers, politicians, and many good people."*

The descendants of those founders continue to live up to the challenge. Later generations included accountants, analysts, and artists. Add to the list the many business executives, engineers (NASA and GM), and MBAs (Stanford and Drexel). The sky was the limit for pilots, a flight engineer, a WAC (Womer's Air Corps), and flight steward. An FBI trainer, operating room nurse, and various types of technicians round out the field. An unending list of accomplished Westside residents could be added to those mentioned on the original plaque.

***

Sanborn Company map, Sheet 95. Westside north end. 1st Street to Strand. Ocean City, NJ 1909.[60]

CHAPTER 2
BIRDS OF A FEATHER

Where people of color settled within the town was the result of many things – choice, money, employment, housing availability, and access. Early builders concentrated most residential development east of The West Jersey Railroad on West Avenue and Pennsylvania Reading Seashore Railroad on Haven Avenue. Westside residential units developed alongside the railroad tracks and spurs amid a mix of light industrial and commercial uses. A large lumber yard sat on the corner of 4th Street and West Avenue. Wagon shops and horse stables defined the neighborhood.

As the town grew, a water tower, sewer plant, and other essential city infrastructure added to the hodge-podge nature of the Westside. With the advent of motorized vehicles came service stations: Jimmy's Exxon Service Center, 4th & West; Rumer's, Carroll's Sinclair, Turner's Mobil, and four stations on 9th Street (Joel's Hess Station, Texaco, Esso, Sunoco). Carroll's and Turner's were minority owned. The Westside with its mix of uses and reasonably priced housing became the area where people of color settled.

Some of the oldest housing stock on the island today is on the Westside. A mix of housing styles eventually spread across the Westside. Single-family homes, small bungalows, boarding houses, and multi-unit housing i.e., Oxford Court, Rose Court, Widows' Row, Cranmer's Row, and Mercer Place provided housing for working class people. Multi-use buildings combining residential use and commercial operations were common. Identifying structurally sound houses scheduled for demolition elsewhere on the island and relocating them to the Westside was also common. The Westside had its own full-fledged hotels. In time, people of color invested in second homes and income properties in the 100 block north of Hotel Comfort extending the northern limits of the Westside.

NEED HOUSES FOR WORKING PEOPLE

B. F. Goetz, Real Estate Agent, Says This Is Crying Necessity Here.

A group of Ocean City men were discussing, a few days ago, the need of houses for working men in this resort for the use of these men and their families all the year.

One of the number was B. F. Goetz, who specializes in real estate north of Sixth street, and who is known to a large number of visitors to this city.

Mr. Goetz said it is a shame the way many working men are running around Ocean City, from agency to agency, trying to find suitable cottages. Every day such people go to his office at Fourth street and Atlantic avenue, he said, adding that there were three women at his office that day looking for such houses.

"Do you know that right now," Mr. Goetz continued, "that right today over 400 working men are earning their living here and spending their money in nearby towns instead of with Ocean City?"

Another member of the party said that one of the causes for this is there are no reasonable rents, and very few unreasonable ones."

Mr. Goetz, who took occasion emphatically to declare that he is not to be called a "realtor," gave it as his view that a number of houses are wanted by the colored people, a committee of colored people having recently called on him and requested him to build some cottages for them.

Ocean City Sentinel, 1922

NEWS OF OCEAN CITY

By MAJOR L. R. THOMAS, Manager of The Daily Press' Ocean City Bureau

COLORED WAITER PURCHASES A FINE PROPERTY.

H. W. Brooks, head waiter at the Oceanic Hotel, purchased on last Saturday of Sutton & Carson their recently built twin cottages, 654-656 West avenue. He will hold them for renting purposes.

Real Estate Broker Darby made the sale.

Colored Waiter Purchases a Fine Property.
The Daily Press Ocean City Bureau, June 1911

Heretofore viable homes have succumbed to monied interests and wrecking crews. Father Time, Mother Nature, urban renewal, and gentrification have taken a toll on a once thriving neighborhood across the Westside evoking memories of yesteryear in the sprinkling of homes that survived.

Sanborn Company map, Sheet 94. Westside south end. Strand to 8th Street. Ocean City, NJ 1909.[61]

Single-Family Housing

As with any American city or town, obtaining a single-family home was a symbol of status. Westside single family housing came in all styles and sizes.

Marie Adams and family, corner 4th Street and West Avenue (house in background). Professional baseball scouts came to Ocean City to give son Jerry Adams a tryout for a spot as a major league catcher. The tryout took place at the baseball field at 5th Street and Bay Avenue. Men in foreground unrelated to Adams Family. Photo c. 1960s.[62]

Mar 19, 1965

GOING DOWN — Among 33 building units being demolished voluntarily by owners under city's community development program is above home at 640 West Ave., in original Urban Renewal project along with 11 other u n i t s known as Kramer's Row in same block.   (Senior Studios Photo)

In 1937, Charles and Florence Sye Sturgis of Salem and Cumberland Counties respectively rented this house at 640 West Avenue after years in the restaurant business in Camden. Following the death of her husband, widow Florence took in her brother, Morris Sye, who spent a brief period in the hauling business before working at a coal yard. 640 West Avenue and nearby Cranmer's Row were demolished in 1965 as part of an urban renewal project. Florence returned to Camden where she died in 1966. Morris moved to Atlantic City where he died in 1970.[63]

Chalmers homestead, 612 Simpson Avenue. Now a summer house for family members.

Thomas Randall Chalmers (1885-abt 1933) and Virgie Hayes Chalmers (1895-1950) owned this 1056 sq. ft. home. The Chalmers branch of the family was from South Boston (formerly known as Boyd's Ferry), Halifax County, Virginia. Thomas was a steelworker in Philadelphia before coming to Ocean City in the 1920s. He worked as a rigger until his early death. The family included fifteen children, eight male and seven female. In 1940, four brothers lived together at nearby 624 Simpson Avenue. Of the eight males, five served in World War II and one in the Korean Conflict. The family name is often referred to as Chalmus.

Alice Emily Cornish Peterson (1894-2003). Photo courtesy of Ocean City Sentinel Ledger, 2003.[64]

Ocean City's Alice Peterson is 108 years old

By CHRISTOPHER SOUTH
Ocean City Sentinel

OCEAN CITY - "I had a quiet life," Alice Peterson said, summing up a life that has seen parts of three centuries.

Peterson, who turned 108 last Friday was born on Feb. 22, 1894, in Sharptown, Md. One of three boys and five girls, only Peterson and her sister Elizabeth Johnson, 97, are still living. According to Peterson, her sister is sensitive about telling her age, but she has no problem telling people how old she is.

"Everywhere I go I tell my age, I don't mind, I'm glad I lived this long." Peterson said.

"Age doesn't mean anything as long as you're healthy," she said.

And Peterson has managed to keep her health for the

Christopher South/Ocean City Sentinel
Ocean City's Alice Peterson smiles after celebrating her 109th birthday on Friday, Feb. 22.

Nathaniel and Alice Peterson and family moved into this bungalow after relocating from their Mercer Place row home where they lived since arriving in Ocean City in the late 1920s. Maryland born Alice Peterson was a 109-year-old widow when she passed away in 2003 having survived her late husband forty-three years. She credited her simple lifestyle, family, friends, and Shiloh Baptist Church with sustaining her as she lived into three different centuries.

Peterson family home, 110 7th Street. Built 1960. Photo c. 2023.

Alvin Thompson came to Ocean City from Millville at about age four. As an adult, he worked as a chauffeur and pile driver while living on the Westside near Powell's Riding Stable. He later lived on Widows' Row. In 1944, now a pinsetter at Stainton's Playland, he and wife Marion Johnson Thompson purchased a big 2.5-story house at 210 West Avenue from Howard S. Stainton for $1 and other good and valuable considerations. Ocean City cottages of the 1920s were decidedly different from what is considered a cottage today. The house once belonged to John Sheppard Trower. Alvin and Marion had no natural children but opened the

In Realtor ad for an 8-bedroom house (cottage) with chauffeur's quarters, 1921.

house to vacationing relatives and family members in need of temporary housing. Marion was named Marion Loretta Johnson at birth. Her middle name was later struck and replaced with Esther. Widowed midlife with no children, Marion gave up the big house to commercial developers. Her brother- in-law located a modest beach block bungalow scheduled for demolition and moved it to 146 Haven Avenue. She painted her house bright yellow. Family history reports Marion receiving a pair of moccasins or a pouch from her Native American mother-in-law, Henrietta Bowman Thompson. The moccasins or pouch were lost when an aging Marion had to leave her bungalow and move in with other family members.

Marion Loretta Johnson certificate of birth.[65]

117

In the 1940s, I loved getting away from Philadelphia and spending time at the shore with Aunt Marion and Uncle Al. They lived in a big house at 210 West Avenue. Early on, it was the only house in the area. Steps led from the street to a porch. The first floor had a living room (I was never allowed to sit in the living room), dining room (Aunt Marion did all her sewing in the dining room), and kitchen (something good was always cooking on the stove). The second floor consisted of six or seven small bedrooms. Students from Lincoln University came to Ocean City for summer work at the Flanders and roomed at Aunt Marion's house. All were quite mannerly and rarely seen because of their work schedules.

Conceptual sketch.
Alvin Thompson, 210 West Avenue.

The rear of the house had an attached shed where Aunt Marion kept a bucket of water. When Uncle Al came in from work, he had to enter through the shed, remove his construction clothing, and freshen up using the bucket of water before entering the house. When I returned from the beach, Aunt Marion required I come in through the shed and wash off all sand. During the war, Aunt Marion had a vegetable garden on the corner of 2nd Street and West Avenue next to the house. She grew tomatoes, corn, and green beans. People stopped to purchase her produce. The Hill family from Philadelphia built a little bungalow next door in later years.

Barbara Potts Bonaparte, August 2023

Every year, Sylvia Henry and I watched the Night in Venice parade from a third-floor window of 210 West Avenue facing the bay.

Irene Rolls Henry, 2022

The Hill family had a summer home at 214 West Avenue with a second building in the rear. Our family rented from the Hills in the 1960s when we were unable to rent a place on Bay Avenue.

Donovan Butler, September 2023

Widow Marion Johnson Thompson's second home at 146 Haven Avenue was sold and demolished. April 2022.

EAN CITY SENTIN

99-5411 OCEAN CITY, NEW JERSEY, THURSDAY, APRIL 28, 1966

Fire Fighters battle blaze in home on Simpson av. Four firemen required treatment for smoke inhalation.—Grainger Photo.

Wayne Thompson, Sr. family home,
737 Simpson Avenue.

Rescuing beach block houses doomed for demolition and relocating them to the Westside was a common occurrence for Sylvester Thompson. He and his crew moved this house from the beach block to Simpson Avenue for his son and daughter-in-law, Wayne and Portia Spruill Thompson.

In 1966, an electrical fire caused extensive damage. The owners restored the house to its original condition.[66]

Firemen Felled Fighting Blaze

Fire caused by a short circuit severely damaged a two-story frame dwelling at 739 Simpson av. late yesterday afternoon.

According to Fire Chief Ferdinand Taccarino, the fire gained headway in a rear utility room while the owners of the house, Mr. and Mrs. Wayne A. Thomson, were out.

It swept upward into an attic and gutted the entire second floor. Firemen were forced to chop holes in the roof of the structure to pour water on the stubborn blaze.

The first floor of the house was damaged by water and smoke. While firemen worked, the Thomsons, who had been called home, toiled with friends to remove much of their living room furniture.

Three firemen were treated for smoke inhalation at the scene of the fire. Damage to the property, according to Taccarino, was "great". He estimated the damage at $6,000.

119

Multi-Family Housing

The earliest multi-family house on the Westside identified to date is the Lomax house, a side-by-side duplex with ties to the city's founding fathers. Preston Lomax purchased the property from city founder Rev. James E. Lake in 1912 with plans to construct residential housing around a community church. Lomax occupied the south side while brother-in-law Rev. Israel Grant Harris occupied the north side. Records indicate the Lomax building and other homes often had rear

Lomax duplex, 632-634 Simpson Avenue

structures suitable for living space. Lomax's early death brought an end to his housing plans. The house still stands today as a duplex.

Emma's,
700 block West Avenue.
Photo c. 1970s.

613 Simpson Avenue duplex.

Ruby Ford at top of stairs,
L-R base of stairs: Unknown,
Theodore, Samuel III, Don
Carl Ford.

Photo c. 1955 courtesy
Samuel Ellis Ford, III

310 West Avenue on right and 312 West Avenue on left.

Owners S. Thompson & Sons, Inc. relocated these apartment buildings from the beach block to their West Avenue site. 312 West Avenue originally sat back from the street. It was later moved forward on the lot. Photo c. 2024.

Multi-Use Housing

A host of small Westside businesses flourished from the 1920s through the 1960s. Most operated from their homes or had space adjoining their homes. No clear distinction between the residential and commercial areas of the Westside existed.

Between 1928 and 1948, William Richard "Dick" Warren (1895-1968) lived on the first floor of Dr. Allen Corson's house at 824 Wesley Avenue on Doctors' Row while working for the doctor as a houseman and gardener. When Dr. John B. Townsend took over Corson's practice, Warren stayed on as houseman for Dr. Townsend but moved to West Avenue.

> *"We moved to a rowhouse on West Avenue around 1948 while I was a toddler. My father opened a restaurant in the house and was known for his barbecue. A couple years later, we moved to a side-by-side duplex on West Avenue owned by Joel Brown Still, a local tailor. Vivian Strawberry's family lived on the other side of the duplex. Mr. Still only wanted one room. My father opened a restaurant downstairs called "Dick's." We belonged to St. Peter's Methodist Church where I worked as a sexton.*
>

William Warren, OCHS class of 1963

Joel Brown Still was a grandson of Dr. James Still, Black Doctor of the Pines. In 1935, Joel ran for Justice of the Peace on the Democratic ticket.[67]

> *"I recall a Joseph (sic) Still, a tall fine-looking, light skinned black man. He was a tailor at Sixth Street and Asbury Avenue.*
>

Bertha Turner. 100 Plus Family Firsts, Sandpaper, Jul 1988.

Dick's Restaurant, 717 West Avenue. c. 1930s. Blanche Mann Gordon Jones on left.

122

Formerly Sample's Restaurant and residence, 101 E. 7th Street.
Restaurant down, residence up. Photo c. 2020

Edward "Pop" Sample was born in Charlotte, North Carolina in 1882. He had years of experience in a kitchen before arriving in Ocean City around 1942. His prior employment included work as a chef on a railroad in Albany, New York during the 1920s and work as a cook for a caterer in Philadelphia in the early 1930s. He was a chef in St. Petersburg, Florida in the late '30s and found work as a chef at the Booth Restaurant after coming to Ocean City around 1942.[68]

By 1948, Pop Sample acquired a building and opened a restaurant on the first floor, lived on an upper floor, and rented rooms to people who came North to work during the summer. Most of his tenants were from Florida. Sample was known for his fried fish dinners and sandwiches. He operated his businesses from the 1940s until his death in Somers Point in 1964 at age 82.

Following Sample's death, David Turner purchased the property and rented it out. It remained in the Turner family until David and his wife, Vernice, both passed away. Heirs to the property improved the building and used it as a rental for several years before selling it in 2013.

Sample house prepped for demolition.
Exterior siding removed. Photo October 2021.

The Turners put a new roof on this house just prior to selling it in 2013. The new owners replaced windows, siding, porch railings, and added decorative stone piers to the lower porch before learning that the building was not structurally sound. Newly installed exterior vinyl siding and interior sheetrock walls were removed before demolition started.

Sample house being demolished, 2021.

Several neighbors (not visible in photograph) watched as demolition contractor Keller took the Sample property down in one day.

"This was an easy one," Keller said. "It had to come down because the foundation was bad, probably some of the effects of SuperStorm Sandy [2012]. The house was built around 1911 and the wood in the old frame structure was weak. That's why the entire building swayed as I took it down section by section."

~Keller, December 2021

Dee's, 712 West Avenue. Three story apartment building with storefront. c. 1974. The Press, 1974

Ace Photography, 424 West Avenue. c. 1990s. Photo c. 2020. Demolished

Melvin and Katherine Stevens property.
100 6th Street. c. 2020

Georgia born Melvin and Kentucky born Katherine Stevens owned a home on the corner of 6th and Simpson Avenue facing what would become the Richard Grimes Recreation Field. Melvin arrived in Ocean City around 1930. He operated a taxi business from the house facing 6th Street while his wife operated a 1950s era restaurant and soda fountain in the attached building facing Simpson Avenue.

In its day, the soda fountain was decorated in hot pink and black with hot pink awnings. There were two coy ponds outside, one under each picture window. Even after the buildings were vacated, a profusion of yellow lilies popped up in the spring of each year. Before the buildings were torn down, clumps of the lilies were dug up and replanted at the homes of area residents.

Stevens' Restaurant & Soda Fountain fronting Simpson Avenue. Adjoining house faced 6th Street.

June Bug's Fish Market, 744 West Avenue.
Sentinel Ledger, 1974.
Fresh fish by the pound, cleaned or uncleaned, or fried fish sandwiches.

Row Housing

Row houses were and are still abundant in many sections of Ocean City. Some are identified as row houses while newer units are referred to as townhouses. Still others have changed to condominium ownership but are row houses nonetheless. All provide affordable housing for working class and middle-class people. Widows' Row, Mercer Place, and the Moore Avenue mini row still present today the way they did years ago, having stood the test of time and many, many storms.

Widows' Row

106th Year, Number 49 Ocean City, N.J. 08226 Thursday, November 20, 1986 Two Sections Price 3

Some of these homes in the 600 block of Haven Avenue may qualify for rehabilitation funding if the city receives an $80,000 Neighborhood Preservation Program grant from the state Department of Community Affairs.

Seek funds to upgrade neighborhood

City Council last Thursday night authorized the administration to pursue an $80,000 grant from the state Department of Community Affairs for neighborhood rehabilitation of the 1½ city blocks bounded by Haven Avenue and the alley between Simpson and Bay

housing units indicates 45 of the 102 substandard dwellings are in that zone.

According to the narrative description to accompany the grant application, the neighborhood is sandwiched between two business zones, including the heaviest commercial spot

dinance in February 1985, Council changed the nature of the code to limit new development to permitted uses unless variances were obtained.

According to Gideonse, rezoning the area aims to preserve it as a residential neighborhood.

Widows' Row, west side 600 block Haven Avenue. Built between c. 1910. Sentinel Ledger, 1986

Haven Avenue is only two blocks long in the area of Widows' Row (600 block and 700 block) dead-ending at the City's dedicated open space called The Strand (park) on the north and 8th Street on the south. It is a mix of residential and commercial uses along a former railroad bed in an area prone to flooding. In days past, passenger trains and freight trains ran through Haven Avenue. 1986 plans to upgrade the neighborhood through a state grant were scuttled when the proposal failed to address the needs of residents being displaced. The houses have required repeated restorations from heavy flooding but remain essentially the same as when constructed. With the demolition of two homes on the south end, only nine of the original eleven homes remain on Widows' Row, four of which African Americans still own.

Train photos courtesy Ocean City Historical Museum

"Pennysmasher" headed north along Haven Avenue. c. 1950s

Railroads running through West Avenue and Haven Avenue.
Sanborn Company maps. Sheet 94, 1909.

Mercer Place

Mercer Place sits between 6th and 7th Streets running perpendicular to Bay Avenue. Built by the same person who built Widows' Row on Haven Avenue, the fifteen houses are similar in style and function to Widows' Row[69]. The houses still stand as of this writing. Photo c. 2020.

Rev. Jerkins and Juanita Moore, Westside matriarch, at Shiloh Baptist Church.[70]

Centenarian Mother Moore came to Ocean City in 1955 from Amelia County, Virginia. She married Jesse Moore, a Mercer Place resident, and joined nearby Shiloh Baptist Church.

Out of a US population of approximately 336,997,624, in 2021 there were 89,739 centenarians (age 100+) or a prevalence of 0.027%.[71]

West Avenue Row

Unnamed rowhouse. West side 700 block West Avenue. The Press, November 1974.

Moore Avenue Mini Row

The mini row of houses at 737, 739 and 741 Moore Avenue includes St. James A.M.E. Church parsonage at 737 Moore Avenue on the north end of the row. The houses still stand. Photo c. 2020.

131

Cranmer's Row

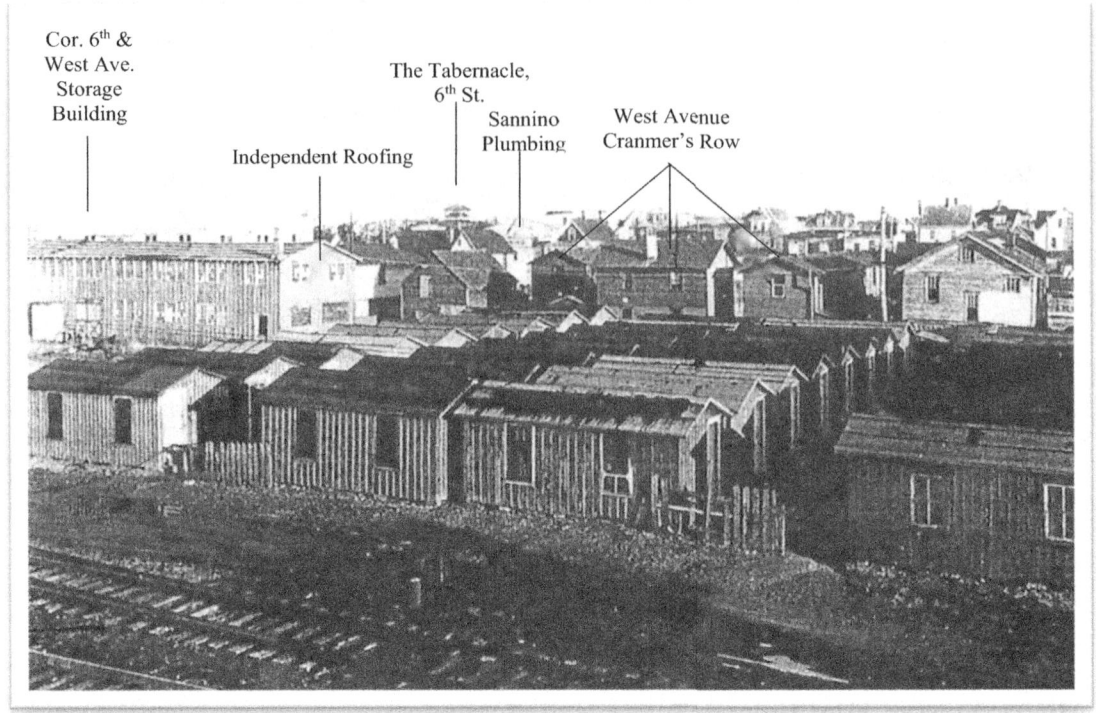

Cor. 6th &
West Ave.
Storage
Building

The Tabernacle,
6th St.

Sannino
Plumbing

Independent Roofing

West Avenue
Cranmer's Row

Cranmer's (sic Cramer's) Row, 600 block between 6th & 7th Streets on West Avenue viewed from Haven Avenue looking east. Pennsylvania Reading Seashore Lines tracks in foreground.[72] Photo courtesy Ocean City Historical Museum.

Lillian Cranmer owned the rental housing known as Cranmer's Row (incorrectly called Cramer's Row locally). Two rows of small starter houses sat perpendicular to West Avenue with an open area between the rows and common bathrooms along the alley. Fencing surrounded the houses. The houses were demolished in 1965 as part of an urban renewal project.

Oxford Court

Three attached houses in the 700 block of West Avenue built perpendicular to the street comprised Oxford Court. The Geranium Temple of Lady Elks No. 469 (Daughter Elks) owned the houses. Residents included Earl Polk in 1928, Richard Barton in 1930, Henry Martin, Mae Brown, Lena Williams, and Sis Fogan. The row has been torn down. No photograph is available.

Rose Court

Rose Court, named for its owner, was located on the west side of West Avenue between 7th and 8th Streets. The houses no longer exist. No photograph is available.

Hotels, Guest Houses, Rooming Houses, and Boarding Houses

Hotel Comfort and The Thomas Hotel (also known as the Washington Hotel/Pink Hotel, E. J. Benning Hotel) were full-fledged Westside hotels. Other establishments on the Westside referred to as hotels are more appropriately categorized as guest houses, rooming houses, or boarding houses.

The area of the Westside north of the Strand and remote from the Central Business District developed as a middle class and upper middle-class neighborhood. Rev. and Mrs. Samuel J. Comfort owned Hotel Comfort at 2nd Street and Bay Avenue near the terminus of the West Jersey Railroad opposite Steamboat Landing. Rev. Comfort, an early pastor at Tabernacle Baptist Church, was a colleague of John Trower and Booker T. Washington, two influential men of the time. Hotel Comfort anchored the north end of the Westside. *"Let's just say they kept the hotel very elite,"* says Barbara Potts Bonaparte who visited the area regularly during the 1940s.

Rev. Samuel J. and Maggie Shaw Comfort Ocean City land holdings

201 Bay Ave.	Hotel Comfort	Lot 13 Sec. B	1901
35th & Wesley Ave.		Lot 908 Sec. H	1911
225 Bay Ave.	Guest House	Lot 19 Sec. B	1923
229 Bay Ave.		Lot 20 Sec. B	1925
237 Bay Ave.	Boatyard	Lot 22 Sec. B	1925
37th & Central Ave.		Lot 796 Sec. H	1925
1st & Simpson Ave.		Lot 204 Sec. B	1926
3rd & West Ave.		Lot 74 Sec. A	1926

Louanna A. Shaw Ocean City land holdings

4th & Haven Ave.		p/o Lot 18, 19, 20 Sec. B	1922
229 Bay Ave.		Lot 20 Sec. B	1925
201 Bay Ave.	Hotel Comfort	Lot 13 Sec. B	1930
225 Bay Ave.	Guest House	Lot 19 Sec. B	1930
237 Bay Ave.		Lot 22 Sec. B	1930
37th & Central Ave.	Vacant lot	Lot 908 Sec. H	1930
1st & Simpson Ave.		Lot 204 Sec. B	1930

George Walker Williams Ocean City land holdings

213 Bay Ave.		Lot 16 Sec. B	1953
217 Bay Ave.	Bay View Guests	Lot 17 Sec. B	1953
221 Bay Ave.	Servant Outbuilding	Lot 18 Sec. B	1953
201 Bay Ave.	Hotel Comfort	Lot 13 Sec. B	1957
Simpson Ave.	Railroad R.O.W.	½ L.110 all L. 111	1962
225 Bay Ave.	Guest House	Lot 19 Sec. B	1972

Aerial view portion of 100 block and 200 block Bay Avenue.
Visible are Hotel Comfort, Bay View Guest House, and 225 Bay Avenue rooming house directly
above boat mast. Photo courtesy Williams family and Donovan Butler, September 2023.

Hotel Comfort, 2nd and Bay Streets, opposite Steamboat Landing.   Ocean City, N. J.

Hotel Comfort under ownership of Rev. Samuel J. Comfort. c. 1914.
Photographic Collection. Hotels Book 8. Ocean City Historical Museum.

201 Bay Avenue. Rev. Samuel J. and Maggie Comfort purchased this corner lot from city founder James Lake in 1901. There the Comforts owned and operated the elite Hotel Comfort. One of their early guests was renown author and educator Booker T. Washington. By early January 1930, facing financial hardship as the economy declined into the Great Depression, the Comforts appointed Maggie's sister, singlewoman and teacher Louanna Shaw, trustee for their six Ocean City properties.

Louanna was able to sell some holdings and mortgaged the hotel and a large guest house to First National Bank Ocean City for an amount in excess of $6000. By 1940, the bank was insolvent. Creditors forced a sale. The only bid tendered was $100 by an administrator for the creditor. The administrator then instructed the sheriff to sell the assets to Louanna's brother, Harry Shaw, for $100 who sold it back to Comfort in 1946 for the same $100. The Comforts both died in 1952 within four months of one another naming Louanna Shaw heir to all property. Louanna sold Hotel Comfort to George and Annie Mae Williams in 1957 for $26,000.

Williams family. L-R: George Millage, Annie May, George Walker, Jane V. Facebook photo.

George Walker Williams was an entrepreneur at heart. As a teenager in Waynesboro, Georgia, he put his movie projector to work and charged neighbors five cents to watch silent films. When he and his employer at a pharmacy in Waynesboro had differences, George and his teenage bride, Annie Mae Hankerson, packed up their young son and moved to New York City where George worked as a dining car waiter.

Still a young man in the 1920s, his New York real estate investments allowed him to provide housing for railroad porters at his numerous Harlem properties. George advanced to head dining car waiter on the New York Central Railroad. The family moved to a house overlooking Yankee Stadium. In the 1940s, the Williams family moved to Yonkers, New York.

In the 1950s, George began investing in property in Ocean City after suffering financial losses in Woodbridge, Middlesex County, New Jersey, an affluent bedroom suburb of New York City. During World War II, patriotic Williams granted a government-industry partnership an easement through one of his properties in Woodbridge for the construction of two cross-country petroleum pipelines from Texas to the East Coast.

The Little Big Inch line crossed Williams' land buried in a ditch four feet deep and three feet wide. It carried gasoline, heating oil, diesel oil, and kerosene critical to the war effort. After the war, the government auctioned off the pipelines as surplus. Newly formed Texas Eastern Transmission Corporation, created specifically for the sale, submitted a winning bid of $143,127,000.

> *"Before the two pipelines began transporting oil, German submarines had sunk so many tankers that many Caribbean Island beaches were seriously polluted with oil. Now, it cannot be stated too forcefully. American oil, which amounted in all to 6 billion barrels out of a total of 7 billion barrels consumed by the Allies for the period of World War Two, brought victory! Without the prodigious delivery of oil from the U. S., this global war, quite frankly, could never have been won."*
>
> *Historian Keith Miller. Big Inch Pipes of WWII*[73]

> *"The government and oil companies reaped millions while my patriotic grandfather received $40 for an easement that rendered his encumbered lot in Woodbridge undesirable and the adjoining lot undersized and unbuildable. He fought for years, but to no avail. He determined to protect his Ocean City investments by purchasing several adjacent properties."*
>
> *Michael Williams, grandson of George Walker Williams*
> *Telephone conference call August 16, 2023*

The 1950s introduced a new era on the Westside with development of the sparsely settled north end setting the pace. In 1953, New York investor George Walker Williams and Annie Mae Hankerson Williams, generally referred to as "Big Daddy" and "Mother" by family members, purchased the Bay View Guest House and several vacant lots on the ocean side of the 200 block of Bay Avenue near Comfort. The Comfort, Shaw, and Williams families then owned most of the properties on the east side of the 200 block of Bay Avenue, including several income-producing guest houses.

In 1957, following the close deaths of both Comforts, Louanna Shaw, sister-in-law and heir of Rev. Comfort, sold Hotel Comfort to Williams who eventually amassed six properties in the same block. The hotel continued to operate under the Comfort name, but Comfort's traditional oysters, clams, and homemade ginger beer became a thing of the past. Reservations for Hotel Comfort were booked through their nearby Williams Bay View Guest House.

"Mother handled the bookkeeping while Big Daddy who had only an eighth-grade education did menus. The hotel served grits and chicken wings for breakfast. Friday was steak day. Family members worked as waitresses. Mother came complete with her social circle from Harlem and Yonkers known as Annie Mae and her Satellites."

Jane Williams Foster, granddaughter of George and Annie Williams, August 26, 2023

Annie Mae on right with her Satellites.
Photo courtesy Carol William-Pullins, 2023.

217 Bay Avenue, Williams Bay View Guest House. In 1953, George and Annie Mae Williams completed their first Ocean City acquisition acquiring three adjoining properties on Bay Avenue from builder Frederick Myers. Included in the deal was 217 Bay Avenue which became the Williams Bay View Guest House and base of operations for future real estate investments. Prior to the Williams purchase, Nathan and Frances Freeman operated their Bay Villa Laundry from this location.

Annie May Hankerson Williams proprietor, Williams Bay View Guest House. 217 Bay Avenue.
To the north in background is Hotel Comfort, 201 Bay Avenue. Photo c. 1955.
Photo courtesy Carol William-Pullins, 2023.

Bay View guest house Depression dining room suite. Furniture of same style as that in Hotel Comfort and guest houses at 217 Bay Avenue and 225 Bay Avenue. Photo courtesy Dr. Melvin Williams.

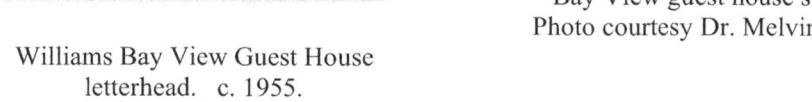

Williams Bay View Guest House letterhead. c. 1955.
Photo courtesy Carol William-Pullins, 2023.

Bay View guest house sideboard.
Photo courtesy Dr. Melvin Williams.

Annie Mae in white gloves and purse securing hat. Photo courtesy Carol William-Pullins, 2023.

Photos courtesy Carol William-Pullins, 2023.

Hotel Comfort with servants' quarters at rear. George W. Williams proprietor.
Williams moved the service building to 221 Bay Avenue. Photo c. 1957.

Hotel Comfort and sedan.

Hotel Comfort under the management
of George Walker Williams.
Viewed from south side.

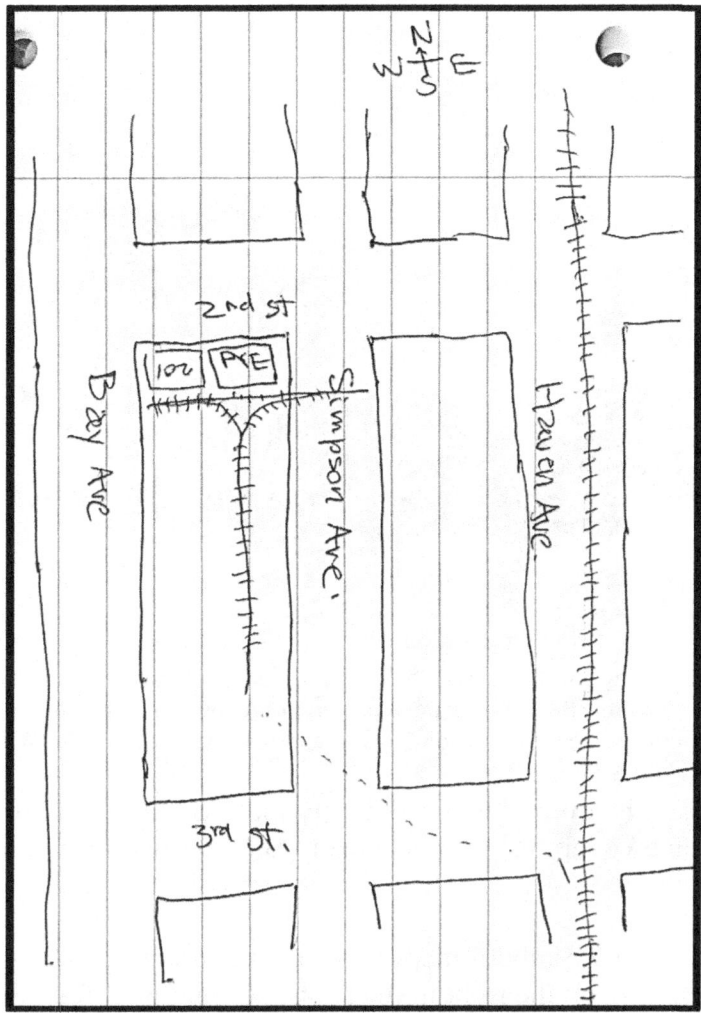

Out and back railroad reversal track. Sketch by Robert A. Butler, August 2023

In the late 1930s, John Pye (Pop Pye) built his home on the corner of 6th Street and Simpson Avenue not far from the Hotel Comfort. By the time I came along in the 1960s, there was an out and back reversal track on the south side. Trains would head towards the house, curve, and go onto a siding from which they could back up and reverse. A visitor to 6 2nd Street saw a train headlight coming straight towards the house, panicked, and alerted everyone else. The train veered off at the last split second as it angled for the siding track. The regular inhabitants of the house found it hilarious. Pop Pye also never paid for coal. He just picked up discarded half-burnt steam engine coal from the railroad tracks.

Robert Butler, step great grandson of John S. Pye, 2023

L-R: Williams Bay View guest house on far left, servants' quarters relocated from rear of Hotel Comfort to Bay Avenue in center, guest house on far right.
Photo courtesy Larry Richardson, great grandson of George Walker Williams.

221 Bay Avenue. The outbuilding previously located at the rear of Hotel Comfort and used as servants' quarters was relocated to Bay Avenue for use as an additional rental property.

225 Bay Avenue. 1909 Sanborn maps show a structure at 225 Bay Avenue which was likely the building on the right in the above photograph. Rev. Samuel Comfort purchased the building in 1923. Facing hard times in early 1930, he appointed his sister-in-law, Louanna Shaw, trustee of his Ocean City holdings. The Comfort and Shaw families worked together to hold onto the property using it for rentals and family vacations. In the 1930s, Louanna rented the building to gardener William Alves and wife Viola Harmon Alves, Ocean City Old Timers, who resided there and sold florist goods from the property.

When the property was eventually sold at sheriff's sale in 1940, Louanna's brother, Harry Shaw, purchased the property and held it until selling it back to Rev. Comfort in 1946. World War I sergeant and New York Central Railroad waiter Robert Given Shaw and his wife Olivia vacationed at the house when not cruising from California to Hawaii or travelling first class to Lisbon, Portugal aboard a luxurious Italian ocean liner. In 1972, years after the death of both Comforts and Louanna Shaw, George and Annie May Williams purchased the property from Louanna's estate through her executor, brother Clarence F. Shaw.

142

Dr. Jane V. Williams, 135 Bay Ave. Summer house photo and still image from 8mm film.
Photos courtesy Larry Richardson, great grandson of George Walker Williams

Philadelphia pediatrician Dr. Jane V. Williams, daughter of George and Annie Mae, purchased a large summer home on Bay Avenue north of her parents' holdings. This house sits at the back of the lot surrounded by newer construction and is still standing as of this writing.

Robert and Phyllis Murray owned a vacation cottage at 140 Simpson Avenue.

Photo courtesy Carol Williams-Pullins

The Bakers had a house on the northwest corner of 2nd Street and Simpson Avenue. Mr. Baker owned a large public relations firm in Philadelphia. He was disabled but walked to the marina every day. The property was landscaped with stones that required periodic weeding.

"The lady who lived in the house always asked neighborhood kids to pull weeds out of the stones. She reminded me of a gypsy."

Rev. Drena Garrett Money, 2023

Mrs. Baker used to ask us kids to pull weeds but was hard pay. She always wore a scarf wrapped around her hair rollers.

Donovan Butler, 2022

With Hotel Comfort as the anchor, the Westside slowly expanded northward into the 100 block. The Sargents had a vacation home on the north end but kept their yacht at an Atlantic City marina. Mr. and Mrs. Hill, owners of a moving company in Philadelphia, built a cottage at 214 West Avenue with a rental building in the rear. The Bell family converted a single-family home at 3rd Street and West Avenue into a duplex. Each summer they rented one side and used the other as a vacation home. Jennings and William Bell served on the Ocean City Beach Patrol.[74] The quiet north end of the Westside became a mecca for folks looking to escape the hustle and bustle of big cities.

Buck's Rooming House. Photo courtesy Ocean City Historical Museum.

"As early as 1928, Henry and Rose Buck operated a rooming house at 951 West Avenue where they rented to hotel and restaurant service workers."
Evangelist Angela Graham (1933-2022)

Bolden's Guest House. 742-744 Moore Avenue.

Bolden's Guest House is just one block south of the Lomax duplex. It was considered upscale for the time. This duplex still stands today much the same as in years past although it has recently been converted to condominium units.

John Carroll's Rooming House, 658 Haven Avenue (to the right of Mobilgas sign). c. 1940s.

John and Mildred Carroll operated a large rooming house and hauling business from their house on the northwest corner of 7th Street and Haven Avenue adjacent to the Pennsylvania Reading Seashore Railroad. Clarence Reynolds and Joe Harvey drove trucks for the hauling business. Carroll also operated a Sinclair Gas Station at 6th Street and West Avenue. In the early '20s, widow Ida Hill Bush boarded at Carroll's and operated an ice cream store from that location.[75] By the late '20s, she had remarried and opened Ida J. Dossar Employment Agency.[76] During the '40s, she operated a bakery at 7th and Haven Avenue.[77]

Sam Esposito had family on the Westside but boarded at Carroll's in the 1950s. A clothes presser by trade, he was known for sleeping long hours on the rooming house porch.[78, 79]

His dog was always at his feet. The house was on a busy corner, so had Sam ever been awake, he had the perfect spot to watch the trains go by, see who was going to St. James A.M.E. church on Sunday, who was going to Turner's pool room, who was using the mailbox on the corner, and who frequented Bridget's corner store. Or perhaps he just enjoyed talking to Carroll's boarders and listening to the music that emanated from the house during weekend dances.

Carroll died at age 56. Widow Mildred was among the masses at Jim Jones' Peoples Temple and who died at Jonestown, Guyana in 1978.[80]

THE WASHINGTON HOTEL   COLORED   6TH AND SIMPSON AVENUES   OCEAN CITY, N. J.
EVERY ROOM AN OUTSIDE ROOM, WITH RUNNING WATER   MEALS   REFRESHMENTS
CHAS. BRYDSON, PROP.   PHONE 591

Washington Hotel, corner 6th Street and Simpson Avenue.
Photo courtesy Paul W. Schopp. SoJourn, Vol. 5 No. 2, Winter 2020/2021

The original name of the Washington Hotel was the Thomas Hotel. In 1925, William and Ida Thomas had the upscale hotel built specifically for Colored people who were excluded from White establishments during the Jim Crow days of the 1920s. When the Great Depression hit and the Thomases were unable to pay the mortgage, Millville National Bank foreclosed on the hotel and another income property which had been pledged as security.

Years later, Charles and Sarah Brydson purchased the hotel from the bank and changed the hotel name to the Washington Hotel. The Brydson's painted the hotel bright pink, resulting in the name Pink Hotel. The last owner of record was E. J. Benning, who purchased it at auction in the 1960s when the bank foreclosed on widowed Sarah Brydson. It was renamed the Benning Hotel and was listed in The Negro Motorist Green Book, a guidebook for African American travelers with a list of hotels, boarding houses, taverns, restaurants, and service stations that catered to people of color. The Rose Court condominiums now stand on the former site of the Thomas/Washington/Benning Hotel.

Affordable Housing

Peck's Beach Village Low Income Housing.

In the 1960s, in order to meet State mandates, the Ocean City Housing Authority erected forty units of low-income rental housing at 4th Street and Haven Avenue. This project was the subject of much controversy between those supporting the introduction of low-income housing and those who feared a loss of property value. Rozelia Cobb was a strong advocate for the project. Ultimately, State mandates compelled the City to build the units.

The selection of a hot pink color for the entire project opened the door for those in opposition to again criticize the project, suggesting that the selected color was totally out of character for Ocean City and was intended to draw negative attention to the project. Today, the houses have been repainted a soft seashore blue. The sixty-year-old flood prone housing will be demolished and replaced with sixty newly constructed units in order to satisfy terms of 2018 court settlement with the State.

SENTINEL-LEDGER

ERSEY, THURSDAY, FEBRUARY 3, 1955   Publication Office Sentinel-Ledger Building, 8th st. and Haven av.   PRICE:

Bid on

Committee of 6 to Pick West Side Housing Site

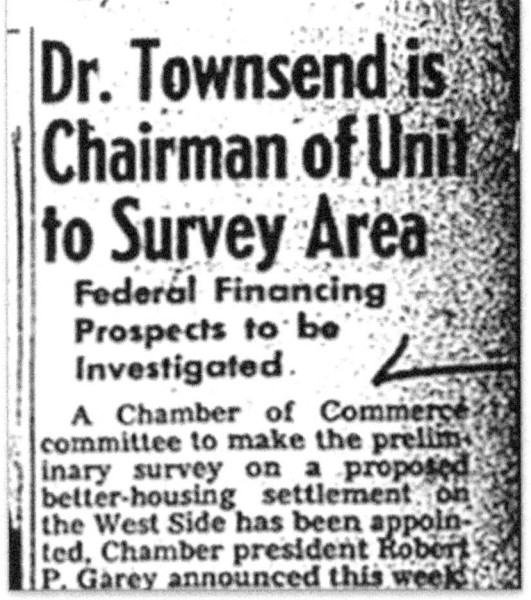

Dr. Townsend is Chairman of Unit to Survey Area

Federal Financing Prospects to be Investigated.

A Chamber of Commerce committee to make the preliminary survey on a proposed better-housing settlement on the West Side has been appointed, Chamber president Robert P. Garey announced this week

John B. Townsend, Edna Mae Thomas, John Trout, John Devine, Haney Lloyd Chattin, Richard Mayer selected to sit on the citing committee for a proposed Westside housing project.[81]

$7,000 Per Unit Cost Seen For Housing Project

C. of C. Group Polls West Side Citizens For Suggestions

Chamber of Commerce promoters for the proposed West Side low-cost housing project this week went prospecting for ground upon which to locate the planned 30-unit development.

which the builder would be the major stockholder.

Mr. Lindsey told the meeting that the units could be constructed for approximately $7,000 each, and rented at $50 a month on a 30-year lease. At this price, each dwelling would contain a living room, combination dining room-kitchen, bath, and three bedrooms, with all facilities, excepting heat.

Eight residents of the area, representing civic and social interests, attended the meeting to offer opinions on the project. They were designated at a committee, headed by Miss Edna Mae Thomas, to poll residents regarding preference of size, architecture and location, and whether prospective residents would rather buy or rent the units.

The sub-committees are to report back at another meeting of the full Chamber body Wednesday night.

Ocean City Sentinel-Ledger, February 1955

Peck's Beach Village viewed from the interior courtyard. Houses front on the courtyard, 2021.

The rear of Peck's Beach Village faces local streets, 2021.

Part of the Peck's Beach project included Senior Citizen Housing as seen looking north from 4th Street toward the interior parking area, 2021.

Rear of senior citizen housing, 2021.

In July 2021, the City relocated seniors to the expanded Bayview Manor, a high-rise senior citizen complex at 6th Street and West Avenue. The Peck's Beach Village units were demolished and replaced with fifteen 3- and 4-story apartment buildings on two sites for a total of sixty new units and a community building. The first floor of each building is to be dedicated to parking, storage, and utilities.[82]

An excavator's gaping claw demolishes one of the old homes at Pecks Beach Village.[83]

Section 8 Housing

In 1972, the City opened ten units of Section 8 Low Income Housing in the 200 block of Haven Avenue. The houses were built at a cost of $10,000 each and sold for $17,000 with ten-year closed mortgages that could not be paid off in less than the stipulated ten years. In order to qualify, a family was required to have at least one child. Investment in this type of single-family, low-income housing reaped rewards for the new owners who were able to build equity in their investment while improving housing conditions in the area. From these ten houses eventually came lawyers, schoolteachers, school superintendents, nursing directors, and several business owners. The proud residents referred to this block of homes as the Gardens of the Westside because of the well-manicured lawns. Most lawns were lost when the houses had to be elevated following SuperStorm Sandy in 2012.

Army veteran Levern Granger is one of the original owners of Section 8 housing.

> *"Know why so many southerners moved to Ocean City? In Marion, South Carolina where I was born, we worked picking cotton for $3 a day. Money goes further in the South. It gave us money for school clothes, but there was no withholding of taxes, no Social Security, no welfare, no healthcare, no safety net. For $15 per trip, my father, Peter Granger, transported people by bus back and forth from South Carolina to Ocean City for summer work. Some decided to stay. We all came here looking for a chance to do better."*
> *Levern Granger interview, Haven Avenue, July 2021 and June 2024.*

Section 8 housing looking south from 2nd Street, 2021.

Section 8 housing looking north along Haven Avenue. Individually owned and maintained, 2021.

Other Housing

Several prominent buildings outside the boundaries of the Westside provided housing for people of color.

Cresse Mansion, 800 Wesley Avenue. Photo courtesy Ocean City Historical Museum.

Lewis and Cecelia Cresse owned the mansion with servants' quarters known as Cresse Mansion. Bank teller Lewis Cresse became President of First National Bank of Ocean City, President of Ocean City Title and Trust, and Mayor of Ocean City. Willard Drain(e) lived in the servants' quarters the few years he worked as a butler for the Cresses. Drain(e)'s sister-in-law, singlewoman Ethel Pierce, worked and lived at the mansion between 1920 and 1930. Years later, the mansion became the Riverboat Club, a membership only club with a long and storied history.

Roger D. Cooper (1888-1964) houseboat, 11th Street and bay.
(Depiction of Mississippi riverboat likely similar to Cooper houseboat.)

Roger Cooper spent his later years living in a houseboat on Ocean City's back bay. He was said to be related to the wealthy and well-bred DuPont family. Cooper was born in New Orleans around 1888 and grew up on the Mississippi River riverfront. He came to Ocean City around 1905 and worked as a teamster while boarding with Elizabeth Schenck on Central Avenue. Later, he moved to a Westside rooming house and worked as a machinist.

When Baldwin Locomotive in Eddystone, Pennsylvania went into business providing locomotives and armaments to the United States and allied forces during World War I, Cooper was one of their early hires. By 1935, he was a self-employed boat machinist working for the Bartine Boat Yard at 11th and the Bay. Boat machinists Bartine Turner, Roger Cooper, and Charles Wright each lived in privately-owned houseboats anchored at 11th and the Bay adjacent to boat yard property. Cooper's World War II registration lists him as Indian. He was a member of Tabernacle Baptist Church during the 1930s and died in Somers Point in 1964.

An apartment over Kabat Men's Shop served as home to Daniel L. Henry (1942-2006), OCHS Class of 1960. Richard Kabat hired impeccably dressed Dan Henry as a salesman, the first person of color to work in sales in Ocean City's downtown business district. Kabat's was an upscale men's stop offering suits hand tailored on site. Clients referred to the store as a little New York on Asbury Avenue.[84]

Kabat Men's Shop,
720 Asbury Avenue

Chatterbox Restaurant. Outside the Westside at 9th Street and Central Avenue.[85]

The soda fountain at the Chatterbox made the restaurant a favorite after school spot for Ocean City students until the fountain closed in 1970. When the owners rented apartments on the upper floor, Victor Humphrey (1947-2022) rented one of the non-traditional rental spaces. He lived there until proposed renovations forced him to relocate.

Disappearing Housing

Several Westside homes inhabited by people of color have succumbed to emigration, gentrification, or the effects of Mother Nature.

Recent Demolitions

D. Henry, 307 West Ave.

Robert and Phyllis Murray vacation cottage, 140 Simpson Ave.

Murray photos courtesy Donovan Butler, June 2024

Robert and Phyllis Murray purchased a small vacation cottage at 140 Simpson Avenue in the 1950s for about $30,000. Son Sidney Murray sold the property in $2024 for $800,000. Demolition commenced shortly thereafter. As of this writing, piling have been installed for a new house.

Sold – Extant

As younger generations move more frequently due to current economic factors, the housing market, and remote work, the ability and desire to live in or maintain original family homes has decreased. Existing families have opted to sell their properties to reap the financial benefits of high land and property values on the island.

W. Boyer, 644 Haven Ave.

L-R: I. Carter, 106 E. 6th St. and
J. Richardson, 104 E. 6th St.

J. Motley, 221 Simpson Ave.

D. Turner, 727 Moore Ave.

W. Brown, 11 W. 7th St.

R. Ford, 11 W. 7th St. rear

B. Hughes, 611 Simpson Ave.

Original Family Ownership – Extant

Few homes are maintained by the original families that owned them, passed down from one generation to another.

C. Spence, 741 Moore Ave.

E. Money, 201 Simpson Ave.

S. Thompson, 625 Haven Ave.

***

Walk a Mile In My Shoes

If I could be you, if you could be me For just one hour If we could find a way to get inside Each other's mind If you could see you through my eyes Instead your ego I believe you'd be, I believe you'd be surprised to see That you've been blind Walk a mile in my shoes Walk a mile in my shoes Yeah, before you abuse, criticize and accuse Walk a mile in my shoes Now there are people on reservations And out in the ghetto And brother there, but for the grace of god Go you and I If I only had the wings Of a little angel Don't you know, I'd fly to the top of a mountain And then I'd cry, cry, cry Walk a mile in my shoes Walk a mile in my shoes Yeah, before you abuse, criticize and accuse Walk a mile in my shoes Walk a mile in my shoes Walk a mile in my shoes Yeah, before you abuse, criticize and accuse Walk a mile in my shoes

Elvis Presley, "Walk A Mile In My Shoes" song lyrics.[86]

CHAPTER 3
THE ELEPHANT IN THE ROOM

"The impact (of racism) is pervasive and deeply embedded in our society—affecting where one lives, learns, works, worships and plays, and creating inequities in access to a range of social and economic benefits—such as housing, education, wealth, and employment."

U.S. Center for Disease Control's Racism Disparities Report[87]

Racism on the South Jersey shore runs deep, long, and wide, ebbing and flowing like tides pushed by ever changing winds. It is often predictable, but sometimes rears its ugly head when least expected. Ocean City racism was quiet and covert. Institutional racism existed in housing, education, health, and employment. Redlining, racial steering, and bank lending practices controlled the housing market.

Discrimination and segregation in Ocean City were not by law (de jure), but simply discrimination and segregation in fact (de facto). The range of jobs open to Blacks was extremely limited, forcing many into service sector jobs abundant in the resort. Others chose self-employment in a variety of occupations needed in the community. For years, skilled trade unions were closed to Blacks, again forcing people of color into service-related jobs.

In 1910, Scotch Hall Sanitorium of the time, at 5th Street and Wesley Avenue opened as a sanitorium for "the well, the invalid, and the elderly". Originally the 1880s home of city founder Ezra B. Lake, it was closed to people of color who gave birth at home with the assistance of a doctor or midwife. During the 1920s, the sanitorium became a birthing hospital but remained closed to people of color.[88] It was not until well into the 1930s when hospital services in Somers Point became available to Blacks.

Movie theater managers, not police, directed Blacks to the balcony. Lifeguards, not police, quietly enforced segregation at the town's beaches. Homeowners insisted visiting Blacks be received at the back door. In time and under pressure to change, outright racism and discrimination in the job market yielded to tokenism, "the practice of making only a perfunctory or symbolic effort to do a particular thing, especially by recruiting a small number of people from underrepresented groups in order to give the appearance of sexual or racial equality within a workforce."[89, 90] Locally, employers reserved certain front of the house service jobs for fair complexioned Blacks (e.g. elevator operator).[91] Change came slowly. Theatres, restaurants, and schools relaxed discriminatory practices. Beaches opened up in the 1950s.

Ocean City people of color acquiesced to these restrictions and limitations wary they were fighting a losing battle. With the introduction of new laws in the 1960s, racism slowly diminished or went underground. There were no riots, no dogs, no fire hoses. Racism was a difficult truth. It remained the proverbial elephant in the room.

Know It When You See It

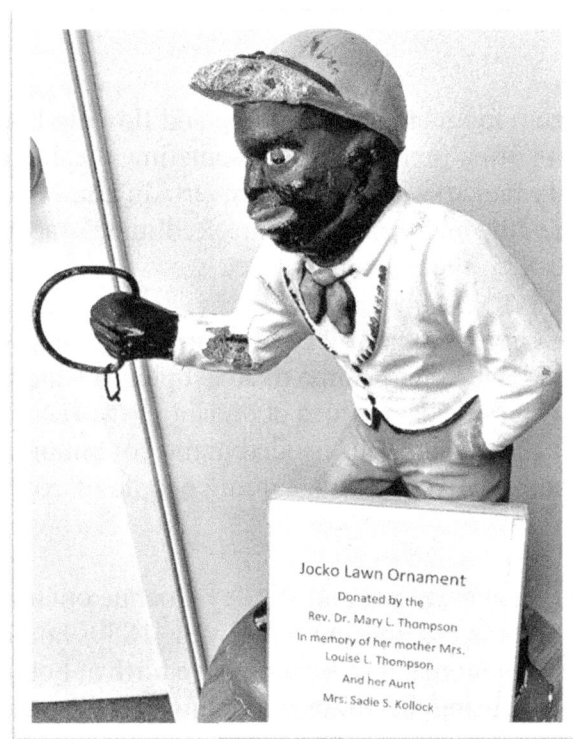

Lawn jockey at the African American Heritage Museum of Southern New Jersey, Newtonville, Buena Vista Township, New Jersey.
Ralph E. Hunter founder and president.

Photo courtesy Alva Thompson

The legend of "Jocko, the lawn jockey." During the Revolutionary War, Tom Graves and his twelve-year-old son Jocko volunteered to serve in George Washington's local militia. Because Jocko was too young for battle, Washington assigned Jocko to tend the horses and keep a lantern burning as a guide to returning soldiers. On Christmas eve 1776, General Washington and his army set out to cross the Delaware but were caught in a blizzard that delayed their return to camp that night. The following day, having defeated the British, General Washington returned to camp only to discover Jocko frozen to death still clenching the lantern. Washington commissioned a statue called "The Faithful Groomsman" to stand at his Mount Vernon estate in honor of Jocko Graves.

"Over time, the statue's original form changed, and its original story was forgotten. The statue became known as "The Lawn Jockey" and by the mid-nineteenth century was usually depicted as the racial "Sambo" character with very dark skin and big protruding lips. It was also often used as a hitching post for horses and made of cast iron, while others were used as ornaments for front lawns."[92]

Blackpast.org

Some accounts claim the statue was used to signal Underground Railroad station stops. According to these accounts, an American flag in the hand of the statue signaled runaway slaves that it was safe to stop at that home. Also, dressing the statue in a striped shirt meant that a fugitive slave could obtain a horse. A blue sailor waistcoat meant the station master could deliver the fugitive to a port and a ship.

When there was nothing better to do, a group of kids from the Westside gathered and took off in search of lawn jockeys, which could usually be found along Bay Avenue. If we found one, someone would muster the courage to knock it over. We ran away laughing, content that we had done a good deed.

Loretta Harris for the Westside kids

"I knocked on the doors of Whites who had lawn jockeys and explained how offensive they were. Sometimes it worked."

Whitney Butler, December 2021

After the American Civil War (1861-1865), most southern states, and later border states, passed Jim Crow laws that denied Blacks basic human rights. The laws existed for about 100 years and were meant to marginalize African Americans, denying them the right to vote, hold jobs, get an education, or take advantage of other opportunities. Those who attempted to defy Jim Crow laws often faced arrest, fines, jail sentences, violence, and death.

While northern states may not have had such laws, many of the practices prevailed, nonetheless. It is not clear how, but the minstrel character named "Jim Crow" became a kind of shorthand for the laws, customs, and etiquette that segregated and demeaned African Americans from the 1870s into the 1960s.

Thomas Dartmouth Rice, an actor born in New York, is considered the "Father of Minstrelsy." After reportedly traveling to the South and observing slaves, Rice developed a Black stage character called "Jim Crow" in 1830. With quick dance moves, an exaggerated African American vernacular and buffoonish behavior, Rice founded a new genre of racialized song and dance—blackface minstrel shows—which became central to American entertainment in the North and South.

"I Want to Break Free"[93, 94]

White performers in blackface played characters that perpetuated a range of negative stereotypes about African Americans including being lazy, ignorant, superstitious, hypersexual, criminal, or cowardly. Several characters in minstrel shows became archetypes, as described in the University of Florida's digital exhibit, "History of Minstrels: From 'Jump Jim Crow' to 'The Jazz Singer'." Some of the most famous were Rice's "Jim Crow," a rural dancing fool in tattered clothing;[95] the "Mammy," an overweight and loud mother figure; and "Zip Coon," a flamboyant-dressed man who used sophisticated words incorrectly.[96]

Actor Al Jolson in blackface in the 1927 film 'The Jazz Singer.[97]

Religious Discrimination and Separation

Ocean City newspaper articles of the late 1800s and early 1900s describe numerous interactions among Blacks and Whites in religious endeavors. They worshiped together in the same church, if not from the same pew. Rev. Dr. William Creditt, Rev. Samuel J. Comfort, and John Trower from Tabernacle Baptist Church arranged joint events with their White counterparts. Creditt spoke at First Methodist Church on more than one occasion. Rev. Israel Grant Harris of Shiloh Baptist Church and Rev. Samuel J. Comfort from Tabernacle Baptist were active in local civic activities. A commonplace practice for Blacks organizing new churches was to acquire church structures being retired by White congregations for little or no money and relocate the structures to the Westside. Elected city officials supported efforts of Westside residents to build a strong religious community.

ILY REPORTER.

ONDAY, JULY 15, 1895.   **NO. 13.**

The colored women who promenade the boardwalk are entitled to protection. It is reported that lately several of them have been grossly insulted by young men.

Youth harassed Colored women enjoying a stroll on the boardwalk following Sunday service.
Daily Reporter, July 1895

Over time, Ocean City became more a patchwork quilt than woven fabric, each patch a distinct group of newcomers bringing their own ambitions and anxieties, hopes and fears, characteristics, and characters. Wittingly or unwittingly, with the growth of the city, biases and prejudice crept into all walks of life: housing, employment, education, social life, and religion, giving rise to the saying heard around the country, "The most segregated time in the United States is Sunday morning at 11:00 a.m."

Postcard of Blacks strolling at 9th Street and the Boardwalk, Ocean City. c. 1908

Photo courtesy Carol Kearney, 2021

Social Discrimination

Well intentioned, unwitting racism found its way into Ocean City life, as evidenced by newspaper accounts of local events showcasing a type of engrained minstrelsy.

BOYS AND NOISE AT PROGRESSIVE LEAGUE

The Annual Father and Son Event Held by League— 300 Present

Boys, noise, was the big feature of the Third Annual Father and Son night held by the Young Men's Progressive League in their quarters at the Hann Building Monday night. For several days previous to the big event, youngsters of the town were buttonholing every League member asking if he had a boy to take along.

Some members put in their appearance with one colored boy and two white boys or vice versa. This annual affair of the League for the entertainment of the boys is not restricted to color or creed and those men who did not have boys to bring went out into the highways and byways and brought in somebody elses boy.

Chronic pessimists and leather-faced individuals habitually addicted to the frown that won't come off, giggled and roared with laughter at the comical antics of over 300 boys who were the guests. The affair included contests of every conceivable nature from a nail driving contest to the double shuffle by a group of colored lads.

The contests and prize winners were as follows: recitations, Howard Gordon, first prize, and Ferdinand Taccrino, second. Talking, Jacob Sannino and Ralph Davis. Toe wrestling, Frank Grozier, Jr., and Horace Regan. Indian wrestling match, Langford Simms and Edward Turner. Wheelbarrow race, Charles Adnezzio and Howard Gordon. Three-legged race, Ira Bashay and Mark Barclay. Potato race, Ernest Rolfi and Howard Garrison. Sack race, Frank Lanzara and Robert Stevens. Jigging for colored boys, Paul Stewart and Clarence Reynolds. Shoe scramble, David Schantz and Charles Stevenson. Blindfold boxing, Joseph Costello and John Stewart. Nail driving, Frank Grozier and Victor Gifford. Cracker eating, Albert Jones and Lonni Newcomer. Pie eating, Edward Clayton and Ferdinand Taccrino. Apple bobbing, Louis Johnson and Wm. Davis.

The prizes consisted of flashlights, Ever-sharp pencils, boxes of candy and tooth brushes.

Boys and Noise at Progressive League. Ocean City Sentinel Ledger, 1922.

Systemic racial segregation existed in formal and informal social events and activities.

OCHS prom 1944. Friends forever. L-R: standing Aaron Edward Harvey, Dewitt Roland Harmon. Sitting Sarah Frances Oliver, Gloria Llewellyn Henry.

"This picture is from Gloria's senior prom in 1944, the last year Ocean City High School held segregated proms. Both couples were high school sweethearts who became lifelong partners. Dewitt and Gloria witnessed Ed and Sarah's marriage.

Marion Harmon, daughter of Gloria and Dewitt

167

Native's Night in O.C., full of shared memories

By ED WISMER
Ocean City Sentinel critic

OCEAN CITY – It was the summer edition of Native's Night at the Historical Museum on Thursday, Aug. 24. Museum President Fred Miller welcomed a respectable audience to the museum, whether they were genuine Ocean City natives or former shoobies who have become year-rounders.

Those who attended shared a wealth of memories of old time Ocean City. Many of the stories were centered around the old Central Avenue School which has also served as police headquarters since 1966.

The program was designed to give snowbirds and visitors who were unable to attend the winter edition of Native's Night an opportunity as well as to accommodate the folks who settled here belatedly, after coming here from Manayunk, Pottstown or Robbinsville and thus missed out on the joys of having been reared here.

Miller displayed a number of projected pictures of the past glories of Ocean City, particularly the schools. The first picture was of the old two-story wooden structure that was the town's first school. Built in 1903, it housed seven grades and was the biggest school in Cape May County. The town grew so fast that, in 1906, a new and larger building had to be built and it also served as the high school. It is that school that became the police facility.

In 1924, Ocean City High School opened at Sixth Street and Atlantic Avenue, directly across Atlantic Avenue from the new Ocean City High School. Many of those gathered at the museum recalled the auditorium, gym and the swimming pool.

Natives recalled that Ocean City had segregation too, but many were unaware that it existed. Shocking to many was the story of Sing Lee and his family. Lee operated a laundry at Ninth Street and Atlantic Avenue. Due to an unspoken quota system for Asians, when the eight children came of age and married, they had to settle elsewhere to avoid increasing Ocean City's Asian-American population. Many who grew up here were unaware of what went on in Ocean City as recently as the early 1960s.

Ed Wismer, Ocean City Sentinel Critic. Ocean City Sentinel, August 31, 2006

Segregated Accommodations

The city playground at 8th Street and Haven Avenue served the entire Westside community when people of color were not welcome elsewhere. Children from 2nd Street to 7th Street walked south to the Haven Avenue entrance. The lesser number of children between 8th Street and 10th Street used the 8th Street entrance. In the 1950s, locals considered the Haven Avenue entrance near the Scout Cabin the main entrance and the 8th Street entrance the back gate. Well intentioned improvements to the playground in later years upgraded the 8th Street entrance to welcome visitors with an ornamental gate and memorial brick installation. Plans left a cyclone fence on the Haven Avenue side, relegating the Haven Avenue entrance to a "back door." Officials installed a much-needed new playground further north.

8th Street playground. 8th Street entrance facing supermarket.

8th Street playground. Haven Avenue entrance near scout cabin facing community.

169

Victor Hugo Green (1892-1960)

Born in Manhattan, New York and reared in Hackensack, New Jersey, Victor Hugo Green was a postal employee and travel writer who penned his first ten page "Negro Motorist Green Book" in 1936 as a pocket guide for Blacks negotiating Whites only policies in New York City. Unwelcome in restaurants, hotels, etc., the guide listed places where Blacks could safely eat, sleep and purchase gas.

Standard Oil's sponsorship agreement with Esso (known today as ExxonMobil) gas stations across the country made the original Green Books available for purchase at a cost of $0.25. The guide was largely unknown to Whites. The motoring public purchased upwards of 15,000 copies of the Green Book per year.[98] Subsequent editions of the 1940s and 1950s included thousands of national and international listings. Ocean City listings are included in at least one of the books.

The Negro Motorist Green-Book est. 1936. 1940 ed. Victor H. Green Publisher, New York City[99]

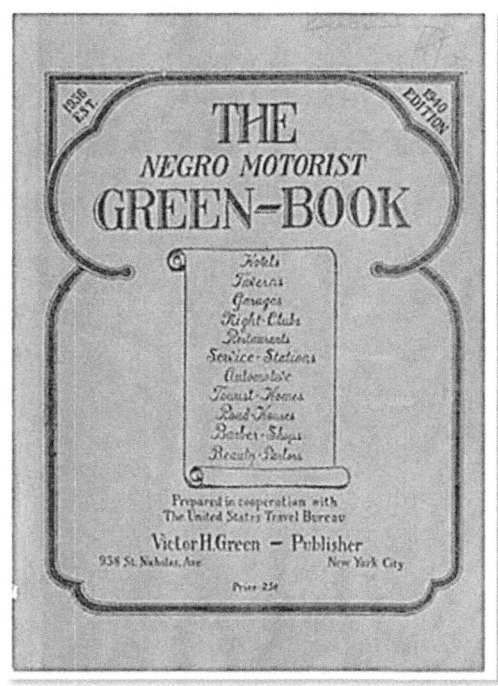

The Negro Motorist Green Book, 1940

The Negro Motorist Green Book, 1947

The Negro Motorist Green Book and
International Travel Guide, 1949

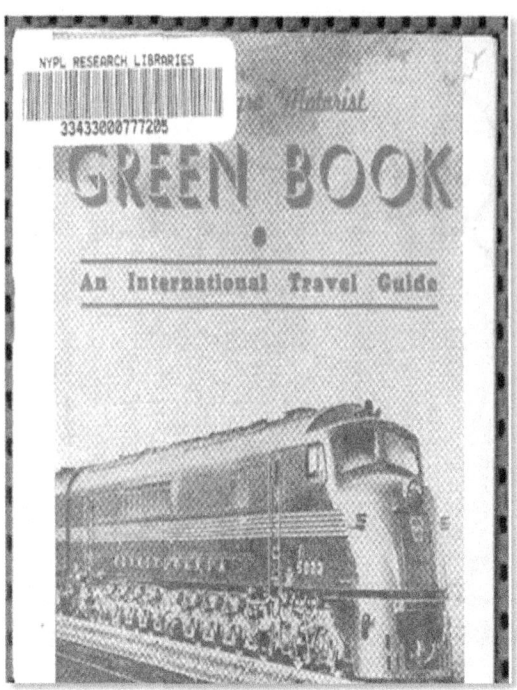

The Negro Motorist Green Book,
1951 Railroad Edition

The Negro Travelers' Green Book,
1953 Airline Edition

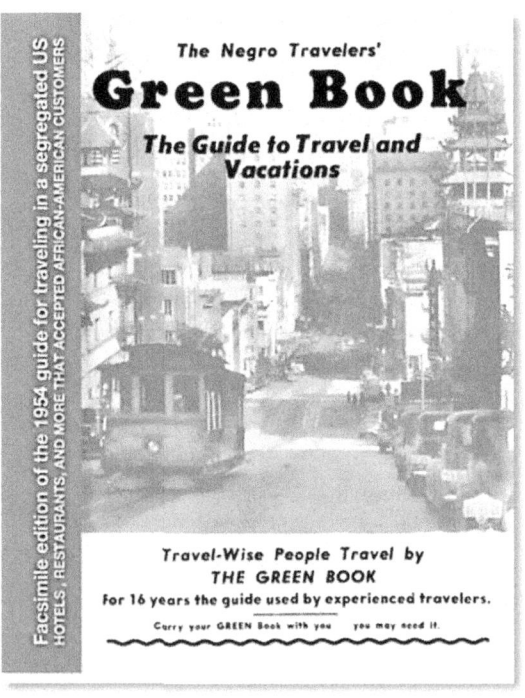

The Negro Travelers' Green Book, The Guide to
Travel and Vacations, 1955 Edition

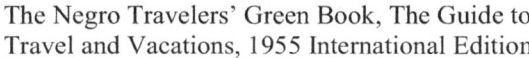

The Negro Travelers' Green Book, The Guide to Travel and Vacations, 1955 International Edition

The Negro Travelers' Green Book, Fall 1956 Edition

Segregated Beaches

Beaches up and down the east coast were segregated. Oak Bluffs on the island of Martha's Vineyard off Cape Cod in Massachusetts has its Inkwell. Atlantic City, another Atlantic coast barrier island off South Jersey, has its Chicken Bone Beach. A little further south, Ocean City off the Cape May peninsula had its own beach designated exclusively for Blacks.

The Ocean City beach was never labeled with a derogatory ethnic name, at least not one that was used openly. It was just the Black Beach (Beach #7) between 5th Street and 6th Street. These three beaches all tell a similar story.

The Inkwell

In the late 1800s, Methodist and Baptist Christian revivals at camp meeting association gatherings attracted visitors to Oak Bluffs on Martha's Vineyard. This became the first summer religious camp established in the United States[100] As the population of the island grew, developers saw the opportunity to cash in on pilgrimages to the Tabernacle. Martha's Vineyard became a popular vacation spot for the affluent who often brought their African American servants to the island with them. Discrimination was very much a part of island life causing African Americans to seek places where they could feel comfortable. Unwelcome on other parts of the island, they tended toward Town Beach, now known as Oak Bluffs, where the only chill they felt was the cool breeze blowing in from offshore. Some say it was local Whites who dubbed the beach "The Inkwell" while others say the Blacks who bathed there affectionately embraced the name.

Today, Oak Bluffs is one of several famous historic African American resort communities along the Atlantic coast having hosted actor Paul Robeson and singer Ethel Waters. Well-to-do year-round Black residents, middle class Blacks who purchased before prices skyrocketed, and trendy vacationers populate the beach. If you make it to the Inkwell by 7:30 a.m. any day of the week, you can bathe with the Polar Bears, a group of locals and visitors who socialize and take an early morning plunge.

Chicken Bone Beach

Chicken Bone Beach, a segregated beach at the end of Missouri Avenue in Atlantic City, became the unofficial Black beach during the 1930s. Blacks and Whites had shared all city beaches since the founding of the resort some 80 years earlier. In 1928, hotel owners in Atlantic City with properties on the beach told city officials, "They had a problem." White patrons were complaining about Black people on the beach and in the ocean in front of their hotels. An executive from the Ambassador Hotel wrote to a public official, "The Georgia Avenue side of the Convention Hall would be a logical place for colored bath houses." In a meeting between leaders of the two races, Blacks were advised that it was in the best interest of all that Negroes patronize the beach where the colored lifeguards would be placed. The north side of town, a place already inhabited by thousands of African Americans who worked in hotels and other Atlantic City businesses, would be the area for Black people to "patronize" the shore town. City owned oceanfront property near the Convention Hall would be the area where "colored" lifeguards would be stationed. No strong-arm methods were used, and the matter was resolved "amicably."[101]

Most of the patrons of Missouri Avenue beach were families on day trips. Unable to dine in restaurants, Black beachgoers packed picnic baskets with food and snacks. Fried chicken was a favorite as it kept well. Workers who cleaned up the discarded bones are said to have nicknamed the area Chicken Bone Beach. Here, regular folks could rub elbows with entertainment stars on the beach during the day and see show-stopping performances in the entertainment district at night. Hotels, restaurants, and bars quickly sprang up to serve Blacks. Celebrities like Sammy Davis, Jr. frequented the beach. Sammy's mother, Elvera "Baby" Sanchez Davis was a retired Apollo Theater dancer and stage actress who worked as a barmaid at Grace's Little Belmont on Kentucky Avenue in Atlantic City following her New York City career.[102]

Jim Crow racial segregation laws were never officially enacted in Atlantic City. With the passage of the 1964 Civil Rights Act, all Atlantic City beaches were again open to everyone, but Chicken Bone Beach remained the preference of Blacks for years to come. Today, a sign and wooden proscenium memorialize Chicken Bone Beach, which is sandwiched between Playground Pier Mall and Jim Whelan Boardwalk Hall. Blacks now congregate at the Inlet at an area they call "The Inkwell."

And Now, a Lily-White Ocean.
To the Editor of the AFRO:

A letter, written by a Kentuckian, was published in a white daily here, and asked that colored people be kept out of the ocean where white people are supposed to bathe.

Colored people have been going in at that particular place for many years without any complaint, but since so many whites have come up from the deep South, we have lots of trouble with them.

So far no steps have been taken by the white people, but it is high time that the colored people got ready for trouble.

CLARENCE MOTLEY,
Ocean City, Md.

Correction: Article was about Ocean City, NJ[103] written by Westside resident Clarence Motley

The Black Beach

Like Martha's Vineyard, Methodists founded Ocean City as a seaside resort for religious camp meetings. There were no people of color on the island at the city's founding, but the Still family arrived in 1884, just five years later. The population mix changed slowly, and in 1928 the city hired Alvin Thompson as the first Black on the Ocean City Beach Patrol. He was assigned to Beach #7 which became the beach for Blacks.

There were no signs designating Beach #7 for Blacks. There were no known laws or statutes prohibiting Blacks from using other beaches and no proclamation ending the discrimination. Lifeguards enforced the separation between races. The practice gradually faded away sometime around the late '50s. Today, the beach is the site of a parking lot and volleyball court with only Ocean City old timers remembering the carefree days of fun at the Black Beach.

"We frequented the beaches at 1st Street and 2nd Street not far from Pop Pye's house. In the late 1960s, someone called the cops to have us removed."

Donovan Butler meeting, Ocean City Library. December 2021.

Call It Out

"In the 1920s, Floyd Scott of Ocean City attended a meeting advertised as a meeting of young Christian men. It was held upstairs over a drug store at 9th Street and Asbury Avenue. After the host explained the purpose of the meeting, a meeting of the KKK, all visitors were asked to stand. Those visitors who intended to join were told to sit. By inference, those still standing were being asked to leave. Floyd Scott never went back."

Mary Jane Scott Bullock
Conversation at Ocean City Community Center, August 2018

"I never had any problems."

Richard Grimes (1918-2014), Ocean City Old Timer

Josephine A. Kapus. 100 Plus, School Days, Ocean City Gazette, 1986

Abbott's Drug Store ad, Ocean City Sentinel Ledger, July 29, 1932

"I looked forward to going back to school in September. In those days there was a lot of prejudice, but things are much better now."

Mable Thompson Griffin (1920-2009), Ocean City Old Timer

Josephine A. Kapus.100 Plus, School Days, Ocean City Gazette, 1986

"You know, years ago, long before that, black people who came to work for the summer had to leave by Labor Day. They could only stay for the summer."

Mildred "Millie" Peterson, OCHS Class of 1948

Historical Museum Celebrates 4th Annual Natives Night, Ocean City Gazette, 1999

"I remember my black classmates being some of my best friends. We didn't know anything different then. There was no racism."

Sonia Forry

Historical Museum Celebrates 4th Annual Natives Night, Ocean City Gazette, 1999

"We had good athletes but no scholarships. No one said, 'Nate, you're good at math.' I wanted to go to college, but the guidance counselor said, 'Well, Nate, I don't know if you can do it.' If you didn't have a parent stand up for you, you were lost. I was told I would have to leave Ocean City to find opportunities. I served on the safety patrol in 5th grade. As an end-of-the-year treat, safety patrol members were treated to a movie at the Village Theatre. A police officer stopped me from entering. "You have to go upstairs on the balcony," said the policeman.

Nathan Davis, OCHS Class of 1955

Ocean City Historical Museum Lecture, Segregation to Success. Ocean City Gazette, Sep 2011

Swimming Pool Given Its Periodic Cleaning

By STEVE CAKE

Ocean City High's swimming pool has a new look. The pool was cleaned by Charles Bakley, one of the school's maintenance men, on January 12. It has been changed from a dark green to a light blue.

The pool is one of the features of which O. C. H. S. can be exceptionally proud. It is 40 feet long and 22 feet wide. At it's shallow end it holds three feet of water, while there is 10 feet at the deep end.

Twice a day chlorine tests are made to determine whether there is a shortage of chlorine in the pool. The water is changed regularly.

Each time it is filled, 45,000 gallons of water are used. It is also heated and circulated daily.

Twice every month a sample is taken to Atlantic City to be checked for bacteria.

Swimming Pool Given Its Periodic Cleaning. Ocean City Sentinel Ledger. February 1955.

Perhaps the most egregious insults happened at school. Oral history holds that Westside children were being denied the opportunity to swim in the high school pool. A group of influential men from the Westside called the Progressive Four petitioned the school board on behalf of the children.

John Lyles, Pete Peterson, Abe Collins, Sylvester Thompson, George Mason, Obie Moore, and Tim Spruill are mentioned as being part of the Progressive Four at varying times. It is unclear which men were in the group that approached the school board, but the school responded by allowing boys, and later girls, to swim the last two periods on Friday afternoons, a boys group and a girls group. The school then drained the Olympic sized pool every weekend. Being rather naïve children, we did not realize all that was going on and simply enjoyed the chance to swim in the pool.

"It was after World War II, and I was in elementary school. They used to take us to the high school swim. Talk started spreading about separating Blacks and Whites. Dad (Nate Davis Sr.), Pete Thompson, Ed Turner, and Leonard Wiggins heard the talk. They had words with the coaches, brothers John and Fenton Carey. Everyone agreed to let the children decide. We kids had no problem swimming together."

"Wayne (Thompson) and Louie (Davis) were tight growing up. They always managed to get into something. Mom gave me the job of taking a little black book to the teacher every day so the teacher could record what Louie had done. One day as I approached the classroom, I saw Wayne struggling to free himself from a chair where Ms. Mowen had lassoed him to the chair using rounds and rounds of string. I kept walking. Also, Roland Wiggins was a child prodigy on the piano and became a lifeguard. He was not allowed to attend the beach patrol ball but was asked to provide the entertainment."

Nathan Davis, Jr., OCHS Class of 1955
Interview, Egg Harbor Township, September 22, 2022

"I was the only black in my afternoon kindergarten class at Central Avenue Elementary School. When one of my classmates celebrated a birthday, White students were lined up two by two and went to party. Not knowing what else to do, I followed. We arrived at a home where the White students played games and sat at a table for ice cream and cake. I was set aside. At the end of the party, I was asked if I knew my way home and was sent off on my own. A man saw me standing on a corner crying and stopped his car to help me. He drove me to 7th Street and West Avenue and dropped me off on the corner near my home at 719 West Avenue."

Vivian Strawberry, OCHS Class of 1958
Telephone conversation April 10, 2023

"There were unspoken rules on where Blacks could and could not go. We understood we were not welcome at the Youth Center, so we did not go. On the contrary, I was surprised when the owner of the Boxwood near 3rd Street and Atlantic Avenue allowed me in during my senior year of high school."

Vivian Strawberry, OCHS Class of 1958
Telephone conversation April 10, 2023

"Janet Turner, Loretta Thorne and I were seniors in high school when a group of White boys spat on us."

Janet Motley Cline, OCHS Class of 1962
Telephone conversation April 2023

"There was an occasion where a group of White boys jumped Black boys after school because some White girls had given their photos to the Black boys. School officials knew about the incident but did nothing."

Janet Motley Cline, OCHS Class of 1962
Telephone conversation April 2023

"Word filtered out around high school that the college prep science teacher did not want women or Blacks in his class. I took it anyway. Let's just say it did not go well even though I scored at the 98th percentile in national science aptitude tests. His arbitrary grading system was demoralizing. Mom was unable to get him to relent. It was a life-altering experience that resulted in my changing my career path. I sometimes wonder what kind of scientist I could have been."

Loretta Harris, OCHS Class of 1963

178

Flanders Hotel want ad.
Ocean City News, September 1925

"Eddie Turner and I planned a post Labor Day swim at the Flanders. We purchased tickets and proceeded to the pool whereupon the manager intercepted us saying, 'You cannot go swimming.' 'But, but, we thought ....,' they replied. 'Today, the pool is for members only,' the manager insisted. Eddie and I got the message. Blacks were not welcome. Years later when I was an Ocean City policeman, I was called to the Flanders to handle a situation where a guest had died of natural causes in one of the hotel rooms. Upon arrival, the manager instructed me that the body must be taken out via the back of the house service elevator. Remembering my treatment at the hotel many years earlier, I got my revenge. I instructed the rescue squad take the body out via the front of the house guest elevator and through the front lobby full of flabbergasted guests."

William Warren, OCHS Class of 1963
Telephone interview. October 13, 2021

Flanders Hotel pool[104]

"I regularly visited the Flanders Hotel and enjoyed being chased away. I was particularly delighted to hop into their pool. Oh, to watch the fine folk flee the pool as if a massive sea serpent was lurking about. They could never catch me and had no idea who I was nor from whence I came nor to where I fled.

179

I would get chased away from Harbor House until I pestered the owner's adult son, Geno Solo, into being my friend. One night Rob and I were at the marina directly across the street from our rental at 225 Bay Avenue. Frank Steelman lived upstairs in the marina. It was Steelman's Marina until he sold it to his employees, brothers Dick and Don Sampson. The police, suspicious of our being there, began to interrogate and berate us. Suddenly, Mr. Steelman spoke from his window above informing the police that, "Those boys are allowed to be on the pier, cove, and property AT ANY TIME DAY OR NIGHT."

Whitney Butler, December 2021

"I came to Ocean City from South Carolina. My teacher, Mr. Driscoll, treated me badly. At age sixteen, I wanted to be a model. I was tall, slim, and had a flare for fashion. My mother worked at Stainton's Department Store on Asbury Avenue. It was the biggest and finest store in town. She kept me dressed in the best of everything. Needing career counselling and advice, I went to Mr. Kirk, the School Guidance Counsellor. He advised me that I would be a domestic worker. I said "Okay," but really didn't know what a domestic worker did, so I went to Mrs. Gleason. She said, "Oh, no. You're not going to be a domestic worker. Domestic workers clean up after other people. They do housekeeping for White folks. They scrub floors, do laundry, cook, and clean the house. Most do the grocery shopping and take care of the children too." I thought to myself, "That's exactly what my mother, Minnie Abram, and her friends like Estelle McCall did back in South Carolina. That's how my mom took care of our family and sent my brothers to college." Mrs. Gleason saw that I had a bright future ahead of me. She encouraged me to follow my dreams and called my mother to discuss plans for my future. Mrs. Gleason made sure my mother could get a loan from the bank. My mother and I were approved for a $3,000 loan which I was to pay off in installments of $30.12 a month. In July 1970, I enrolled at Berkley Secretarial and Fashion Design School in East Orange. I was an adult when I learned from former classmates that the Counsellor treated them similarly."

Sophia Abram Bratton (1952-2024), OCHS Class of 1970, August 2023

"In the fall of my senior year in high school, I began the process for applying to college. As a straight A honor roll student in the top 10 of my class, I had planned to apply to several Ivy League or Ivy Plus colleges and universities. Knowing that applicants had to be multi-faceted achievers to be considered for this type of school, I held leadership and membership roles in nearly 20 extracurriculars, had volunteered hundreds of hours, and took advanced level courses including three languages. Although my SAT scores weren't quite as strong as I had hoped, I knew they were sufficient to qualify, and when paired with my academics, other activities, and recent role serving as Miss Ocean City, I should be a strong

candidate. I brought my list of 6 schools to the high school guidance counselor for review, as counselor review and letter of recommendation was standard practice. He struggled to find his words, then told me that my choices were 'ambitious' and that I would need to add at least two 'safety schools' to my list. With no other option, I applied to the two additional schools. The following Spring, I marched into the guidance counselor's office and presented him with a folder containing 8 acceptance letters. He was shocked."

Michelle Harris Anderson, OCHS Class of 1989, May 2024

Growing up in Ocean City was great, but racism was always there - undercover. Simply put, it wasn't a cross burning on a lawn. It was being forced to the balcony in movie theaters. It was being tailed in the local department store until the owner, Howard Stainton, confronted the sales clerk and put a stop to the practice. It was not being able to get a job on the boardwalk. It was the school guidance counsellor telling me I should just sign up with the military and go to Vietnam. It was fighting to open a business in town, a business my partners and I ran successfully for twenty-four years until the building was sold.

Ronald Pennington, OCHS Class of 1971, August 2023

Jim Crow was not reserved for the South, minstrel shows, or film. Atlantic City Electric Company corporate letterhead featured an image of "Elec," a blackface butler. The image was also included in employee handbooks. An updated version of "Elec" appeared in 1940s advertising.

Atlantic City Electric Company dividend payout ad. Ocean City Sentinel, 1930.

Conservation Program ad featuring "ELEC." Ocean City Sentinel Ledger, September 17, 1943

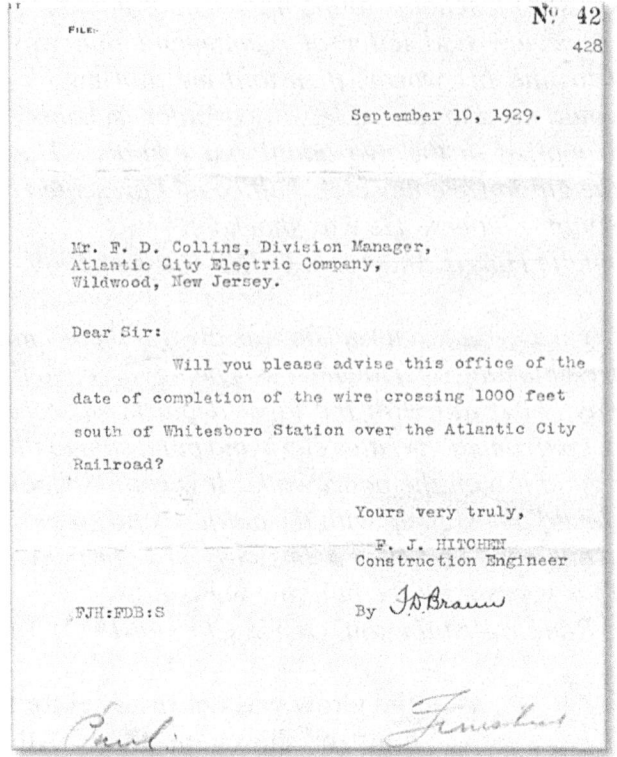

September 10, 1929.

Mr. F. D. Collins, Division Manager,
Atlantic City Electric Company,
Wildwood, New Jersey.

Dear Sir:

Will you please advise this office of the date of completion of the wire crossing 1000 feet south of Whitesboro Station over the Atlantic City Railroad?

Yours very truly,

F. J. HITCHEN
Construction Engineer

FJH:FDB:S   By J.D.Braun

N° 42
428

Internal letter.
Front and reverse sides of communication from F. J. Hitchen, Construction Engineer, to F. D. Collins, Division Manager featuring "ELEC" on back of letterhead.

"ELEC" believes in the COMMUNITY which he serves. Wildwood, NJ. September 1929.

"ELEC"
believes
in the
COMMUNITY
which he serves

The Woman's Christian Temperance Union donated the water fountain outside City Hall to the City in 1915. Its base was marked "For Whites Only." "In the 1950s, Mom (Dorothy Thompson) pulled me away from the fountain when I stopped for a drink of the cool, refreshing water."

Loretta Thompson Harris,
daughter of Dorothy Thompson

"Mom deliberately took me to the fountain for a drink in the 1960s."

Alva Thompson, 2020,
daughter of Dorothy Thompson

Water fountain.[105] Corner 9th Street and Asbury Avenue outside City Hall as it appears as of the writing of this book

By the 1970s, Dorothy was openly taking her grandchildren to the fountain for water. *"She took me there."*

Angela Harris Moore, 2020, granddaughter of Dorothy Thompson

Thoughts on Blue Law,
NAACP, and politics
Editor Ocean City Sentinel-Ledger,
July 1927

Thoughts on blue law, NAACP, and politics

Editor, Sentinel-Ledger: I have just returned from the boardwalk and it can truly be called a disaster area today (Sunday, July 27).

I would estimate that crowds and businesses are off by at least 50 percent. This is a terrible thing to happen to these merchants and we must try and help them.

Two years ago I would have resisted efforts to open this town that I love so much on Sundays. But since it has been open for the better part of two summers, I have changed my mind completely.

There has been absolutely no ill effects from the loss of the blue laws. They are unfair, unjust and unnecessary. It has been proven beyond a doubt that we can still have the same quiet peaceful town without the restrictions of the blue laws.

I issue an appeal to the mayor and every Council member to delay enforcement of the blue laws until the fall when we can vote on this

the Mainland branch of the NAACP, to go to hell!

There is not a fairer or more tolerant city in the U.S.A. for black people to live in, than Ocean City. We live together, we work together and we play together. Any attempt by the NAACP to stir up trouble in this town is so totally uncalled for, it would be obscene.

And I might add that the black leaders and residents of this town should be the first to rise to the mayor's defense on this issue. The Davis family, the Grimes family, the Thompson family and many more longtime black residents should rise to the fore-front on this issue and squash this absurd troublemaker from out of town.

And isn't it disgusting how the three Bittner allies are already voting together to block things. Mr. "do nothing" Videtto is without a doubt the worst Council member we have ever had, and Mr. Jessel is falling right

Stainton's three-story department store opened on July 3, 1940. Ocean City Sentinel-Ledger[106]

"Resort's Big New Department Store Formally Opens Today; Climaxes
Merchandising Career Begun Here 28 Years Ago."

A full-page ad in the newspaper told people what to expect: "STAINTON'S new department store is dedicated to sound principles of offering the finest quality merchandise at reasonable prices, with an efficient, dependable and courteous service."

In 1947, the Stainton's Annex opened behind the department store on West Avenue. It carried furniture, bedding, floor coverings and appliances. It also included Stainton's Toyland where Santa would greet the children and listen to what they wanted for Christmas. Many wanted the Lionel trains they saw displayed in the front of the store.

> *Christmas is supposed to be a time of merriment and good cheer. Every year, area children lined up to see Santa at Stainton's Department Store, recite their wish list, and receive a mesh stocking filled with fruit and candy. As I excitedly climbed up onto Santa's lap in the 1950s to request a Lionel train set, Santa asked, "What's a little Black boy like you want for Christmas?" Good cheer and courteous service?*
>
> *Kenneth Thompson, OCHS Class of 1965, December 2013*

Stamp It Out

Nationally, the '50s gave way to the '60s and all the turmoil of that decade as Blacks fought for civil rights and Whites resisted. Dr. King led The March on Washington for Jobs and Freedom. The assassinations of John F. Kennedy, Martin Luther King, Jr., and Robert Kennedy in quick succession rocked the country.

"The Greensboro sit-ins were a series of nonviolent protests in February to July 1960, primarily in the Woolworth store, now the International Civil Rights Center and Museum in Greensboro, North Carolina, which led to the F. W. Woolworth Company department store chain removing its policy of racial segregation in the Southern United States. While not the first sit-in of the civil rights movement, the Greensboro sit-ins were an instrumental action and also the best-known sit-ins of the civil rights movement. They are considered a catalyst to the subsequent sit-in movement in which 70,000 people participated. This sit-in was a contributing factor in the formation of the Student Nonviolent Coordinating Committee (SNCC)."[107, 108, 109]

protesting racial segregation
Ministers picketing a Woolworth store in New York City to protest racial segregation at the lunch counters of the chain's Southern branches, 1960.
Image: Everett Collection/Shutterstock.com

Ocean City native Janet Motley attended college in North Carolina during the 1960s when race riots erupted. She was one of the protesters beaten and jailed. There were calls asking people to go to North Carolina to support the students who were being badly beaten.

Sit-in at Woolworth's, Greensboro, North Carolina.[110]

"We did not get to North Carolina to support the effort, but we staged a sit-in at Woolworth's segregated lunch counter in Ocean City. It only took one day to compel service; there was no violence. In the 1950s, store clerks followed any group of Black children throughout the stores, sometimes peeking around corners or from behind clothes racks. We found this amusing and scattered in many different directions giving clerks a run for their money. Ironically, while we were being chased from Stainton's Department Store, its owner, Howard Stainton, was a regular visitor at our home. Our father installed all his foundation work."

Loretta and Kenneth Thompson, 2013

Bridge Over Troubled Waters

By the 1960s, most Westside people had televisions and were able to see and hear nightly news reports of racism, segregation, and discrimination. Across the country, simmering pots of anger boiled over into protests, riots, stand-offs, and fighting in the streets.

Ocean City remained quiet. While the NAACP, Student Non-violent Coordinating Council, and Black Panthers protested and marched for equality nationally, the local branch of the NAACP headed by carpenter John C. Little primarily advocated for affordable housing. Open hostilities never erupted.

"The civil rights movement was an organized effort led by Black Americans to end racial discrimination and gain equal rights under the law. It began in the late 1940s and ended in the late 1960s. Although tumultuous at times, the movement was mostly nonviolent and resulted in laws to protect every American's constitutional rights, regardless of color, race, sex, or national origin."[111]

"The Civil Rights Act of 1964, which ended segregation in public places and banned employment discrimination on the basis of race, color, religion, sex or national origin, is considered one of the crowning legislative achievements of the civil rights movement. It survived strong opposition from southern members of Congress and was finally signed into law in 1964. In subsequent years, Congress expanded the act and passed additional civil rights legislation such as the Voting Rights Act of 1965."[112] Slowly, barriers in employment, housing, and education in Ocean City began to fall.

The Fair Housing Act of 1968 made it illegal for lenders to discriminate on the basis of race, color, religion, national origin, sex, handicap, or familial status. The practice of redlining and race steering diminished.

Theater managers no longer forced Blacks to the balcony but allowed them to sit at the rear of the first floor. Restaurants relaxed the practice of seating people of color at the least desirable places, tables next to the kitchen or in high traffic areas. Instead, the cute little table near the window with a view became available.

The Road Most Travelled

A timeline of select local and national events that shaped my personal context of the struggle for freedom and equality for people of color.

1797	New Jersey Society for the Abolition of Slavery
1804	New Jersey Gradual Abolition of Slavery law. Allowed for the children of enslaved Blacks born after July 4, 1804 to be free only after they attained the age of 21 years for women and 25 for men. Servitude act that delayed end of slavery in the state for decades.
1860	***Census lists Dorothy Jackson born 1762 as slave of sea captain Amariah Corson, Upper Township. Dorothy died of old age at 100 yrs. of age in Jan 1862 in Beesley's Point.***
1861-1865	Civil War.
1 Jan 1863	Lincoln's Emancipation Proclamation. Did not free enslaved African Americans in the Northern States. Freed only those in the mostly southern "rebellious states."
19 Jun 1865	Enslaved Blacks in Galveston, TX are last to learn they had been freed via the Emancipation Proclamation. Commemorated now as "Juneteenth."
Dec 1865	13th Amendment to U.S. Constitution ratified. Abolished slavery and involuntary servitude.[113]
Dec 1865	New Jersey bitterly refused to ratify the 13th Amendment.[114]
1865-1964	Jim Crow era. Black Codes re-established via state and local statutes legalizing segregation. Created form of indentured servitude. Controlled work, housing, voting, pay, travel, seizure of children for labor.
24 Dec 1865	Ku Klux Klan formed in Tennessee.
23 Jan 1866	State constitutional amendment abolished slavery in New Jersey. Last northern state in Union to abolish. Parts of state below Mason-Dixon Line. Gradual abolition. Indentured servitude system instituted.
1867	Reconstruction Act. Attempt at democracy in South. Huge Black vote elected Blacks to congress.
1868	14th Amendment to U.S. Constitution. Citizenship guaranteed to those "born or naturalized in U.S." including former slaves.
1870	15th Amendment to U.S. Constitution. Guaranteed voting rights for Black men. Barred voting rights discrimination.[115] Literacy tests imposed by Southerners to disenfranchise Blacks
1879	***Ocean City founded.***
1884	***Jacob Still and family first Blacks to arrive Ocean City.***
1888	Great Blizzard of 1888.

1890	In the South, literacy tests imposed. Grandfather clauses excluded those whose ancestors did not vote in 1860s.
By 1893	*Jacob Still, proprietor Still's confectionery store on boardwalk, brought salt water taffy to Ocean City.*
1893	The Panic of 1893.
1896	*Macedonia United Methodist mission started.*
1896	Plessy v. Ferguson "Separate but equal" facilities enshrined Jim Crow segregation system. 50 years of second-class citizenship.[116] Founding of NAACP, National Urban League. Reformers: Booker T. Washington, W. E. B. DuBois, A. Philip Randolph.
1896	National Association of Colored Women (NACW) founded to promote equality and suffrage for women. Motto "Lifting As We Climb."
1897	*Union Tabernacle Baptist mission started.*
1901	*St. James A.M.E. mission started.*
1912	*Shiloh Baptist Church started.*
1912	*Clarence Turner first Black on OCPD.*
1916	*Newlin Turner first Black graduate of OCHS.*
1916-1970	Great Migration. Economics and segregation drove 6 million from rural South to North, Midwest and West.
May 1917	Selective Service Act signed requiring registration.
7 Dec 1917	*World War I. U.S. declared war on Germany and enters war. Segregated military.*
18 Jan 1919	Paris Peace Conference convened.
Jul 1919	Red Summer. White supremacist terrorism and racial riots occurred in more than three dozen cities across the United States. Hundreds killed. Black WWI veterans defended communities.
Nov 1919	Red Scare "Palmer Raids." Particularly targeted Italian immigrants and Eastern European Jewish immigrants with alleged leftist ties, with particular focus on Italian anarchists and immigrant leftist labor activists. 10,000 people arrested.
1920	19th Amendment. Suffrage for women though states disenfranchised Black women.
1921	Black Wall Street Massacre, Greenwood, Tulsa, OK.
1928	*Alvin Thompson first Black on Ocean City Beach Patrol.*
1929-1939	Great Depression. Oct 29, 1929 market crash: Black Tuesday. End of unprecedented economic prosperity.
Dec 1933	21st Amendment ended national prohibition. O.C. remains dry town.
1933	Franklin Delano Roosevelt's first "New Deal" on banking crisis

1935	National Council of Negro Women founded by Mary McCloud Bethune to pursue civil rights and suffrage for Black Women
1937	Hindenburg disaster. German airship exploded over Lakehurst, NJ
8 Dec 1941	***U.S. declares war on Japan entering World War II following attack on Pearl Harbor. Segregated military***
1945	Jackie Robinson left Negro League Kansas City Monarchs and signed with Minor League Montreal Royals
1947	Jackie Robinson first Black to play in Major League baseball
Late 1940s	***Rayfield Lyles hired O.C. USPS***
Late 1940s	***Richard Grimes hired O.C. USPS***
c. 1946	***Oscar Harmon first person of color hired by Ocean City Fire Department***
Jul 1948	***Executive Order abolishing segregation in U.S. military***
1950s	Civil rights movement started (Rosa Parks, Little Rock Nine)
9 Sep 1957	Civil Rights Act of 1957[117]
1961	Affirmative action policies instituted to assure equal employment opportunities
1962	***Marizita Grimes first Black Ocean City teacher***
12 Jun 1963	Medgar Evers assassination
28 Aug 1963	March on Washington. "I Have a Dream"
22 Nov 1963	John F. Kennedy assassination
2 Jul 1964	Civil Rights Act of 1964[118]
21 Feb 1965	Malcolm X assassination
7 Mar 1965	Bloody Sunday, Edmund Pettus Bridge
13 Jun 1967	Thurgood Marshall named first Black Supreme Court justice
6 Aug 1965	Voting Rights Act of 1965. Removed remaining deterrents to voting. Enacted federal oversight of voter registration.
1965	***Louis Dennis Davis hired by Ocean City Fire Department***
4 Apr 1968	Martin Luther King assassination
6 Jun 1968	Robert F. Kennedy assassination
26 Jun 1978	U.S. Supreme Court rules that affirmative action can be used as a legal strategy to deal with past discrimination.
3 Nov 1983	Martin Luther King Jr.'s birthday becomes a federal holiday
17 Sep 1984	Vanessa L. Williams becomes the first Black Miss America
13 May 1985	Philadelphia police bomb the headquarters of MOVE, a Black liberation group.
Aug 1987	***Michelle Harris selected first Black Miss Ocean City***
Mar 1990	Clarence Thomas nominated Supreme Court justice.
12 Sep 1992	Mae Carol Jemison becomes the first Black woman in space
16 Oct 1995	Million Man March in Washington, D.C.
Aug 2001	***Kara Harmon selected second Black Miss Ocean City***

21 Jan 2009	Barack Obama first Black inaugurated as President of the United States of America
10 Jan 2012	***Rev. Gregory Johnson elected to Ocean City Board of Education and City Council.***
25 Jun 2013	Supreme Court struck down key provision Voting Rights Act of 1965 in nine states[119]
14 Jan 2020	***Antwan McClellan elected to the New Jersey General Assembly representing 1st Legislative District***
21 Jan 2021	Kamala Devi Harris first Black and AAPI woman inaugurated as Vice President of the United States
25 Feb 2022	Ketanji Brown Jackson confirmed first Black female Supreme Court justice
29 Jun 2023	Supreme Court reverses affirmative action policy in college admissions.

In 2023, New Jersey and forty-six other states observed Juneteenth as a state holiday. Also known as Freedom Day or Emancipation Day, the holiday commemorates the day enslaved Blacks in Galveston, Texas learned that they were, in fact, freed by President Abraham Lincoln's Emancipation Proclamation two and half years earlier. The date was June 19, 1865. Juneteenth then is a holiday of celebration and a mournful remembrance of deep injustice and loss.

> *"But we must remember that there were still enslaved Black men and women in New Jersey even after Juneteenth. Imagine, New Jersey's death grip on slavery meant that until December 1865, six months after enslaved men, women, and children in Texas found out they were cheated of their freedom, approximately 16 African Americans were still technically enslaved in New Jersey."[120]*
>
> Noelle Lorraine Williams, Director,
> African American History Program,
> The New Jersey Historical Commission

The 13th Amendment to the Constitution abolishing slavery and servitude did not end racism. Affirmative Action policies of the 1960s opened doors but not minds and are slowly being dismantled. Two steps forward, one step back.

$$***$$

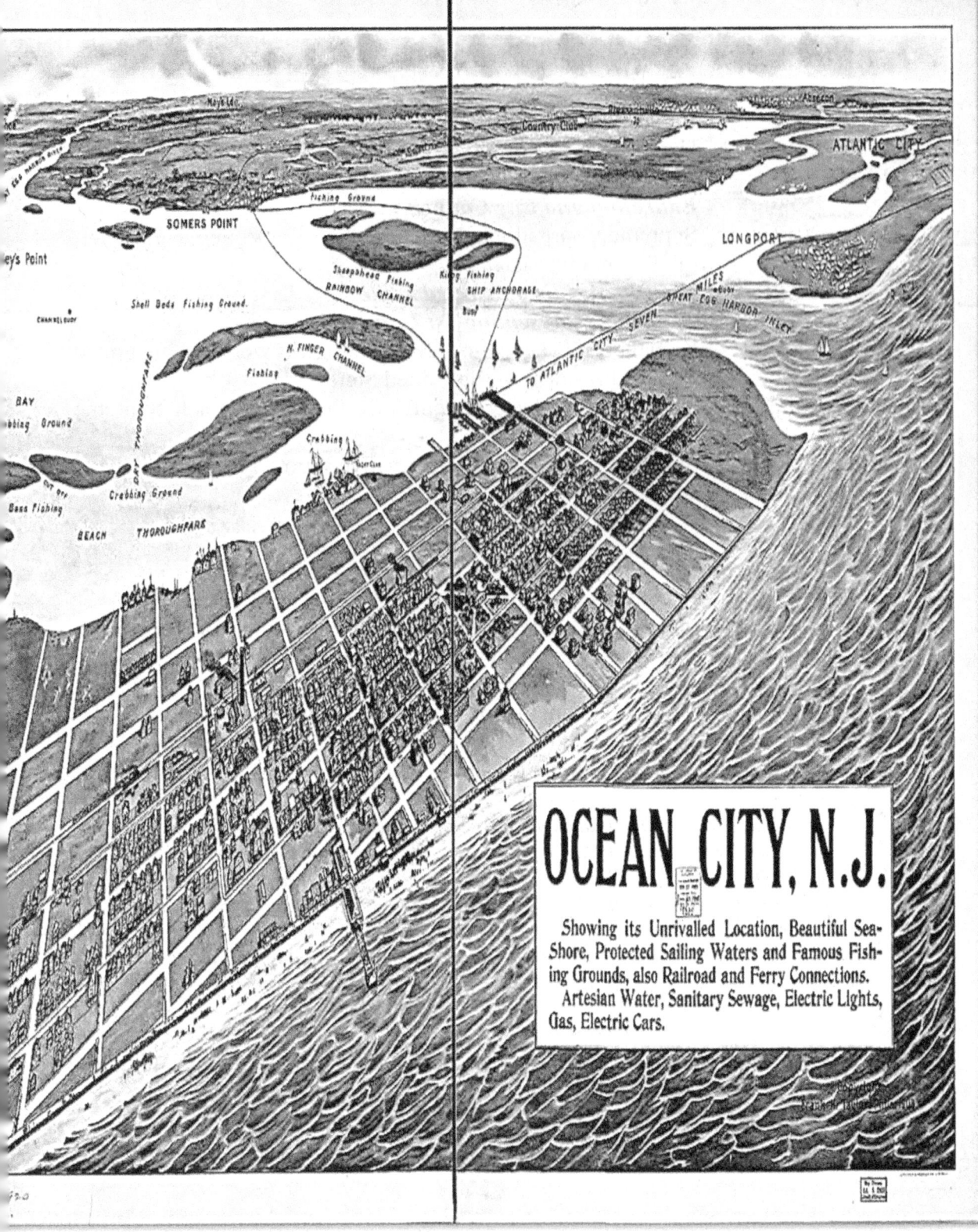

OCEAN CITY, N.J.

Showing its Unrivalled Location, Beautiful Sea-Shore, Protected Sailing Waters and Famous Fishing Grounds, also Railroad and Ferry Connections. Artesian Water, Sanitary Sewage, Electric Lights, Gas, Electric Cars.

1903 aerial of Ocean City's north end. Twelve miles southwest of Atlantic City. Ocean City has 8.5 miles of beachfront, 2.5 miles of boardwalk, and fertile fishing, crabbing, and clamming grounds on the east and west in the Atlantic Ocean and back bays.[121]

Frank H. Taylor, Philadelphia

CHAPTER 4
WATER, WATER, EVERYWHERE

The Beachfront

Some of Ocean City's earliest residents and visitors may have marveled at beach bungalows on wheels and bathers in wool bathing suits.

1908 postcard.[122]

SAVED LIVES OF TWO

Andrew Young Is Hero To Some Summer Cottagers

Andrew Young, colored, chauffeur employed by Frank H. Stewart, Philadelphia business man and a cottage in the Twentieth street section of this city, saved the lives of a man and girl off Twentieth street a few days ago, and those of the cottagers familiar with the conditions look upon him as a hero.

Young was at work on the Stew-

art premises when he heard the cries of a girl bather in the surf. He saw she was in distress and rushed to her assistance. He had to run five hundred feet on the beach before reaching the ocean, and then he was compelled to swim out five hundred additional feet to reach the girl. In the meantime, a male swimmer had seen the girl's predicament and went to her aid. Young got both to tread water as best they could while he pushed and otherwise helped them ashore. Sad to relate, according to neighbors, neither the man nor the woman thanked the colored man for his help.

Andrew Young saves two bathers at 20th Street beach. Ocean City, July 1925.

Mislabeled 1930s postcard titled "6th Street Bathing Beach" with handwritten title "Blacks Private Beach". Ocean City beaches were segregated. Blacks did not have a private beach. The beach between 5th and 6th Streets (Beach 7) was designated for Blacks and protected by Black lifeguards.

May 30, 1931 – Ocean City Beach Patrol Captain Jack G. Jernee hitches a lifeboat behind the Ford Model "A" in front of the beach patrol's winter headquarters at Seventh Street and Haven Avenue. The lifeboat is going to the 10th Street beach where veteran lifeguards Harry Thorning, Ralph Clayton and Marley Fitzgerald are stationed.

Reyn's Garage (later Fred Reiss' Lumber) at 7th Street and Haven Avenue on the Westside was winter headquarters for the Ocean Beach Patrol. Photo courtesy Ocean City Historical Museum.

Ocean City Beach Patrol, Beach #7

Some called it the 5th Street beach, and some called it the 6th Street beach. It all depended on what street you chose to get to the beach. Westside residents coming from north of the Strand typically used 5th Street while those south of the Strand used 6th Street. Officially, according to Ocean City Beach Patrol records, it is Beach 7 between 5th and 6th Streets. Numbers painted on lifeguard stands confirm the designation.

Alvin Leroy Thompson (1901-1959)
First Black on Ocean City Beach Patrol

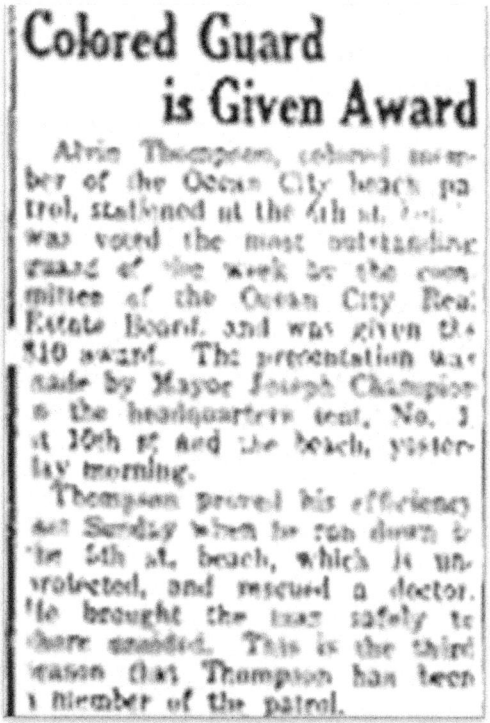

Colored Guard is Given Award. Ocean
City Sentinel Ledger, August 1930

Ocean City founded its beach patrol in 1898. The first African American lifeguard on the Ocean City Beach Patrol was Alvin Thompson who served from 1928 through the summer of 1937. No complete list of Black lifeguards exists. Developing a list is difficult and tedious as Blacks were not named in early listings, were often omitted from photographs and newspaper articles, and excluded from the Annual Beach Patrol Balls.

For years, Alvin worked alone as opposed to the current practice of working in pairs. Though the beach was noted for being the roughest on the East Coast, Thompson never lost a bather. Many of his rescues were so dramatic they were reported in the local newspaper. Local historian Dick Grimes loved to tell the story of how Alvin Thompson and one of the Harris brothers (Archie Harris) left competitors in their wake during swimming competitions.[123] In 1939, Archie and brother Ardmore, a rookie, took third place in the squad rowing competition.

Beach patrol members identified to date:

- Jennings Bell
- William Bell
- Walter Buckholtz
- Irving Carter
- Webster Cooper
- Oscar Harmon
- Archie Haggie Harris
- Marshall Ardmore Harris
- Martin Howard**
- Victor Humphrey*
- Isaac Johnson
- Michael Langley
- Timothy Marable
- Jerome Martin
- Samuel Martin
- John Morris
- John Motley
- Brady Murrel
- Richard Murrel
- Reginald Oliver
- William Reynolds
- Harry Segal 'Sonny' Rolls
- Henry Skipwith
- Howard 'Mickey' Smith
- Junious Stewart
- Robert Smith Stockley
- Harry Swayne
- Alvin Thompson
- Jerry Thompson
- Kenneth Thompson*
- Sylvester Thompson, Sr.
- Sylvester Thompson, Jr.*
- David Turner, Jr.
- Roland Wiggins
- Roger K. Williams

mascot
**unconfirmed*

THE AFRO-AMERICAN, WEEK OF JULY 28, 1934.

OCEAN CITY

By CLARENCE MOTLEY

OCEAN CITY, N.J.—Albert (Al) Thompson one of the life guards along the Jersey coast, has been placed on duty a few weeks earlier this year than last, because of the large number of colored bathers this year. Al is confronted with the most dangerous position along the entire Atlantic Coast.

Clarence Motley, The Afro American, July 28, 1934

L-R: Samuel "Cutie" Martin, Henry Skipwith, Archie Harris, Alvin Thompson. c. 1930s.
Photo courtesy William Griffin.

The first African American lifeguard on the Ocean City Beach Patrol was Alvin Thompson (standing fifth from the left). He was on the patrol from 1928, the date of this picture, through the summer of 1937. No one ever drowned on his watch, although many of his rescues were so dramatic they were reported in the local newspaper. In August 1930, he was voted the most outstanding guard of the week by the Ocean City Real Estate Board and given a $10 award.

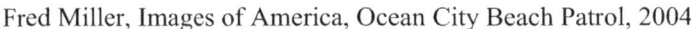

Fred Miller, Images of America, Ocean City Beach Patrol, 2004

Alvin Thompson far right. c. 1930s. Photo courtesy William Griffin.

L-R: Alvin Leroy Thompson and John Isaac Motley. c. 1930s. Photo originally shared by Jul-Ann Peterson Scott, Facebook.com 2021. Photo courtesy Janet Motley Cline.

Photo c. 1937.
10th Street.
Photo courtesy
Ocean City
Historical
Museum
Top row left:
Archie Harris.
Bottom row right:
Alvin Thompson.

Many of the Ocean City lifeguards who were members of the 1938 squad fought in World War II. Three members, Jack Mintzer, John O'Brien, and Norman Blackman, lost their lives in

Fred Miller, Images of America.
Ocean City Beach Patrol, 2004.
OCBP 1938.
Top row left: Archie Harris.
Top row right: Sam Martin.

L-R: World War II veterans Oscar Harmon and Webster Cooper served together on the Beach Patrol after the war. Photo courtesy Tryee Harmon Lawson Eason, July 2019.

Unidentified female with Oscar Harmon. Post WWII.
Photo courtesy Tyree Harmon Lawson Eason, July 2019.

Al Senior took this group shot of the '47 Beach Patrol. Captain Thomas A. Williams, in dark jacket, is seated in the second row. On his left is nurse Margy Reiss Struble, Dr. Willets P. Haines and nurse Ann Thompson. Three mascots huddle in the middle of the front row; the one on the right is Angelo Psaltis, who beca 1958 and is now a lieutenant on the OCBP.

1947 beach patrol included Roger Williams and Howard Martin. Senior Studios photograph.

Courtesy of Fred Miller, Senior Studio, O.C. Historical Museum, O.C. Rowing and Athletic Association

Williams and his squad are smiling because they won their fourth straight South Jersey Lifeguard Championship, winning both the swimming and rowing events. Barney Hungerford won the the doubles rowing race. Below left, the Aug. 1, 1952 issue of the Ocean City Sentinel-Ledger carried a High Noon promotional photo adjacent to an article which reported: "Grace Kelly, is the star playing opposite Gary Cooper in the Strand's weekend attraction, High Noon. Since Miss Kelly was a child she has spent her summers here. The blonde, blue-eyed newcomer to town where he is a marshal." Below, it was during the 1952 Lifeguard Ball that Public Safety Director Laurence P. Lunny presented the South Jersey Lifeguard Championship trophies to, nev Hungerford.

Ocean City Beach Patrol 1952

The Ocean City Beach Patrol 1956

Harry S. Rolls holding son Harry "Buster" Rolls in lifeguard stand.
Note advertisement of 2nd Annual Dance honoring WWII veteran Harold Sumpter (see Chapter 5).
Photo 1948. Photo courtesy Joanne Rolls, daughter of Harry S. Rolls.

Back row bending forward: William "Cut" Reynolds. Standing: Bill Cason, Unknown, Nate Davis, Isaac Johnson in OCBP jacket. Kneeling L-R: Howard "Mickey" Smith in OCBP jacket, Brady Murrel, Unknown, Bill Chalmus, Leroy Grice with cigarette, Unknown, Unknown, Louie Davis, Dickie Murrel in OCBP jacket. Sitting L-R: Willard "Shadow" Boyer in hat. Lying with cigarette in mouth Harry Rolls without his OCBP jacket, Earl "Ninny" Chalmus, child Harry "Buster" Rolls. Lying front white hat: Matthew "Reds" Bacchus. c. 1950s. Photo courtesy Irene Rolls.

Robert Lamont Smith Stockley (1936-1993). Photo originally shared on Facebook by Aline Dickerson B. Milliga.

Howard Webb "Mickey" Smith (1933-2008) Photo courtesy Aline Dickerson B. Milligan.

Timothy Marable (1942-2022). OCHS Class of 1961 Yearbook, The Caravel. Photo courtesy Ocean City Historical Museum.

Jerry Thompson (1942-2016) OCHS Class of 1960.
Jerry Thompson and Timothy Marable formed a team at Beach 7 in the 1960s.

Ocean City Beach Patrol, 1959. Jerry Thompson 2nd row 5th from right.
Photo courtesy Norman Ervine, member OCBP. Senior Studios photograph.

Ocean City Beach Patrol, 1959. Blow-up from full photo above.

Ocean City's surf dash relay team won the second-place plaque at the Cape May County Tournament in 1998. From left to right are Zack Benson, Mike Langley, Bryan Theiss, and Shanin Theiss.

Photo courtesy Fred Miller[124]

Front Row, Left to Right: Cliff Grimes, Dave Robinson, Pat Walker, Larry Hirshland, Pete Downham, Chris Foglio, T.J. Mullineaux, R.J. McAllister, Bill Jenkins. Second Row: Mark Baum, Paul McCracken, John McShane, Craig Wallace, Russ Stevens, Chuck Kaczmarski, Kathy Bourbeau, Alan Lovas, Chris Dollarton, Cricket Frank, Otis Reich, Bill Balchunas, Brian Booth. Third Row: Jim Bradley, Joe Youngblood, Dave Hamilton, Greg Schneider, Fred Mille, Joe Schmitt, Tom Mullineaux, Dr. Joseph R. Tordella, Angelo Psaltis, Bud McKinley, Captain Oliver Muzsaly, Ed Yust, Bill Stull, Bob Amsler, John Saia, Zack Benson, Paul Gallagher. Fourth Row: Ashlea Graham, Elise Thieler, Sandra Wilson, Christy Johnson, Fran Reed, Chris Denn, Mike Hamilton, Doug Schmitt, Kevin Murray, Dennis Swan, Bud Rockey, Ron Kirk, Bill Dorney, Steve Platt, Vannessa Scully, Diane Croft, Stephanie Wilson, Kristie Brown, Sara Griffith, Bryan Theiss. Fifth Row: Bryan Chojnacki, Chris Field, Bob Speca, Pete Davish, Matt Myhre, Eric Bryce, Dave Lippman, Bill Long, Chris Hoeveler, Jake O'Hara, Conor Gorman, Charles Wigo, Nick Dougherty, Cris Southard, Evan Winokur, Greg Browne, Bob Garbutt, Jr., Matt Garbutt, Jeff Garbutt. Sixth Row: Mike Values, Mike Jekogian, Shanin Theiss, Ryan Dunn, Mark McElwee, Drew Muzslay, John Woolery, Jackson Neall, Don Garland, Steve Green, B.J. Gillin, Bob Neary, Taylor Gartland, John Dorr, Brian Kozakowski, Will Freund, Jeff Yachmetz, Heath Muzslay, Kyle Richards. Top Row: Sean McDole, Dave Sadowski, Jay Schiesser, T.J. Caine, Mike Langley, Bill Kazmarck, Jonathon Stephanik, John Stauffer, Andy Toland, Geoff Wilcox, Melissa Koch, Ryan Kavana, Ray Clark, Carolyn Stephanik, Kelly Egan, Greg Fleck, Ed Field, Corby Derr.

Ocean City Beach Patrol 1998. Michael Langley. Ocean City Gazette, September 2, 1998.

The Black Beach, Beach #7

Men on Beach 7. Standing L-R: Lefty Outen, Reds Carney, Flip Clark, Paul Stewart, Ardmore Harris. Bottom L-R: William Strawberry, Alvin Thompson, Harry Carney, Sam Martin, unknown boy. c. 1930s. Thompson family album. Photographer William Mitchell.

Mamie Pride Carpenter (1892-Unk.)[125]

Elizabeth P. Bundy Walker (1911-1985)[126]

L-R: Unknown, Ella Frances Henry with cigarette, Hazel Thompson. c. 1930.
Photo courtesy R. Barry Banks, 2022.

Ella Frances Henry Morris (1904-1939). Photo courtesy R. Barry Banks, 2022.

Jack's Beach Service provided beach chairs and umbrellas for beachgoers. Photo c. 1940.[127]

Jack's Beach Service. Top row center: Floyd Nutter. c. 1948

Guys on Beach 7. Earl Chalmers in tam lying down, Lemuel Brown, Charles Spence
second from right, Roland Wiggins far right kneeling. c. 1940s.
Thompson family album. William Mitchell photographer.

Ladies on Beach 7. Back row L-R: Uknown, Noel Davis, Vivian Henry, Joan Henry, Gloria Henry,
Thelma Oliver, Sarah Oliver. Middle row: Unknown, Unknown, Unknown, Janet Henry, Marjorie
Henry. Front row little girls unknown. Photo courtesy Sonia Henry.
William "Billy" Mitchell photographer.

Regular beach goers to Beach 7. Photo courtesy Jane Murrel Pillow.

Ella Mann Watt (1917-2004). Photo courtesy Blanche Livingston Preston, daughter of Ella.

Rolls family photos courtesy Joanne Rolls

Irene Henry Rolls and
Harry "Buster" Rolls

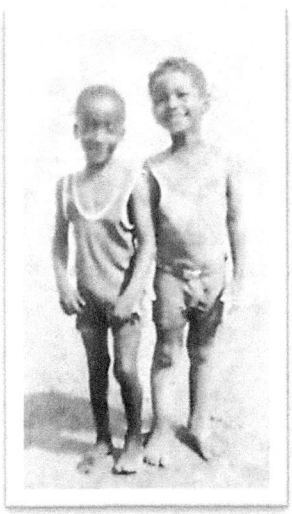

Leonard Leondis Wiggins, Jr. (1925-1996) and
Harry Segal Rolls (1926-1992)

Harry "Buster" Rolls

Harry Segal Rolls (1926-1992)

Lithian "Rocky" Harmon Henry
(1931-2018)
Photo courtesy
Tyree Harmon Lawson Eason

Paul (1914-1982) &
Fanny Stewart (1916-2007)
Ocean City Old Timers
program booklet, 1971

Henry family photos courtesy Sonia Henry

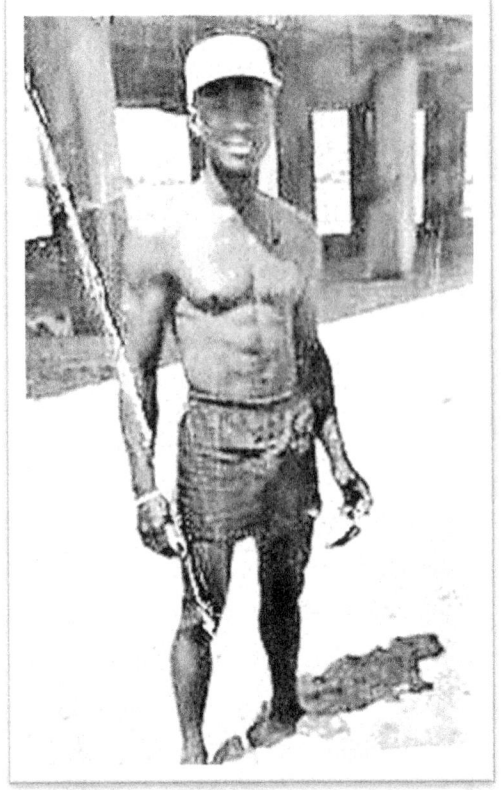

Carl "Mikey" Henry (1928-2014)　　　　Joseph Welton Henry

Vivian "Toogie" Henry (1924-1954)

L-R: Daniel Henry and Joseph Henry

Daniel Lee Henry (1942-2006).
OCHS Class of 1961.

L-R: Wayne Thompson (1938-1998) and
James Hannah (1936-1991) fishing on jetty.

William "Billy" Griffin,
OCHS Class of 1963.
Photo c. 1945
Photo courtesy William Griffin

John Wesley Motley

Jocelyn Alston, OCHS Class of 1963,
and Kenneth Thompson (1947-2015),
OCHS Class of 1965.

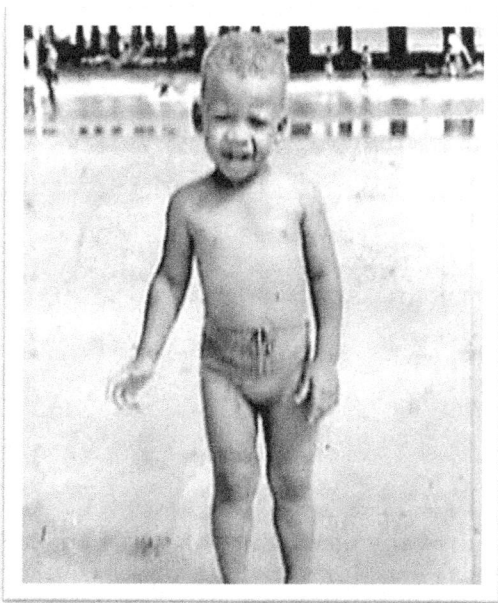

L-R: Jennifer Harvey, Jerry Smith, Jocelyn Alston, Timothy Marable. c. 1960s

Kenneth Homer Thompson. Photo c. 1950.

L-R: Morris Money, Sarah Thompson Money, Unknown, Anita Hayes Ricks, Mable Thompson Griffin, William Griffin, Unknown. Kneeling in front: Ronald Money. Photo courtesy William Griffin.

L-R: Morris Money, Sarah Thompson Hayes Money, Anita Hayes Ricks, Mable Thompson Griffin, William Griffin. Kneeling: Ronald Money. Not Beach 7. Photo courtesy William Griffin

L-R kneeling: Michael Thompson, Pleasantville H.S. Class of 1977; Unknown Philadelphia lad; Alva Thompson, OCHS Class of 1970. L-R top: Tyrone Thompson, OCHS Class of 1981; Wayne "Ricky" Thompson, OCHS Class of 1980.

Sharif K. Thompson, Class of 1996, being baptized near Ocean City Fishing Club's 14th Street fishing pier which was designed and constructed by Sharif's grandfather. Photo c. 2005. Photo courtesy Alva Thompson, mother of Sharif Thompson

Pye descendant photos courtesy Butler brothers

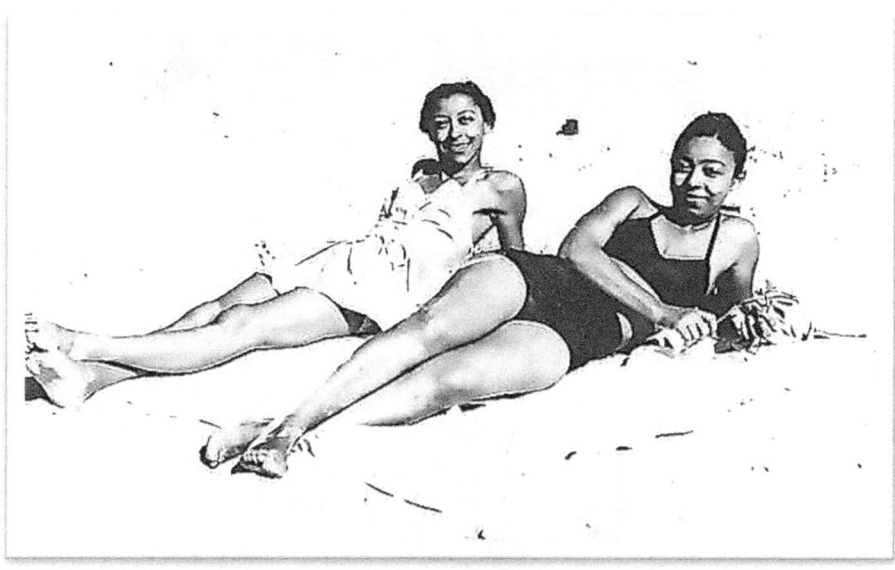

Grace Harris Butler (1927-2008) on left and Blanche Gillis Parker (1912-1976)
vacationed in Ocean City every year. Photo c. 1940s.

Beach 7. Back row: Ralph Parker's sister, Ralph Parker, Blanche Gillis Parker, Unknown,
Helen Gillis Harris. Front row: Phyllis, Juanita, Cheritta, Barbara.

Blanche Gillis Parker

Ralph Parker and Blanche Gillis Parker

Potts family photographs courtesy Barbara Potts Bonaparte

The Potts family lived in Philadelphia and vacationed in Ocean City where they were friends of beach patrol member Alvin Thompson.

Benjamin Franklin "Frank" Potts, Sr. (1908-1991) and son Stephen (1947-2014.

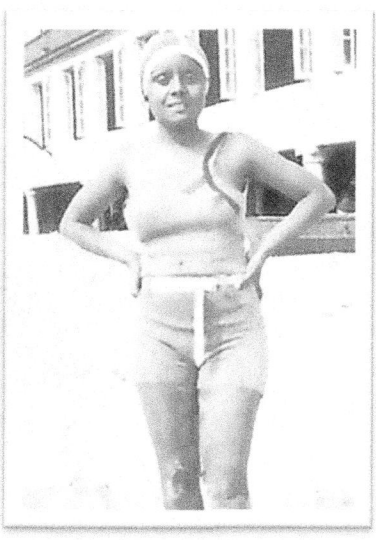

Iva Flowers Potts (1910-1966), wife of Frank, Sr.

Frank Potts and lifeguard Alvin Thompson

Barbara Potts Bonaparte, daughter of Frank Potts

Uncle Al was the first Black lifeguard in Ocean City. I remember him being short but very muscular. 'If you are going to be at the shore, you must learn to swim,' he said. He taught me to swim."

Barbara Potts Bonaparte, daughter of Frank Potts, August 2023

Williams family photos courtesy Carol Williams-Pullins

L-R: George Williams, III;
George Williams, Jr.,
Melvin Williams,
Rowena Johnson Williams

Rowena Johnson Williams
and son George Williams

During beach replenishment projects, wide-circumference pipes laid in 6th Street pumped sand from the bay to the beach. Crude, temporary asphalt mounds created "bridgework" allowing vehicles to cross.

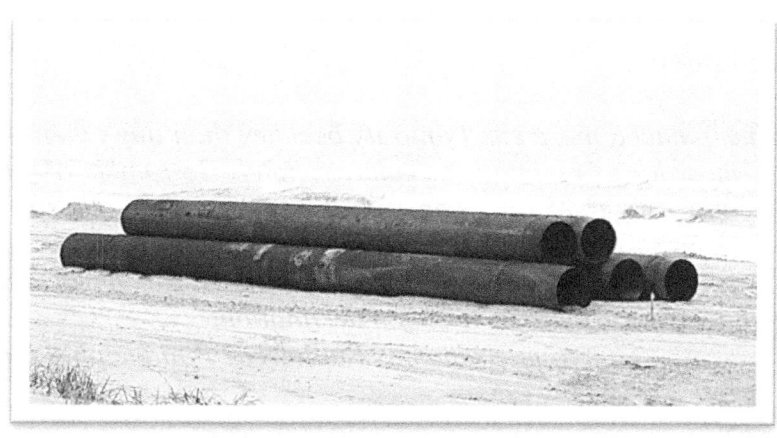

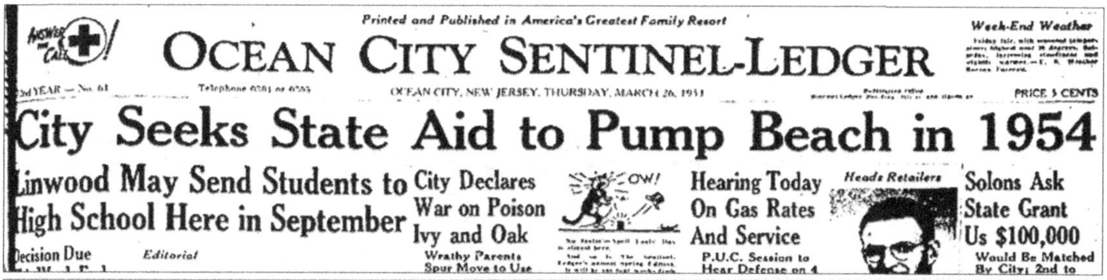

Printed and Published in America's Greatest Family Resort

OCEAN CITY SENTINEL-LEDGER

Week-End Weather

OCEAN CITY, NEW JERSEY, THURSDAY, MARCH 26, 1953 — PRICE 5 CENTS

City Seeks State Aid to Pump Beach in 1954

Linwood May Send Students to High School Here in September

Decision Due

Editorial

City Declares War on Poison Ivy and Oak

Wrathy Parents Spur Move to Use

Hearing Today On Gas Rates And Service

P.U.C. Session to Hear Defense on 4

Heads Retailers

Solons Ask State Grant Us $100,000

Would Be Matched By City; 2nd to

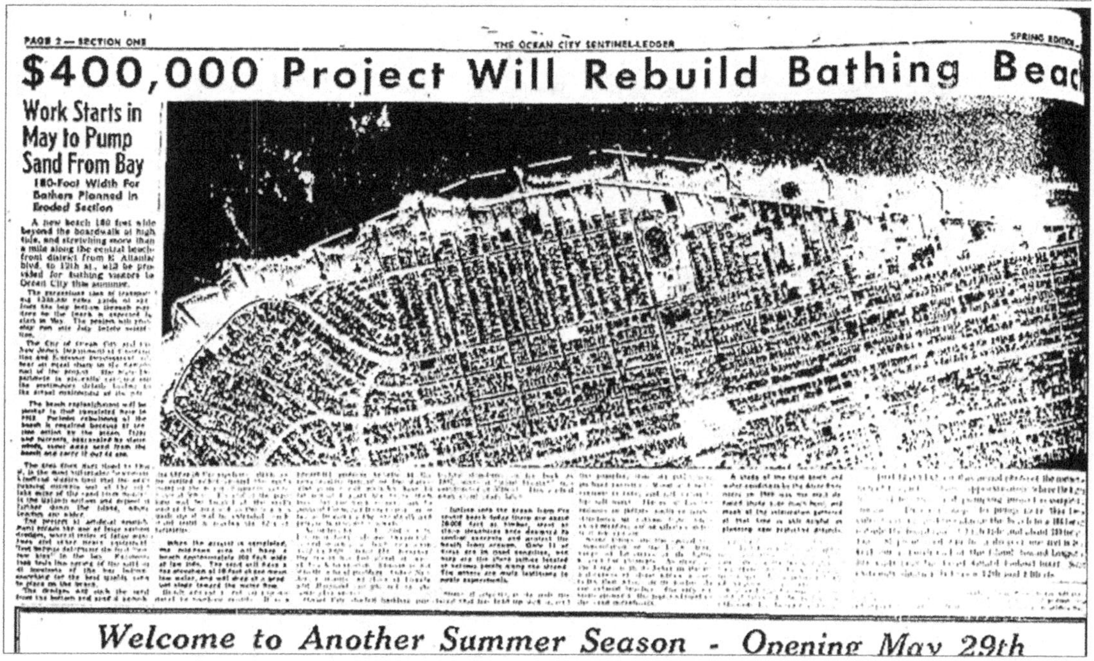

PAGE 2 — SECTION ONE — THE OCEAN CITY SENTINEL-LEDGER — SPRING EDITION

$400,000 Project Will Rebuild Bathing Beac

Work Starts in May to Pump Sand From Bay

180-Foot Width For Bathers Planned In Eroded Section

A new beach 180 feet wide beyond the boardwalk at high tide, and stretching more than a mile along the central beachfront district from E. Atlantic blvd. to 12th st., will be provided for bathing visitors to Ocean City this summer.

Welcome to Another Summer Season - Opening May 29th

"The erosions are still in progress, and unless checked will result in further loss of physical property."[128] That was the conclusion reached in 1922 by a team of experts in a landmark analysis of New Jersey beaches' never-ending battle with the Atlantic. A century later, despite sinking land and rising seas in a warming climate, the beaches fronting $80 billion worth of real estate on the barrier islands have endured.

"New Jersey has pumped more sand onto its beaches than any other state over the last 100 years in order to maintain its approximately 130 miles of Atlantic coast shoreline. Ocean City's total area consists of 10.797 square miles: 6.333 square miles of land (58.66%) and 4.464 square miles of water (41.35%). Ocean City's eight miles of shoreline and two and a half miles of boardwalk make the city a much desired place to live and a favorite vacation destination."

Sam Morris/Thomas Pullin, The Philadelphia Inquirer, 2022

Ocean City beach erosion south of the Music Pier.

The Back Bays

Thoughts immediately go to the beach when Ocean City is mentioned...and rightfully so. But the beach is not the only place where residents and vacationers work, play and while away the hours. The bayfront attracts those who love boating, fishing, crabbing, watching the sun set, or just listening to old salts weave stories of the sea. Lifelong fishermen and clammers pry a living out of the ocean and bays. Marinas, boatyards, and seafood restaurants line the bayfront.

Millville glassmakers Mary & Frank Wheaton owned 1.9+/- acres at 5th and the bay. The property included a large house, docks, tennis courts, and a pool. In the late '50s, Thompson & Sons installed a bulkhead, docks, and piers for the wealthy Wheaton family. That gained the Thompson family permanent access to the property. We were greeted at the front door whenever we requested permission to go crabbing from their docks or use the tennis courts. We were not made to go to the back door, as was the custom. Later generations were granted the same privileges, including use of the pool.

Wheaton estate looking west toward the bay. The City of Ocean City now operates the estate called Bayside. Not visible are tennis courts and swimming pool area.[129]

Docks on bay at former Wheaton estate. The estate is now known as Bayside.[130]

Bay Avenue dock for deep sea fishing boats Silver Spray and Sea Way.
Dick Sampson in shorts and Melton "Butch" Williams. Photo courtesy Larry Robinson.

Capt. Al Burchard was one of several men who ran deep-sea
fishing charters from Ocean City's bayfront.

"My brothers and I spent countless hours on the bayfront. I enjoyed carefree beach days, setting crab traps on piers along the Great Egg Harbor Bay, and bicycling about the island. Rob and I would ride our bikes through the Gardens to just below the Longport Bridge and await the return of the deep-sea fishing boat Silver Spray II. We raced Capt. Al (Burchard) and the Silver Spray back to its home at Steelman's, later Sampson Brothers Marina, right across Bay Ave from our summer rental home at 225 Bay Avenue. Granny would come out on the porch with Don and Mom if she was there. The fishermen who only fished as a business trip from Philly would give us hungry-looking kids their catch. Captain Al would sell us fish. We had fish in our freezer all winter in Philly. Oh, great times!!

I built a wooden raft, but Dick and Don Sampson deemed it unsafe, so they let us boys use one of their dinghies in the lagoon. This brings back memories of Charlie "Boots," the old salt, Art, and Hoxie. My wife of forty years and I took our children to Ocean City when they were coming up. They enjoyed Wonderland Pier and Gillian's Pier just as we had. Our grandson loved vacationing in Ocean City too."

Whitney Butler, step great grandson of John Pye. January 2022

Lemonts Marina,
228 Bay Avenue, Ocean City

"Lemonts on a lazy hot summer day."[131]

"As kids, we didn't have lots of money, so we went along the bayfront checking soda machines for change that may have been left. Sometimes, if you got it just right, you could beat the soda machine out of a free soda. Lemonts had a pay telephone and soda machine. A special touch could get you a soda."

Donovan Butler, step great grandson of John Pye.
December 29, 2021

Michael Williams, Jimmy, Mark Richardson, Melton Williams, Donovan Butler, Larry Richardson. Photo credit Larry Richardson.

Thompson & Sons installing docks at Harbor House, 2nd Street and Bay, 1983.

William Griffin at newly installed Harbor House docks, 1983.

***

Civil War Recruiting Advertisement[132]

CHAPTER 5
UNCLE SAM WANTS US!

Whether as a volunteer or draftee, the military was one avenue for Westside residents to find gainful employment. For many it was the gateway to a world of opportunities. Some families had multiple members who enlisted. Several men and women from the small Westside population found a career in the military.

The law of 1792, which generally prohibited enlistment of Blacks in the Army, became the United States Army's official policy until 1862. The only exception to this Army policy was in Louisiana, which gained an exemption at the time of its purchase through a treaty provision which allowed it to opt out of the operation of any law which ran counter to its traditions and customs. Louisiana permitted the existence of separate Black militia units which drew its enlistees from freed Blacks.[133] The government did not place legal restrictions on the enlistment of Blacks into the Navy because of its chronic shortage of manpower.

The Civil War (1861-1865)

United States Colored Troops

The United States Army began recruiting African Americans between 1862 and 1863 when Union troops were suffering heavy losses. Approximately 186,000 African Americans, free men, and runaway slaves, making up 163 units volunteered for duty as part of segregated units called the United States Colored Troops (USCT).[134] They served in Cavalry, Artillery, and Infantry regiments. They too took heavy losses but are credited with helping turn the direction of the war. African Americans also served in the Union Navy.

From 1863 to 1865, Camp William Penn was a Union Army training camp in Cheltenham Township, Pennsylvania for the USCT. The Union League of Philadelphia funded the camp. Prominent abolitionists owned the land where the camp was built. Over ten thousand recruits were trained in two years.[135]

Civil War Recruitment Advertisement for People of Color[136]

The original gate of Camp William Penn between two residential properties leads to the training camp where thousands of Black recruits were prepared for war.[137]

Camp William Penn Training Camp[138]

U.S. Colored Troops[139]

Civil War Veterans Listing

Though Ocean City's founding in 1879 came years after the Civil War, several Black Civil War veterans made their way to Ocean City and spent their final days living on Ocean City's Westside. Included in this group is Jacob Still, Ocean City's first Black resident and owner of the first salt water taffy store on the boardwalk. Rev. David Wells was a member of Ocean City's Morgan Ranck Post 137 American Legion and a member of The Grand Army of the Republic (GAR), the preeminent veterans' organization formed at the close of the Civil War.

As no burials are permitted on the barrier island of Ocean City, except for John W. Brown, these veterans lie at rest in unmarked graves in unidentified plots in the now defunct Second Cape May Baptist Cemetery in Upper Township. Seaside Cemetery surrounds the defunct Baptist cemetery.

Known Black Civil War veterans who resided in Ocean City:[140,141,142,143]

CIVIL WAR VETERAN	DOB-DOD	UNIT
John W. Brown	1834-1905	U.S. Colored Troops B,127
Joseph Thompson West Finneman	1845-1926	U.S. G,45 Inf. Musician
Jacob Still (aka Stahl)	1833-1901	U.S. Colored Troops B,51
Rev. David A. Wells	1844-1927	U.S. Colored Troops D,41

Civil War Veterans Photo Gallery

John W. Brown (1834-1905). Seaside Cemetery, Upper Township.

Joseph Thompson West Finneman (1845-1926)

Jacob Still (1833-1901). Seaside Cemetery, Upper Township.

David Wells (1844-1927)
Seaside Cemetery Plot No. 3, Grave No. 8 ER, Upper Township
Application For Headstone, David Wells[144]

World War I (1914-1919)

The United States remained neutral for the first three years of World War I. German U-boat attacks on merchant ships and Germany's declaration of war against all ships in the war zone prompted the United States to enter the war in 1917. The Selective Service Act instituted one month later required males between the age of 21 and 30 to register for service. Black veterans of World War I, the Great War, entered a segregated military. The military transported Blacks to the war zone on segregated ships.[145]

146

Ft. Meade, Maryland. c. 1917.

Despite facing segregation and discrimination at home, 2.3 million African Americans enlisted or were drafted into service during WWI believing their service would improve conditions for Blacks in the United States.

> *"Let us, while the war lasts, forget our special grievances and close ranks shoulder to shoulder with our White fellow citizens."*
>
> Dr. W. E. B. DuBois
> *(Harvard education activist, sociologist,*
> *socialist, historian, and author)[147]*

Negro troops on board USS Pocahontas during ship's second trans-Atlantic voyage, 1917.[148]

Black soldiers boarding U.S.S. Shoshone for transport to the war zone.
The ship departed from New York City destined for St. Nazaire, France.[149]

World War I Veterans Listing

Notable African American units to serve in World War I

- 92nd Infantry Division

- 93d Infantry Division

- 366th Infantry Regiment

- 369th Infantry Regiment (Harlem Hellfighters)

- 371st Infantry Regiment

Known veterans of World War I who resided in Ocean City:[150, 151, 152, 153]

WORLD WAR I VETERAN	UNIT	ENLISTED
Harry Tilghman Anderson*		25 Feb 1919
Seymour Holman Barker	51 Co. 13 Bn. 153 Dep. Brig.	20 Jun 1918
John William Bowser	154 Dep Brig	22 May 1918
	Co. K 368 Inf. 92 Div.	15 Jun 1918
William Lemuel Brown		
Charles Cullen Clark, Sr.**	Mess Attendant 3	8 Feb 1919
Samuel Lloyd Doughty	Co. C 511 Service/Engineers	1918
Charles Finneman	Butchery Co. 322, QMC (Colored)	
Timothy Allen Harris		
John Clempton Hughes, Sr.	Co. I, 366 Inf.	26 Apr 1918
Richard Jones	Field Remount Squadron QMC	31 Jul 1918
Joseph John Mitchell, Jr.	Co. I, 59th Pioneer Inf.	31 Aug 1918
Obert "Obed" Reed Moore	154 Dep Brig	17 Jan 1918
Richard Washington Murrel	Co. E 813 Pioneer Inf. (Colored)	4 Aug 1918
Joseph Noel	350th Field Art. Vet Det 92 Div.	30 Jun 1918
Oliver Wallace O'Ferrall	162 Depot Brigade	Mar 1918
Earl Martin Polk		26 Apr 1918
Alphonso Raglin		
Charles Randolph		
Harry Albertis Rolls	Depot Service Co #2C A.S.C.	19 Jul 1919
	Med Det Camp Hosp No. 33	
	Brest Casual Co. 2251 (Colored)	
Marion Stanford Rutter	Depot Serv. Co. 31 A.S.C. Colored	1 Aug 1918
Herbert/Hubert Waters Singleton	154 Dep. Brig.	15 Apr 1918
	Co A 522 Engineers Service Bn.	
	Co A 523 Engineers Service Bn.	
	17 Engineers Service Bn.	
Charles J. Smith		
James H. Smith		
John Streeter		
George Lincoln Sumpter	Co. 51st Engineers 153 Depot Brig.	25 Apr 1917
	Co. D 405 Res Labor Bn QMC	
Fredrick J. Talmadge	Btry. C 19th Reg Field Artillery	14 Aug 918
Otto Wade Thompson	Depot Service Co. #19, A.S.C.	4 Aug 1918
Newlin D. Turner	Co. A 537 Engineers Serv. Bn.	1919
Leonard Leondis Wiggins	Co. L 371st Inf.	18 Jun 1918
Oliver H. Wiggins	HQ Co. 802 Pioneer Inf. (Colored)	21 Jun 1918
Robert Mack Winston	158 Dep. Brigade	2 Sep 1918

Upper Township resident. OCHS graduate.
**Ocean City resident credited to Delaware.*

World War I Veterans Photo Gallery

Seymour Holman Barker (1896-1963)

John William Bowser (1889-1940)
154 Dep Brig. Co. K 368 Inf. 92 Div.

The 92nd Division was one of the African American units cited for notable service. Bowser came to Ocean City in 1928 from Maryland's Eastern Shore. He died in 1940.

John Bowser shipped out from Hoboken in June of 1918 aboard the U.S.S. George Washington.

CHARLES CLARK
Nanticoke chief

Charles Cullen Clark (1894-1971)
Mess Attendant 1st Class[155]

Charles Cullen Clark entered the military from Ocean City in February 1919.[154] He enlisted at the Naval Recruiting Station in Philadelphia as a Mess Attendant 3 assigned to the U.S.S. Glacier. He was discharged in 1919 as a Mess Attendant 1 in Brooklyn, New York. His war service was credited to Delaware.

The U.S.S. Glacier served as a supply ship to the Pacific Fleet until 1918 delivering fresh provisions, stores, ammunition, target material, and mail. It transported personnel and towed target rafts and coal barges on the West Coast, Mexico, and Central America. She made three trips to Europe carrying fresh meats and general stores to naval forces operating in European waters. Her third trip was from New York to Brest, France, returning to Norfolk with a cargo of aviation material and high explosives for New York. She was detached as a Naval Overseas Transport Ship and assigned to the Train Squadron, Atlantic Fleet issuing stores to the Atlantic Fleet and engaging in target practice with the fleet on the East Coast.[156]

U.S.S. Glacier[157]

WW I	WW II	KOREA				ORIGINAL	Suspended MAY 26 1971

1. NAME OF DECEASED - LAST - FIRST - MIDDLE *(Print or Type)*		14. NAME AND LOCATION OF CEMETERY *(City and State)*
Clark, Charles Cullen		Clark Family Cem. @ Millsboro, Delaware

IMPORTANT - Item 18 on reverse side must be completed. See attached instructions and complete and submit both copies.

2. SERVICE NUMBER 434422	3. PENSION OR VA CLAIM NUMBER
War Ser. Cert. No.	

15. This application is submitted for a stone or marker for the unmarked grave of a deceased member or former member of the Armed Forces of the U. S., soldier of the Union or Confederate Armies of the Civil War or for an unmarked memorial plot for a non-recoverable deceased member.
  I hereby agree to take responsibility for proper placement at the grave or memorial plot at no expense to the Government.

4. ENLISTMENT DATE *(Month, day, year)*	5. DISCHARGE DATE *(Month, day, year)*	NAME OF APPLICANT *(Print or Type)*	RELATIONSHIP
Aug. 30, 1917	Feb. 8, 1919	Kenneth S. Clark	son

6. STATE	7. DECORATIONS	ADDRESS OF APPLICANT *(Street address, City and State)*
Delaware		Oak Orchard

8. GRADE OR RANK	9. BRANCH OF SERVICE, COMPANY, REGIMENT, DIVISION	Millsboro, Delaware
MAH1C	Navy – served R.S. at Norfolk, Va. U.S.S. Glacier	SIGNATURE OF APPLICANT Kenneth S Clark DATE 4/16/71

10. DATE OF BIRTH *(Month, day, year)*	11. DATE OF DEATH *(Month, day, year)*	16. FREIGHT STATION
Oct. 29, 1894	April 13, 1971	Millsboro, Delaware

12. RELIGIOUS EMBLEM *(Check one)*	13. CHECK TYPE REQUIRED	17. NAME OF CONSIGNEE WHO WILL TRANSPORT STONE OR MARKER
	UPRIGHT MARBLE HEADSTONE	James & Watson Funeral Home
XX LATIN CROSS *(Christian)*	FLAT MARBLE MARKER	ADDRESS OF CONSIGNEE *(Street address, City and State)*
STAR OF DAVID *(Hebrew)*	FLAT GRANITE MARKER	Main St., Millsboro, Delaware 19966
NO EMBLEM	X FLAT BRONZE MARKER	I HAVE AGREED TO TAKE THE STONE OR MARKER TO THE CEMETERY.

DO NOT WRITE HERE		SIGNATURE OF CONSIGNEE
FOR VERIFICATION	ORDERED 1 0 JUN 1971	James & Watson F.H. per Richard T Watson
B/L 72420	CONTRACTOR Shadow Bronze Co. Kingwood, West Va.	
MAH1 US NAVY/WWI		

DD FORM 1330, 1 NOV 62	EDITION OF 1 DEC 61 MAY BE USED	APPLICATION FOR HEADSTONE OR MARKER

The 813 Pioneer Infantry Regiment consisting of Companies E, F, G, H, I, M, and He served in France in support of Army troops repairing roads, doing salvage work, and the unpleasant task of burying the dead. They trained at Camp Sherman and Camp Mills and were demobilized in July 1919 at Camp Dix.[158]

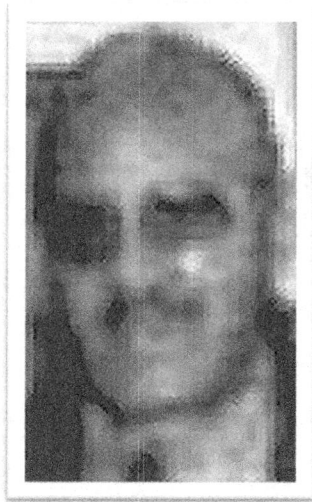

Richard Washington Murrel (1891-1945)
Co. E 813 Pioneer Inf.
Photo courtesy Jane Murrel Pillow

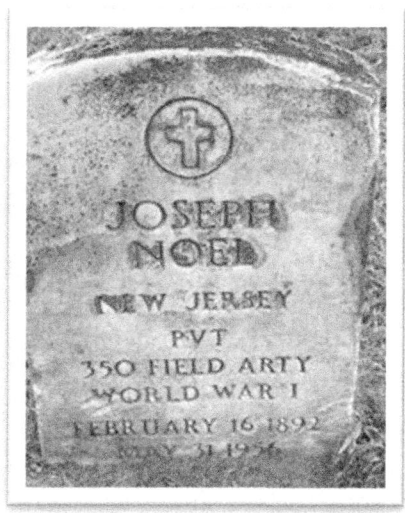

Joseph Noel (1892-1956)
350th Field Art. Vet Det 92 Div[159]

Private First Class Mitchell shipped out of Hoboken aboard the Leviathan during WWI. He returned on the same ship a year later having advanced to Corporal. Both of his sons served in WWII.

Joseph John Mitchell, Jr. (1884-1975)
Co. I 59th Pioneer Infantry

Richard Washington Murrel was aboard the U.S.S. Pocahontas when it embarked from Hoboken, NJ September 1918 bound for France.[160]

USS President Grant was a split superstructure, six mast ship originally built in Ireland for the Hamburg-Amerika Linie. With the outbreak of World War I in 1914, she sought refuge in New York. She remained inactive until 1917 when the United States entered the war, seized the USS President Grant for the Navy, and commissioned her as a transport ship. In 1919 after several trips transporting Joseph Noel and other soldiers to and from the war zone, the ship was decommissioned and transferred to the Army.

Oliver Wallace O'Ferrall (1892-1955)   Ernest Bernard O'Ferrall (1904-1993)

Oliver O'Ferrall was known locally as Oliver W. O'Farrell. The Ocean City Old Timers club established a scholarship to recognize his dedication to family and contributions to his church and community at large. The discovery of variations in the family name produced new information.

Tall, slender Oliver O'Ferrall reported his place of birth as Belleville, Illinois when he registered for the draft in 1917. When he enlisted in the Army, he was a single man, age 25 with no natural children, working as a cook and caring for his deceased brother's children (Ernest Bernard and Robert Fletcher O'Ferrall).

Oliver later owned a catering business in Philadelphia. Both nephews served in the military. Ernest became a laboratory chemist. In 1940, Robert resided at the Larchmont Hotel, 11th Street and Ocean Avenue in Ocean City, and owned Fletcher's Church Dining Service in Philadelphia. Another nephew, namesake Oliver Wallace O'Ferrall born 1923, was lead singer for nationally acclaimed recording artists, The Silk Tones.

Otto Wade Thompson (1890-1957)
Depot Service Co. #19, A.S.C. (Colored)
Photo courtesy William Griffin

Otto came to Ocean City from Millville with his family while a teenager. He was employed at the Radjon Company when he was drafted into the military.

Following his discharge, he worked in road construction before joining his father's express delivery business. Oral family history indicates he was a volunteer bell ringer for the Salvation Army. His name is listed on the World War I memorial plaque at Ocean City's Memorial Park.

Otto Wade Thompson departed from Bordeaux, France Jun 1919 aboard the U.S.S. Scranton transport ship destined for Hoboken, NJ.[161]

NO IMAGE
AVAILABLE

Newlin Turner was the first Black to graduate from Ocean City High School. He was a member of American Legion Morgan Ranck Post and is listed on the World War I memorial plaque at Ocean City's Memorial Park.

Newlin D. Turner (1895-1932)
OCHS Class of 1916

Newlin D. Turner returned from Europe aboard the U.S.S. Mt. Vernon which arrived in Hoboken in 1919.[162]

Harry Albertis Rolls (1892-1964)
Photo courtesy Joanne Rolls, granddaughter.

Harry returned to New Jersey from Brest, France on the U.S.S. Imperator.

U.S.S. Imperator Brest, France to Hoboken July 7, 1919.
By JMReid1220 - Own work, CC BY-SA 4.[163]

Harry Albertis Rolls was scheduled to return from the war zone aboard the U.S.S. Noordam on June 25, 1919, but was struck from departing passenger list and reported sick in hospital.[164]

Charles J. Smith, Sr. (1911-1990)
Photo courtesy
Aline Dickerson Bennett Milligan

Charles J. Smith military grave plaque.[165]

Leonard Leondis Wiggins (1892-1977)
Co. L 371st Inf.
Photo courtesy Nathan Davis, Jr.

Leonard Wiggins was drafted into the noted African American 371st Infantry Regiment from Millington, Kent County, Maryland as part of the automatic replacement draft. He departed New York in August 1918 aboard the U.S.S. France headed for France, returning to Hoboken in February 1919 aboard the U.S.S. Leviathan. The unit gained fame when Corporal Freddie Stowers, also of the 371st Infantry Regiment, was posthumously awarded a Medal of Honor, the only African American awarded the medal for actions in World War I.[166]

Leonard Wiggins was transported to France aboard the U.S.S. France in 1918.[167]

U.S.S. Leviathan in New York Harbor.[168]

Leonard Wiggins returned stateside from France aboard the U.S.S. Leviathan arriving at Hoboken, New Jersey.

Wiggins returned stateside aboard the U.S.S. Leviathan.[169]

Robert Mack Winston (1887-1961)

Winston resided in Philadelphia at enlistment. He served in the 158th Depot Brigade at Camp Sherman in Ohio from September 2, 1918 to December 5, 1918. The brigade received and organized recruits and outfitted them with uniforms, equipment, and initial military training in preparation for war on the front lines in France.

Conversely, the brigade received soldiers returning home at the end of the war and processed their discharges. Winston did not see service overseas. He applied for veterans' compensation in 1935 from his 632 West Avenue address in Ocean City. Winston is buried at Beverly National Cemetery in Burlington County, New Jersey.

Spanish–American War (Apr 1898-Dec 1898)

The Spanish–American War was a brief armed conflict between Spain and the United States. The United States declared war on Spain when Spain sank the battleship U.S.S. Maine in Havana Harbor in Cuba on February 15, 1898 leading to U.S. intervention in the Cuban War of Independence. The war ended with the signing of the Treaty of Paris in December of that year.[170]

Spanish-American War Veterans Listing

SPANISH-AMERICAN WAR VETERANS[171]	OCCUPATION	SOURCE
James A. Ingram	Cement worker	1930 census
Samuel C. Stewart	Hotel waiter	1930 census

World War II (1939-1945)

President Franklin D. Roosevelt signed the Selective Training and Service Act (the draft) into law September 16, 1940. All men between the ages of 21 and 45 were required to register. While there were wartime drafts during the Revolutionary War, the Civil War, and World War I, this draft was different in that it was the nation's first peacetime draft.[172]

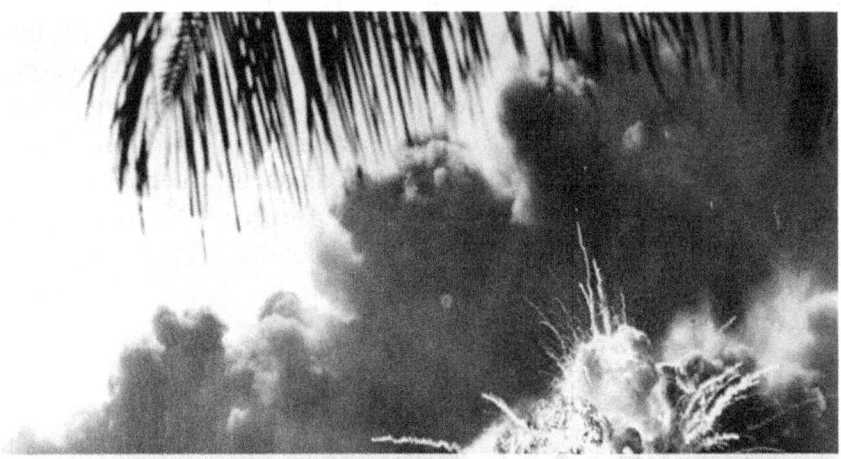

The Attack on Pearl Harbor

On December 7, 1941, the U.S. naval base Pearl Harbor was the scene of a devastating surprise attack by Japanese forces that would push the U.S. into entering WWII. Japanese fighter planes destroyed nearly 20 American naval vessels, including eight battleships, and over 300 airplanes. More than 2,400 Americans (including civilians) died in the attack, with another 1,000 Americans wounded.

"World War II exposed a glaring paradox within the United States Armed Forces. Although more than 1 million African Americans served in the war to defeat Nazism and fascism, they did so in segregated units. The U.S. military reinforced the same discriminatory Jim Crow policies that were rampant in American society. Black servicemen rarely saw combat and were largely relegated to labor and supply units. White officers commanded the units.

Several African American units proved essential in helping to win World War II, with the Tuskegee Airmen being among the most celebrated. But the Red Ball Express, the truck convoy of mostly Black drivers, was responsible for delivering essential goods to General George S. Patton's troops on the front lines in France. The all Black 761st Tank Battalion fought in the Battle of the Bulge, and the 92nd Infantry Division fought in fierce ground battles in Italy. Yet, despite their role in defeating fascism, the fight for equality continued for African American soldiers after World War II ended. They remained in segregated units and lower ranking positions well into the Korean War.

> *"The arrest, beating and blinding of African American veteran Isaac Woodard by Batesburg, South Carolina police on February 12, 1946— hours after he was honorably discharged from the United States Army, and while still in uniform—caused a national furor and helped inspire Harry Truman's move to desegregate the military."*[173]

> *"My stomach turned over when I learned that Negro soldiers, just back from overseas, were being dumped out of army trucks in Mississippi and beaten," Truman said. "Whatever my inclinations as a native of Missouri might have been, as president I know this is bad. I shall fight to end evils like this."*[174]

In 1947, Truman became the first president to address the National Association for the Advancement of Colored People (NAACP). In his speech at the Lincoln Memorial, Truman said, *"It is my deep conviction that we have reached a turning point in the long history of our country's efforts to guarantee freedom and equality to all of our citizens."*

In 1948, President Harry Truman issued an executive order intended to eliminate racial segregation and discrimination in the armed forces. Truman issued the order in contradiction of his White supremacist upbringing. The last all Black military units were disbanded during the first half of the 1950s.[175]

Tuskegee Airmen

In 1939, the Civilian Pilot Training Act was signed authorizing civilian schools to train military pilots. A last-minute amendment provided for the inclusion of African Americans though there were restrictions on the number of Blacks accepted into the Army Air Corps. Tuskegee Institute in Tuskegee, Alabama was among the Black colleges approved to provide training. Two years later, under pressure from the Black community, the War Department finally formed an all-Black unit of pilots, the 99th Pursuit squadron, with several other units following shortly thereafter.

P-51 plane flown by Tuskegee Airmen.

First Lady Eleanor Roosevelt, a supporter of civil rights, was instrumental in gaining recognition and acceptance of the Tuskegee Airmen as pilots when she asked a Tuskegee Airman to give her a forty-minute aerial tour of Tuskegee Airfield in a single engine, two-seater Piper Cub. Her strong endorsement of the pilot's abilities paved the way for Black airmen in the still segregated military.

Included as Tuskegee Airmen are 1,000 men who graduated as trained pilots of the 2,400 aviation cadets who entered the program. The group also includes more than 16,000 other men and women who became navigators, bombardiers, mechanics, crew chiefs, radiomen, technical inspectors, welders, painters, nurses, cooks, clerks, typists, and others required to support the mission.

Tuskegee Airmen, World War II[176]

"The Tuskegee Airmen distinguished themselves in combat, flying hundreds of missions over wartime Europe, including 179 bomber escort missions. They are credited with destroying more than 260 enemy planes in the air and on the ground, as well as enemy vehicles and ships. They earned three Distinguished Unit Citations, 96 Distinguished Flying Crosses and many other medals. At least 150 gave their lives during the war, including 66 killed in action."[177]

New Jersey Monthly Magazine

Red Ball Express

During World War II, hundreds of Black soldiers were drawn from the Army Quartermaster Corps to form the Red Ball Express, a truck convoy system of predominantly African American drivers that served as the supply route for Patton's Third Army. The Army Transportation Corps taught men to drive. The men carried critical supplies inland from St. Lô, France to twenty-eight American divisions that had broken through the beaches of Normandy and were racing across Western Europe in pursuit of retreating German forces.

The treacherous 700-mile route was marked with red balls so the drivers wouldn't get lost. Shell fragments, barbed wire, and empty C-ration cans that littered the roads routinely shredded truck tires. Wandering livestock and starving civilians begging for food stood in the path of the convoys. Overloaded trucks tipped and flipped, sank into the mud of country roads, and veered into ditches as drivers nodded off at the wheel from lack of sleep. When trucks broke down, the drivers fixed them and ran them again.[178]

Red Ball Express, Belgium by Sgt Bill Augustine. Post-Work: W. Wolny.[179]

Red Ball Express[180]

761st Tank Battalion, the "Black Panthers"

The 761st Tank Battalion was a majority Black unit formed in 1942 when the military was still segregated. The battalion had thirty Black officers, six White officers, and six hundred seventy-six enlisted men. Baseball star Jackie Robinson was one of the Black officers. Time spent in court battles because of his refusal to relinquish his seat on a military bus prevented Robinson from seeing action in Europe. The 761st took the nickname "Black Panthers."

In October 1944, the Black Panthers became the first African American tank squad to see combat in World War II fighting in France and Belgium. They were one of the first American battalions to meet the Russian Army in Austria and broke through Nazi Germany's Siegfried line allowing General George S. Patton's troops to enter Germany. The 761st participated in four major Allied campaigns including the Battle of the Bulge where an Allied victory turned the tide of the war in favor of the Allies earning four campaign ribbons.

The Black Panthers fought their way further east than nearly every other unit from the United States, receiving 391 decorations for heroism. The men were awarded eleven silver stars, sixty-nine bronze stars, and some 300 purple hearts.[181, 182, 183]

761st Tank Battalion, the "Black Panthers"[184]

761st Tank Battalion, the "Black Panthers"[185]

92nd Infantry Division, the "Buffalo Soldiers"

American Indians possibly coined the term Buffalo Soldiers and gave it to Black soldiers who were sent to control the Native Americans in the West after the Civil War. The name was one based out of respect for a worthy enemy. Or the name may have come from the coats they wore fashioned from animal skins. Buffalo Soldiers were used in several peacetime activities at home and abroad.

The 92nd Infantry Division was initially formed in 1917 and consisted of 15,000 Blacks from across the country who took the nickname "Buffalo Soldiers" as a tribute to the Buffalo Soldier regiments who had been sent to fight the American Indians in the 1860s. White senior officers led this Black unit of enlisted men and junior officers. The 92nd was made a part of the 93rd Infantry and fought alongside the French during World War I. The unit was demobilized after World War I. The 92nd was reactivated for World War II and began combat training in October 1942. They went into action in Italy in the summer of 1944. Of the 909,000 Black Americans selected for duty in the Army during World War II, only one Black division, the 92nd Infantry, saw infantry combat in Europe. The vast majority of African Americans in uniform were assigned to segregated construction or supply units or placed in units that performed unpleasant duties such as graves registration. After years of pressure from the Black community, the United States government rescinded its policy of excluding African American soldiers from combat. On July 30, 1944, the first wave of Buffalo Soldiers, the 370th Regimental Combat Team, landed at Naples, Italy to the cheers of Black American soldiers from other service units.

92nd Infantry Division "Buffalo Soldiers"[186]

92nd Infantry Division "Buffalo Soldiers"[187]

Buffalo Soldiers logo
Courtesy U.S. Department of Defense[188,189,190]

Exercise Sage Brush

Between October 31 and December 15, 1955, the United States Army conducted field trials called Exercise Sagebrush. Some 140,000 Army and Air Force troops deployed to twenty-five areas in Louisiana in an exercise to test the readiness of United States forces to respond to a simulated atomic attack. The exercise included a Sky Cavalry, a combination of an 82nd Airborne reconnaissance group and a Transportation helicopter unit. [191]

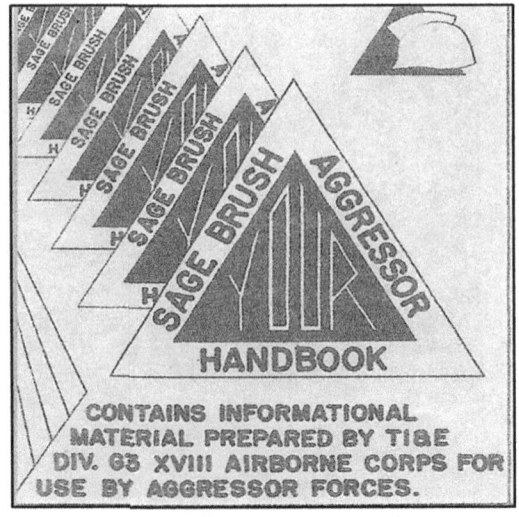

The primary goal was to test a newly developed 280mm atomic cannon, Atomic Annie, a military unit that could fire a cannon more than twenty miles and give the United States the ability to deliver an atomic weapon from air or land.

The exercise totally disrupted daily life for residents. It took years to repair Louisiana infrastructure destroyed in the simulation. Ocean City's 82nd Airborne ranger Pvt. Richard Evans of Camp Polk, Louisiana participated in the exercise. [192]

World War II Veterans Listing

Many Westside residents served in World War II (1939-1945). Listed are men and women residing in or attending school in Ocean City at the time of enlistment, i.e. Upper Township residents. It also includes those living elsewhere at the time of enlistment who later moved to Ocean City. Most notable is the number of men from the Chalmers family who joined the military. Of the fifteen children in the family, eight male and seven female, five males served in World War II, and one served during the Korean Conflict. It was with entry into the military that the Chalmers name transitioned from Chalmers to Chalmus.

WORLD WAR II VETERANS[193, 194]	ENLISTED	BRANCH
Ira D. Anderson	13 Sep 1943	Army
Charles James Anderson		Navy
Paul Thomas Anderson	7 Feb 1941	Army Tuskegee Airman
Eugene Armstead	15 Sep 1943	Army Quartermaster Corps
Andrew Edward Barton	14 Dec 1945	Army Air Force
Frederick Ignatius Barton	4 Sep 1942	86th Aviation Squadron
Richard Evans Barton	13 May 1943	Corps Engr Searchlight Co.
Franklin Alexander Bland	27 Jul 1942	Army Branch Immaterial
Samuel Leon Brown	5 Nov 1942	
Irving Lucius Carter	13 Jun 1942	Army Branch Immaterial
Earl Vincent Chalmers/Chalmus	18 Apr 1941	Army Branch Immaterial
Wilburt Andrew Chalmers/Chalmus	27 Jul 1942	Army Branch Immaterial
Willis Randall Chalmers/Chalmus	22 Mar 1943	Army
Francis Calvin Chalmers/Chalmus	19 Aug 1943	Army
Norman Whiticar Chalmers/Chalmus	21 Dec 1944	
Emanuel Pruitt Clark	22 Sep 1944	Army
Webster Claudius Cooper	22 Mar 1943	Army
Alfonso Joseph Dickerson	6 Apr 1945	Army
Walter Parker Doughty	1 Nov 1945	Army
William Vernel Fladger	19 Sep 1942	Army Branch Immaterial
Wilbert Gerald	13 Jul 1943	Army
Homer Washington Gillis	16 Sep 1942	Coast Guard Comm.
John Lycurgus Arthur Gillis	23 Jan 1943	Army Branch Immaterial
Raymond Griffin		
Leroy Nathaniel Grice	23 Jul 1943	Army Quartermaster Corps
Richard Sydney Grimes	11 Jun 1941	Army Air Corps
Charles Robert Harmon, Sr.	8 Mar 1944	Co. C 1st Bn IRTC
Dewitt Roland Harmon	22 Apr 1943	Army
Oscar James Harmon, Jr.	24 Oct 1942	Army Air Force
Theodore Robert Harmon	23 Sep 1941	Army Branch Immaterial
Archie Haggie Harris, Jr.	23 Jul 1943	Army Air Force Aviation Cadet
Marshall Ardmore Harris	13 Dec 1940	Army Branch Immaterial

WORLD WAR II VETERANS	ENLISTED	BRANCH
Aaron Edward Harvey, Jr.	22 Apr 1943	Army
Herbert D. Harvey	27 Jul 1942	Army Branch Immaterial
Carl Leroy Henry	3 Mar 1942	Navy
Ross Dee Humphrey	Career	Army
Norrece Thomas Jones, Jr.	14 May 1942	Army Branch Immaterial
Sylvanus Wiley Leatherbury	27 Jul 1942	Army Branch Immaterial
Lemuel Thomas Lewis, Jr.	27 Feb 1942	Army Quartermaster Corps
James L. Lyles	27 Jul 1943	
Rayfield Charles Lyles	30 Nov 1940	Army Branch Immaterial
Talmadge Lyles	27 Jul 1942	Army Branch Immaterial
Jerome Martin	29 Jun 1942	Army Branch Immaterial
Samuel Saunders Martin	27 Aug 1942	Coast Guard
Joseph Samuel Mitchell	15 Sep 1943	Army
William Sylvester Mitchell		Army
Joseph Mobley	22 Oct 1943	Army
Arthur Marvin Money	27 May 1942	Army Branch Immaterial
Charles Amos Money		
Daniel Tildon Orvis Money	13 Aug 19142	Army Branch Immaterial
Morris Layton Money	3 Nov 1943	Navy
Howard Wendell Morgan	17 Mar 1941	Army Branch Immaterial
Lawrence Motley	22 Apr 1943	Army
William Wesley Neil	8 Mar 1944	Army
Reginald Eugene Oliver	16 Sep 1942	Coast Guard Special Weapons Group, 11th Def. Btn.1st Marine Amphibious Corps
Leonard Nathaniel Outen	16 Mar 1942	755 Chemical Depot Co.
Earl Alfonzo Polk	15 Nov 1943	Army
Clarence S. Reynolds	15 Jun 1943	
Harry Segal Rolls		Navy
Charles Lewis Spence	7 Aug 1942	Army Branch Immaterial
Paul Edward Stewart	6 Jan 1944	Army
Joel Brown Still	11 Jun 1942	Army Co. D 743 MP BN
George Lukason Sumpter	25 Apr 1942	Army
Harold Cornelius Sumpter	29 Jul 1941	Army 776 Q.M. Corps*
Philip Howard Sumpter	8 Jan 1942	Army Branch Immaterial
Edward Clarence Turner	18 Nov 1943	
David Robert Turner	27 Jul 1942	Army Air Forces
Eugene Elemule Watts	16 May 1945	Army Mil. Police Corps
Floyd Leonard Watts	14 Jul 1943	Army
Leonard Leondis Wiggins, Jr.	17 May 1945	Army QM Corps
Roland A. Wiggins		Air Force Band
Roger K. Williams	21 Jun 1944	Navy STM 2/C
Nathaniel Harry Winston	13 Aug 1942	Army Branch Immaterial

*Killed in action

Note: Branch Immaterial was a designation given to enlistees who were not assigned to specific units at the time of enlistment.

World War II Veterans Photo Gallery

Charles James Anderson
1923-2004)
Photo courtesy
Patricia Anderson, daughter

Ira D. Anderson (1910-1978. Photo taken on
7th Street east of Haven Avenue. Home of
beautician Lottie Singletary in background.
Photo courtesy William Griffin.

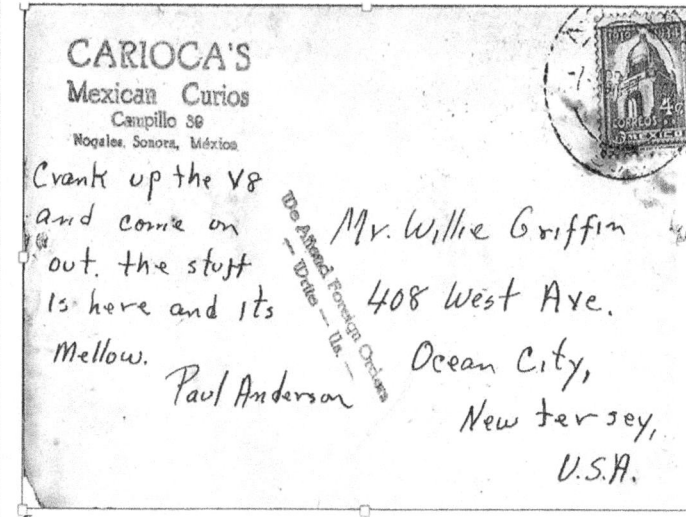

Paul Thomas Anderson (1917-2003)
Photo courtesy William Griffin.

Ira and Paul Anderson lived in Tuckahoe in Upper Township, a sending district to
Ocean City High School. The Andersons were considered Ocean City guys.

William Dick "Griff" Griffin (1918-1984) on left with Ira Anderson. Griff's car in the background.
Photo courtesy William Griffin, son of William Dick Griffin.

Service Men and Veterans

Ocean City Man Home from Bitter Fighting in Korea

Much Decorated Sergeant, After Nine Years in Service, Decides to Make the Army His Career

An Ocean City veteran of nine years in the Army, including some of the hottest action in Korea, is now back home on a 30-day leave.

He is Sgt. Richard Barton, nephew of Mrs. Louisa Pollard, 210 7th st. Upon completion of his leave here, he will return to active duty at the Airborne Heavy Drop School, Fort Lee, Va.

SGT. BARTON entered the Army in May, 1943, and thereafter was in action in the Pacific theatre for 22 months during World War II, serving in the Philippines, New Guinea and Australia.

After the war he returned to the States and served with the 82nd Airborne Division four years.

In September, 1950, he transferred to the Rangers and attended the Ranger school at Fort Benning, Ga. Upon graduation and qualification as an Airborne Ranger he was sent into combat in Korea with the 2nd Airborne Infantry Company.

This unit was assigned to the 7th Infantry Division and was in action at the Chosen Reservoir, Tangyang Pass, Heartbreak Ridge and the airborne assault at Munson-Ni.

Sgt. Barton was wounded at Tangyang Pass and spent three months in an Army hospital at Osaka, Japan.

* * *

DURING THE NINE YEARS of service he has accumulated a vast assortment of decorations, including the Purple Heart, Combat Infantry Badge, Bronze Star and V Device and four unit citations.

Some of the others are the Philippine Liberation Ribbon, Philippine Independence Ribbon, Philippine Presidential Unit Citation, Korean Presidential Unit Citation, U. S. Presidential Unit Citation, American Theatre Ribbon, World War II Victory Ribbon, Korean Campaign Ribbon, United Nations Ribbon, Japanese Occupation Ribbon, Green Combat Leaders Tabs, Meritorious Unit Citation, Parachute Wings with Star, the French Furreggure, and the Good Conduct Ribbon.

Sgt. Barton is a member of the

SGT. RICHARD BARTON

Harold Sumpter Post No. 6061, Veterans of Foreign Wars, of this city. He expects to remain in the Army as a career.

Burglar Fined $200; Jailed 18 Months

A $200 fine and 18 months in prison was imposed late last week on James Levand, 23, of Cape May, who pleaded guilty in county court to charges of breaking and entering.

A fisherman, he was arrested for twice breaking into a Cape May store and the Elks home. Prosecutor Albert M. Ash said that Levand had a previous conviction for illegally wearing a soldiers' uniform.

Richard Evans Barton (1925-1973). 82nd Airborne, Ranger. Member Howard Sumpter Post No. 6061, Veterans of Foreign Wars. Ocean City Sentinel Ledger, 13 Mar 1952.

Samuel Leon Brown (1914-1992)   Earl Vincent Chalmers/Chalmus (1917-1982)

"Earl drove a truck in the Army during World War II and was part of the Red Ball Express. There was another man named Dave who summered in Ocean City. In 1947, a wealthy man gave Dave a 1931 sixteen-cylinder Cadillac convertible."
Douglas Longenecker, June 28, 2018, Ocean City Historical Museum

Charles Cullen Clark, Jr. (1924-1978)

Charles Cullen Clark, Jr. was born in Ocean City, New Jersey in 1924. He was the son of World War I veteran and Nanticoke Indian chief Charles Cullen Clark, Sr. Charles, Jr. descended from a long list of Nanticoke chiefs originally from Indian River (now known as Millsboro, Delaware). Records indicate Charles Jr. entered World War II at age seventeen. He died at the Portsmouth, Virginia Naval Hospital at age forty-eight where he was a recorded as a Vietnam veteran. His service was credited to Delaware.

Emanuel Pruitt "Flip" Clark (1915-1987)

"Flip" Clark was born in Ensley, a large city neighborhood incorporated into Birmingham, Alabama in 1910. "Flip" and his brother, Jet, came to Ocean City in the late 1920s with their mother Cora. After serving two years in the Army, Flip sought work at a dry-cleaning establishment while Jet worked as a presser for Talese Town and Country on Asbury Avenue. Cora and her second husband, William Reynolds, added two more children to the family, daughter Willette who married William Strawberry and outstanding high school athlete William "Cut" Reynolds, Jr.

Walter Parker Doughty (1923-1980)
OCHS Class of 1943

L-R: Homer Gillis (1921-2012) and John Lycurgus "Kirk" Gillis (1924-2020). Pre-war. 6 2nd Street, Ocean City. c. 1941.

"I remember Uncle Kirk's World War II stories from the "CBI Theatre of War" (China, Burma, India).

Driving convoy trucks on the Burma Road in the dark with no headlights for fear of being strafed by Japanese air patrols. Seeing trucks fall off the narrow cliff roads and having to keep going, low gear, creeping up the hills. Gurka soldiers with long, curved knives slitting the Japanese soldiers' throats from behind. Don't even LOOK at Gurka women!"

John Lycurgus "Kirk" Gillis
as told to nephew, Robert A. Butler

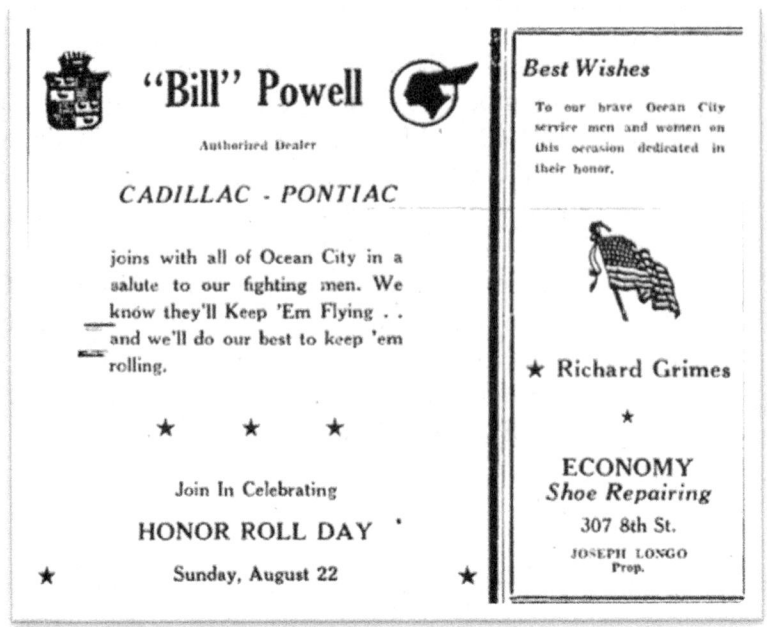

Tributes to veterans on Honor roll Day, including Richard Grimes.
Ocean City Sentinel Ledger, 1943.

Richard Sydney Grimes (1918-2014)
News of Our Men and Women in Uniform. Ocean City Sentinel Ledger, August 20, 1943.

Harmon photos courtesy Marion E. Harmon, daughter of Dewitt Harmon

Dewitt Roland Harmon (1924-2010). OCHS Operation Recognition, 2002.

Harmon on left.   Harmon on right

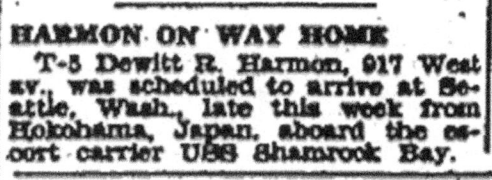

Harmon on left.   Ocean City Sentinel Ledger, 1946.

273

State of New Jersey

Distinguished Service Medal

AWARDED TO

STAFF SERGEANT OSCAR J. HARMON JR.

CITATION

The Governor of the State of New Jersey, Christine Todd Whitman, under the authority of 38A:15-2, New Jersey Revised Statutes, awards the Distinguished Service Medal to Staff Sergeant Oscar J. Harmon Jr. for distinguished meritorious service in ground combat during World War II in the Asiatic Pacific Theater of Operations.

CHRISTINE TODD WHITMAN
GOVERNOR

Distinguished Service Award

Oscar James Harmon, Jr. (1922-2005) on left.
Unidentified man on right.
OCHS Operation Recognition, 2002.
7th Street and West Avenue.
Photos and obituary courtesy Tyree Harmon
Lawson Eason, daughter of Oscar.

Oscar "Hop" Harmon, a Nanticoke Native American, was born in Ocean City. He attended local school and was a five-letter athlete in high school. "Hop" loved horses and spent summers during the 1930s working as a groom for Powell's Stables.

Oscar served four years in the Army Air Corps during World War II. After discharge, he took and passed the Ocean City Fire Department entrance exam, becoming the first person of color to pass the exam. Segregation and discrimination led to a short-lived career with the Fire Department. Discouraged, "Hop" left the department in 1946 to pursue a career playing semi-pro football in Boston, Massachusetts. He returned to New Jersey in the late 1940s taking a summer job on the Ocean City Beach Patrol. In the off season, he worked for Chitty's Upholstery in Somers Point, raised and sold pigs, and did private work for Philadelphia's Wanamaker family, owners of Wanamaker Stores.

He was known locally as "The Fishman," selling his catch of the day in the Ocean City area. For a time, Oscar installed propellers on helicopters for government contractor Chez Vault in Stratford, Connecticut. His last thirty-seven years of employment were with Dee Lumber Company of Linwood, New Jersey, first as a truck driver and later as a Shipping/Receiving foreman. After retirement in 1984, Oscar enrolled at Atlantic County Vocational Technical School in Mays Landing where he received certifications in Tailoring, Electrical Work, and Auto Mechanics.

Oscar joined Mt. Zion Baptist Church in 1993 becoming a dedicated worker in several ministries leading to his ordination as a Deacon. He was a lifetime member of the American Legion Post #81 in Pleasantville and Veterans of Foreign Wars (VFW) of Cardiff. Oscar was the first Black councilman in Egg Harbor Township.

VFW membership card.

State of New Jersey

STATE HOUSE, TRENTON, N.J.

ASSEMBLY COMMENDATION
By Assemblyman **JEFF VAN DREW**

WHEREAS, Assemblyman Jeff Van Drew, as the duly elected representative of the First Legislative District, is pleased to honor and congratulate

Oscar Harmon

on the occasion of receiving a High School Diploma during

Operation Recognition

WHEREAS, This distinguished Veteran placed his country before all else, and courageously served his military duty, while giving up the privilege of completing his education; and,

WHEREAS, The citizenry of the First Legislative District, through their elected representative, recognize this distinguished individual as an inspiration to all and whose heroism and achievements help us glimpse a future of hope and promise; and,

WHEREAS, Through sacrifices, hard work and dedication this individual has brought honor and pride to the citizens of the State of New Jersey; now, therefore,

Be It Known To All That The Undersigned Hereby Honors:

Oscar Harmon

upon receiving his High School Diploma during Operation Recognition

November 11, 2002

and extends sincere best wishes for continued happiness and success.

JEFF VAN DREW
Member of the General Assembly

State of New Jersey

THE SENATE AND GENERAL ASSEMBLY
STATE HOUSE, TRENTON, N.J.

JOINT LEGISLATIVE RESOLUTION
By Senator GORMLEY and Assemblymen LeFEVRE and BLEE

WHEREAS, The Senate and General Assembly of the State of New Jersey are pleased to join in honoring and saluting Staff Sergeant Oscar J. Harmon Jr., an esteemed member of his Township of Egg Harbor, Atlantic County, community, who received the New Jersey Distinguished Service Medal at the Cherry Hill Armory on June 15, 2000; and,

WHEREAS, The State of New Jersey's highest military award, the Distinguished Service Medal has been presented to Oscar J. Harmon Jr. for his meritorious service as a member of the United States Army Air Corps during World War II; and,

WHEREAS, Oscar J. Harmon Jr. served his country with honor and valor, demonstrating his love for America and his steadfast commitment to protecting the security of the United States; and,

WHEREAS, Oscar J. Harmon Jr.'s selfless acts during the performance of his duties have exemplified true patriotism and a concern for others; and,

WHEREAS, It is both proper and fitting for the members of this Legislature to pause in their deliberations to praise the United States Army Air Corps career of Staff Sergeant Oscar J. Harmon Jr. and to commend him as a man of outstanding character and exceptional determination; now, therefore,

Be It Resolved by the Senate and General Assembly of the State of New Jersey:

That this Legislature hereby honors and congratulates Oscar J. Harmon Jr. for receiving the Distinguished Service Medal, New Jersey's highest military award, acknowledges his unparalleled determination and sense of duty in serving our country, and extends to him this Legislature's sincere best wishes; and,

Be It Further Resolved, That a duly authenticated copy of this resolution, signed by the Senate President and the Assembly Speaker and attested by the Senate Secretary and the Assembly Clerk, be transmitted to Oscar J. Harmon Jr.

Attest:

Dolores A. Kirk
Secretary of the Senate

Linda Metzger
Clerk of the General Assembly

President of the Senate

Speaker of the General Assembly

277

ARCHIE HAGGIE HARRIS .IR

Archie Harris Now Studies Flying

Archie Harris, husky Ocean City negro athlete, who set a world discus record while at Indiana University, is now in basic training as a pre-aviation cadet at Keesler Field, Miss.

Harris is the son of Mrs. Mary N. Harris, of this city, and served for a number of years on the Beach Patrol. He was graduated from Indiana and had been teaching physical education at a southern school before entering the service.

Keesler Field track fans are trying to drum up competition with other Air Force outfits, remembering the time when Archie threw the platter 174 feet 8¼ inches for an unofficial world record at the NCAA meet at Stanford in 1941.

Archie Haggie Harris, Jr. (1918-1965)
Tuskegee Airman. Military Service Feb. 1,
1945 – Nov. 12, 1946. Second Lieutenant,
617 Bomb Squadron (M) 447th Composite Gp.
Tactical Air Command.
Died Oct 29, 1965 in New York City, NY.

Archie Haggie Harris pre-aviation cadet
Ocean City Sentinel Ledger, October 15, 1943

Archie Harris, Jr. is an Ocean City legend who distinguished himself as an athlete at Ocean City High School and went on to become an Olympic candidate in the discus throw. He also excelled at the shot put and played football at Indiana University. Following college, he joined the Army where he became a Tuskegee Airman. Nearly 1,000 fighter pilots trained as a segregated unit at an air base in Tuskegee, Alabama. Not allowed to practice or fight with their white counterparts, the Tuskegee Airmen of the 617 Bomb Squadron painted the tails of their North American P-51 Mustang airplanes red. When the pilots of the 332nd Fighter Group painted the tails of their P-47's red, the nickname "Red Tails" was coined. Bomber crews applied a more effusive "Red-Tail Angels" sobriquet. Unable to break the color barrier preventing Blacks from becoming commercial airline pilots, Archie pursued a career in teaching in Harlem after his military service.

Archie Haggie Harris, Jr.
Beverly National Cemetery
Burlington County, New Jersey

Aaron Edward Harvey, Jr. (1925-1996)

Ross Dee Humphrey
(1917-2005)
Army Field Sergeant

Ocean City native Aaron Harvey served two years in the military during World War II. After discharge from the Army, he married his high school sweetheart, Sarah Frances Oliver. Shortly thereafter, he joined the Ocean City Police Department.

Carl Leroy Henry (1928-2014). OCHS Class of 1945.

Norrece Thomas Jones, Jr. (1919-2009)

Norrece T. Jones, Jr., a longtime administrator at Cheyney University in Pennsylvania, died at a retirement community in Germantown, Pennsylvania. He was 90 years old. Jones was born in South Carolina but reared in Ocean City. While an undergraduate at Hampton University in Virginia, he was a CIAA champion boxer. The Army recruited Jones during World War II. He became a Master Sergeant and served in France and Italy. Jones finished his undergraduate work at Hampton University and studied business administration at the Wharton School of the University of Pennsylvania. In 1948 he was hired as a bookkeeper at Cheyney University. After a career of 35 years at Cheyney, he retired in 1983 as Vice President for Fiscal Affairs.

Sylvanus Wiley Leatherbury (1909-2004)

Crisfield, Maryland native was living at 638 Haven Avenue when he registered for the draft, as required of all men in his age group. He claimed a conscientious objection but was drafted into the Army in July 1942 nonetheless. Leatherbury received a disability discharge on September 27, 1943. [195]

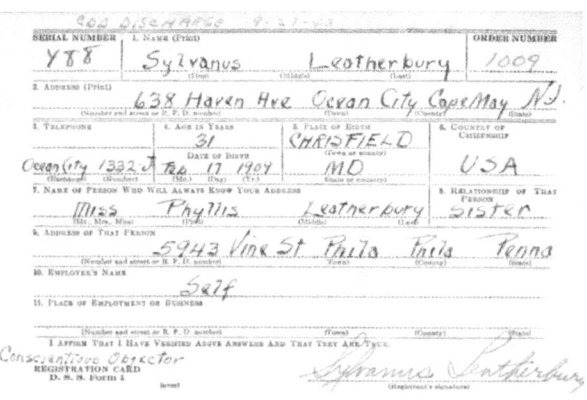

Lemuel Thomas Lewis, Jr. (1919-1983)

Samuel Saunders Martin (1917-1987)

Lemuel suffered brain damage in a World War II non-combat service-related accident resulting in reconstructive surgery that required a permanently implanted plate in his head. While he was able to function normally, he qualified for military disability. Lem was a hyper type of person who walked everywhere he went at a pace hard to match.

Charles Amos Money
(1914-1997)

Howard Wendell Morgan
(1918-2012)

Lawrence Motley (1924-1996)

Leonard Outen (1921-1960)

Harry "Sonny" Segal Rolls (1926-1992). OCHS Class of 1943.

Charles Lewis Spence (1921-1987).
Pleasantville High School Yearbook

Paul Edward Stewart
(1914-1982)

Resort Woman Has 3 Sons, All To Be In U. S. Army

If the Sumpter family is any criterion, the United States should win the war in a hurry.

Mrs. Mary Sumpter, colored, 622 Bay av., Ocean City, is believed to hold the record here so far by having two of her three sons already in Uncle Sam's rapidly growing army, and the third son scheduled to don a uniform January 15.

"I'm very proud of them all," she said today, "but I naturally feel a great deal of concern, too."

ONE SON NOW CORPORAL

Her second son, Harold Sumpter, 23, was drafted into the army last July 29 and was stationed most of the time since then at Fort Belvoir, Va. He was advanced to the rank of corporal, and recently transferred to another post, but his mother hasn't heard where. He has taken an examination for it.

The youngest son, Philip, 22, was an orchestra musician in New York and just entered the service at Fort Dix last week as a private. He is awaiting assignment.

OLDEST SON ENLISTS

George, Jr., 25, oldest of the family, recently passed an examination for postal work, but changed his mind and enlisted. He will enter the service on the 15th.

The boys come by army duty naturally, as their father, George, Sr., was a veteran of World War I and belongs to Morgan Ranck Post, American Legion. He is an apartment superintendent in Washington, D.C. Mrs. Sumpter is employed in the home of Mr. and Mrs. Burdette Tomlin, Plata pl. and Atlantic

Daily Sentinel Ledger article on George, Philip, and Harold Sumpter in Army, January 8, 1942.

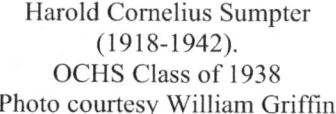

George Sumpter (1916-1995)
Photo courtesy William Griffin

Harold Cornelius Sumpter (1918-1942).
OCHS Class of 1938
Photo courtesy William Griffin

Philip Howard Sumpter (1920-1989)
Photo courtesy Philip Sumpter, Jr., May 2022

Harold Sumpter, son of George Lincoln and Mary Lucinda Johnson Sumpter, was a star athlete at Ocean City High School and Xavier University in New Orleans. He enlisted in the Army in 1941. On August 8, 1942, while attempting to rescue a fellow soldier from drowning in a Waycross lake, the fellow soldier panicked causing both men to drown. Sumpter was scheduled to go on furlong August 9 to come home to Ocean City. Major George A. Nelson, a commanding officer of the Army Air Forces Training Center in Atlantic City, presented Sumpter's mother with a posthumous medal and citation for her son's heroism.[196]

Harold Sumpter, World War II memorial plaque at Ocean City's Memorial Park.

Harold Sumpter Post No. 6061, Veterans of Foreign Wars. 718 Bay Avenue, (Elks' Home, 618 Bay Avenue) Ocean City. The Sentinel, 1946.

Colored V.F.W. Post Is Organized Here

Instituting services were held Sunday at the Elk's Home, 718 Bay av., for Harold Sumpter Post No. 6061, Veterans of Foreign Wars, of this city.

There were several state, county and district officers of the V.F.W. present for the ceremonies. Mayor Clyde W. Struble and Commissioner Edward B. Bowker also were guests and made congratulatory remarks.

The instituting officer was District Deputy Parsons, of Rheims Post No. 564, Atlantic City. Other speakers were Mrs. Parsons, Rev. Mayo and Mr. Donaway, all of Atlantic City.

Floyd Leonard Watts (1922-2004)
Photo courtesy Nathan Davis, Jr., Macedonia
United Methodist Church Historian

Dr. Roland Wiggins (1932-2019)
OCHS Class of 1949 senior photo

Pianist Roland Wiggins played in an Air Force band during his time in the military. Famed jazz and R&B trumpeter and vocalist Donald Byrd was among the many bandmates of Dr. Wiggins.[197]

David Robert Turner (1910-1972)
6th Air Cargo Respply Sq. Army Air Forces

WW I	WW II	KOREA		#U.S. GOVERNMENT PRINTING OFFICE: 1971–24803/422-726		ORIGINAL
1. NAME OF DECEASED - LAST - FIRST - MIDDLE *(Print or Type)*				14. NAME AND LOCATION OF CEMETERY *(City and State)* Seaside Cemetery, Palermo, N.J.		
TURNER, David Robert				IMPORTANT - Item 18 on reverse side must be completed. See attached instructions and complete and submit both copies.		
2. SERVICE NUMBER 32 077 270		3. PENSION OR VA CLAIM NUMBER ??		15. This application is submitted for a stone or marker for the unmarked grave of a deceased member or former member of the Armed Forces of the U. S., soldier of the Union or Confederate Armies of the Civil War or for an unmarked memorial plot for a non-recoverable deceased member. I hereby agree to accept responsibility for proper placement at the grave or memorial plot at no expense to the Government.		
4. ENLISTMENT DATE *(Month, day, year)* 27 Jul 1942		5. DISCHARGE DATE *(Month, day, year)* 12 Dec 1945				
6. STATE N.J.		7. DECORATIONS See discharge		NAME OF APPLICANT *(Print or Type)* Vernice Z. Turner		RELATIONSHIP Wife
8. GRADE OR RANK Cpl	9. BRANCH OF SERVICE, COMPANY, REGIMENT, DIVISION AC-AUS, 6th Air Cargo Respply Sq			ADDRESS OF APPLICANT *(Street address, City and State)* 727 Moore Ave., Ocean City, N.J.		
10. DATE OF BIRTH *(Month, day, year)* 18 Jul 1910		11. DATE OF DEATH *(Month, day, year)* 7 Jun 1972		SIGNATURE OF APPLICANT *Vernice Turner*		DATE 9 Jun 1972
12. RELIGIOUS EMBLEM *(Check one)*		13. CHECK TYPE REQUIRED UPRIGHT MARBLE HEADSTONE		16. FREIGHT STATION Ocean City, N.J. 08226		
XX	LATIN CROSS *(Christian)*	FLAT MARBLE MARKER		17. NAME OF CONSIGNEE WHO WILL TRANSPORT STONE OR MARKER John T. Newman		
	STAR OF DAVID *(Hebrew)*	XX	FLAT GRANITE MARKER			
	NO EMBLEM	XX	FLAT BRONZE MARKER	ADDRESS OF CONSIGNEE *(Street address, City and State)* 08222 508-2nd Ave., Beaslous Point, N.J.		
DO NOT WRITE HERE				I HAVE AGREED TO TAKE THE STONE OR MARKER TO THE CEMETERY.		
FOR VERIFICATION 25 SEP 1972		ORDERED 8 NOV 1972		SIGNATURE OF CONSIGNEE *John T. Newman*		
B/L Z-5573266		CONTRACTOR Maz Mon. Service				
DD FORM 1330, 1 NOV 62		EDITION OF 1 DEC 61 MAY BE USED.		APPLICATION FOR HEADSTONE OR MARKER		Form Approved Budget Bureau No. 22-R205

Military Headstone Application

Roger Williams
(1925-2008)

Photo courtesy Thompson family album   Photo courtesy Blanche Livingston Preston

Florida native Roger Williams lived between Florida and Ocean City. He joined the Navy from Ocean City. His implanted gold tooth, a fashion statement in his native Florida, makes for easy identification. Roger served on the Ocean City Beach Patrol and operated a Chinese restaurant in Ocean City following his military years.

Roger Williams in Navy attire. 7th Street east of Haven Avenue.

Background: L-R: Turner's Mobil sign, Carroll's Rooming House, railroad cross arms, Fred Reiss Lumber, edge of Lottie Singletary's home and beauty shop.

Cold War Era (1945-1991)

"The Cold War was a state of geopolitical tension after World War II between powers in the Eastern Bloc (the Soviet Union and its satellite states) and powers in the Western Bloc (the United States, its NATO allies and others). Historians do not fully agree on the dates, but a common timeframe is the period between 1947, the year the Truman Doctrine, a U.S. foreign policy pledging to aid nations threatened by Soviet expansionism was announced, and either 1989, when communism fell in Eastern Europe, or 1991, when the Soviet Union collapsed. The term 'cold' is used because there was no large-scale fighting directly between the two sides, but they each supported major regional wars known as proxy wars".

Secretary of Defense William S. Cohen approved a Cold War Recognition Certificate for award to all members of the armed forces and federal government civilian employees who faithfully served the United States during the Cold War era, Sept. 2, 1945 to Dec. 26, 1991.[198]

Cold War Veterans Listing

COLD WAR VETERANS	BRANCH	SERVICE
Louis Dennis Davis	Army	1956-1958
Theodore Charles Ford	Air Force	1955
Bernard W. Morris, Jr.	Army	Unk. -1957
Clarence Jackson Motley	Air Force	
Keith Allen Murrel	Army	
Raymond Timothy Stephens	Army	1946

Cold War Veterans Photo Gallery

Louis Dennis Davis (1938-2020).
Wearing fireman's uniform.

Theodore Charles Ford. OCHS Class of 1955.
Featured in Military section.

Here's Local Soldier, As He Really Looks

Introducing an Ocean City soldier now in basic training at Fort Dix. A former city employe, is the son of Mr. and Mrs. B. W. Morris, 450 West av. Due to an error by the Army, The Sentinel-Ledger last week published a picture of another man, released by the Fort Dix public information office and improperly identified as Morris.

Bernard W. Morris, Jr. (1929-2010)

Keith Allen Murrel.
OCHS Class of 1975

Clarence "Sonny" Jackson Motley

Clarence was known to childhood friends as "Sonny." Together the boys tried all the mischievous things young boys do. To keep him out of trouble, his parents sent him off to boarding school. Afterwards he joined the Air Force as a Military Policeman and was assigned to President Jimmy Carter's detail. Following military service, he became a deputy sheriff in San Antonio. Pennsylvania, New Jersey, California, Colorado, and Texas have all been home to Sonny. He now resides in Colorado.

"When I was caught scaling the fence surrounding the Flanders Hotel pool, a pool off limits to people of color, my dad decided it was time for me to get out of town."
Clarence Motley, October 2023.

Raymond Timothy Stephens
(1927-2003)

Christopher D. Robertson,
OCHS Class of 1978

Christopher served in the Navy from 1978 to 1984 where he was an analyst crew member on a Lockheed P-3 Orion patrol plane and a search and rescue swimmer.

Christopher D. Robertson. Crew member Navy P-3 Orion.

Korean Conflict (1950-1953)

The Korean War was a conflict between the Democratic People's Republic of Korea (North Korea) and the Republic of Korea (South Korea). In 1950, the United States military was actively working to rebuild portions of South Korea and train its standing army when North Korea invaded the South.

The United States responded to calls from the United Nations to support Korea. Fighting raged for three years leaving many casualties but no resolution to the conflict.

Korean Conflict Veterans Listing

KOREAN CONFLICT VETERANS	BRANCH	ENLISTED
Allen Benjamin Chalmers/Chalmus	Air Force	1952
Samuel Ellis Ford, Jr.	Air Force	1952
Norman Kenneth Ford, Sr.	Air Force	1952
Nathaniel Graham	Army	1953
Charles Edward Harris	Air Force	1950
Ross Dee Humphrey	Army	
John Arthur Oliver, Jr.	Air Force	1950
Brady Murrel	Air Force	1953
Richard "Dickie" Washington Murrel, Jr.	Army	
Timothy M. Murrel	Air Force	
Howard "Mickey" Smith		
Donald Michael Still	Air Force	
Robert Lamont Smith Stockley		
Blanche Lillian Young Still	Air Force	

Korean Conflict Veterans Photo Gallery

Richard W. "Dickie" Murrel (1929-2004)

?esort Man Enters ?ir Mechanics School

A/3c BRADY MURREL

A/3c Brady Murrel, 21, son of Mr. Marion W. Murrel, 734 West av., has entered the Aircraft Mechanics School at Sheppard Air Force Base, Texas, home of the largest technical school of this type in the world.

During his specialized training as a student at Sheppard he will receive intensive training designed to provide him with the thorough knowledge and basic skills required in servicing, inspecting and maintaining aircraft currently used by the United States Air Force.

Airman Murrel attended Ocean City High School prior to his enlistment in the Air Force on May 15.

Brady Murrel (1932-2013)
Ocean City Sentinel Ledger, October 1, 1953

Timothy M. Murrel (1930-2015)
OCHS Class of 1951

Howard Webb "Mickey" Smith (1933-2008).
Photo courtesy
Aline Dickerson B. Milligan, sister

Robert Lamont Smith Stockley (1936-1993)
Photo originally shared on Facebook by
Aline Dickerson B. Milligan, sister

Donald Michael Still
(1933-2011)

Blanche Lillian Young Still
(1934-2005)

Donald and Blanche Still. Both veterans.

Raymond H. Preston (1935-2019)
Photo courtesy
Blanche Livingston Preston, wife

Vietnam War and Vietnam Era (1955-1975)

The Vietnam War was a twenty-year civil war between North Vietnam supported by the Soviet Union and China and South Vietnam which was supported by the United States and other non-communist allies. The war was the result of North Vietnam's attempts to unite the country under communist rule.[199]

Between 1961 and 1966, Black males accounted for about 13 percent of the U.S. population and less than 10 percent of military personnel but almost 20 percent of all combat-related deaths. That disparity would decline before the war ended, but the racial tensions at home began to insert themselves into the military in Vietnam, damaging unit morale.[200]

Vietnam War and Vietnam Era Veterans Listing

Overall, 310 men from the City of Ocean City fought in the Vietnam War. To date, twenty-three Ocean City resident men and women of color have been identified as Vietnam or Vietnam era veterans. Of the thirteen Black males in Ocean City's Class of 1965, eight were drafted into the military for service in Vietnam.

VIETNAM WAR / VIETNAM ERA VETERANS	ENLISTED	BRANCH	CAREER
James Edward Abram		Army	
Charles Baker	1963	Army	
Ronald 'Barry' Banks	1965	Army	
Nathan Logan Banks	1965	Army	
Bruce Banks	1968	Army	
Walter J. Buckholtz, Jr.	1953	Air Force	
Charles Cullen Clark, Jr.	1947	Navy	Career
Don Carl Ford		Air Force	Career
Norman Kenneth Ford	1952	Army	
Alphonsa Gayle	1965	Army	
Levern Granger		Army	
Willie Earl Granger	1965	Army	
Gary James Harmon	1968	Army	
Charles Edward Harris	1951	Air Force	Career
Stanley Harris	1968	Army	
Alma Maxine Henry Glenn	1955	WACS	Career
Daniel Lee Henry	1961	Army	
Victor Dunare Humphrey	1965	Air Force	
Charles Jordan	1972	Army	
Timothy Marable		Marines	
Clarence Jackson Motley		Air Force	
Timothy M. Murrel		Air Force	
Alexander Pratt			
Rowell			
Harry Thomas Selby	1965	Air Force	
James Talmadge	1965	Army	
Kenneth Homer Thompson	1965	Army	
Anthony V. Washington	1966	Army	

Vietnam War and Vietnam Era Veterans Photo Gallery

James Edward Abram (1945-2020)

Charles Baker (1945-2023)
OCHS Class of 1963

Banks family photos courtesy R. Barry Banks

Ronald Barry Banks, OCHS Class of 1965
"Cooking my birthday dinner – Vietnamese rice."

Ronald Barry Banks

Nathan Logan Banks,
OCHS Class of 1965

Bruce Allen Banks,
OCHS Class of 1968

Walter was more commonly known as Buckholtz or "Bucky." He was an all-around athlete who lettered in football, basketball, and track while finding time for glee club and student council. His military career took him to Vietnam, the Philippines, and Japan. Bucky owned and operated Bucky's foods while stationed in California. After his 1972 retirement from the military where he was a Personnel Equipment Specialist, he managed Food Services at Bally's Casino in Atlantic City until 1996. His last employment was with Anchor Security Services in Long Island, New York after which he retired to Maryland to be near family.

Walter James Buckholtz, Jr.
(1932-2015). OCHS Class of 1951

Charles Cullen Clark, Jr.
See World War II.

Victor Dunare Humphrey (1947-2022)
OCHS Class of 1965

Harry Thomas Selby (1931-1997)
OCHS Class of 1951

Anthony V. Washington (1947-2014)
OCHS Class of 1965

Charles Edward Harris (1933-2010)
Communications, Strategic Air Command
Photo courtesy Angela Harris Moore, daughter

Da Nang during 1968 Tet offensive

Harris was awarded the Air Force Commendation Medal for service as Communications Supervisor during the Vietnam 1968 Tet offensive. Post-military retirement, he served as a NJ state police dispatcher and later as a casino security captain. He served as a Democratic Committee person and volunteer poll worker for Upper Township.

Henry family photos courtesy Sonia Henry

Alma Maxine "Mackey" Henry Glenn. OCHS Class of 1955.

Alma Maxine "Mackey" Henry Glenn boarding a plane with colleagues.

Daniel Lee Henry (1942-2006). OCHS Class of 1960.

Daniel Lee Henry, Vietnam   Alexander Pratt. OCHS Class of 1961.

Levern Granger

Willie Earl Granger (1946-1968)
OCHS Class of 1965

Sgt. Willie Earl Granger was killed in action in Vietnam in August 1968. He is memorialized on a wall plaque at Ocean City's Memorial Park. He is believed to be the first Ocean City resident killed in Vietnam.

Levern Granger, Willie's brother, says, *"I'm trying to get the spelling of Willie Earl's name corrected on the wall plaque. It reads "Sgt. Willie E. Grainger." Grainger with an "i" was our slave name taken from the owners of Grainger Chewing Tobacco. When our great great grandparents were freed from slavery in the tobacco fields of Mullins, South Carolina, they dropped the "i" and took the name Granger. The plaque needs to be changed."*

Levern Granger interview, Haven Avenue, July 2021

NO IMAGE
AVAILABLE

Charles Jordan served in the 82nd Airborne Division, an airborne infantry division of the United States Army specializing in parachute assault operations into denied areas "responding to crisis contingencies anywhere in the world within 18 hours."[201]

Charles Jordan, OCHS Class of 1971

Kenneth was drafted into the Army after high school graduation. Having hunted large and small game since receiving a Blunderbuss at age fourteen, Kenny qualified as a Sharpshooter while in boot camp.

He was sent to Germany where he reported to the Adjutant General. One of his special memories was being assigned to escort Muhammed Ali on a tour of Germany.

Kenneth Homer Thompson (1947-2015)
OCHS Class of 1965

Kenneth Thompson, Germany. Ft. Dix boot camp graduation. Photo courtesy Ronald Barry Banks.

First Gulf War (Kuwait, Persian Gulf) (1990-1991)

The First Gulf War lasted from August 1990 until February 1991.

First Gulf War Veterans Listing

FIRST GULF WAR VETERANS	ENLISTED	BRANCH
Don Carl Ford – See Ford family feature		
Tyrone Samuel Henry – See Ford family feature		

Afghanistan War (2001-2021)

The Afghanistan War lasted from October 2001 to August 2021. On September 11, 2001, surprise attacks on United States sites by al-Qaeda forces from Afghanistan-backed Taliban forces controlling the country, triggered retaliatory strikes from the United States. Al-Qaeda was defeated in just months, but the battle to take down the Taliban and restore rule to the Afghan people continued for 13 years.

Afghanistan War Veterans Listing

AFGHANISTAN WAR VETERANS	ENLISTED	BRANCH
Anthony Thompson	1994-2014	Navy

Afghanistan War Veterans Photo Gallery

Anthony Thompson, OCHS Class of 1990.

Lt. Col. Anthony Thompson in the cockpit.

Anthony Thompson entered the Navy in 1994 with a degree in Mechanical Engineering from Temple University in Philadelphia. He retired from the military as a Lieutenant Colonel after twenty years piloting Lockheed's P-3 Orion where he patrolled coastlines in pursuit of enemy boats and submarines. The P-3 is a four-engine, turboprop anti-submarine and maritime surveillance aircraft developed for the United States Navy, primarily for maritime patrol, reconnaissance, anti-surface, and anti-submarine warfare. Its distinctive tail stinger or "MAD" boom is used for the magnetic anomaly detection (MAD) of submarines.

Anthony's overseas patrols included flights over Kosovo, Bosnia, and Herzegovina. He was stationed in Kandahar, Afghanistan and at Balad Air Base, a joint air base with the Iraqi Air Force in the Sunni Triangle 40 miles north of Baghdad. Thompson chose retirement from the military over an offer to work as a Navy liaison to the Pentagon.

U.S. Navy P-3C

Underside of U.S. Navy P-3C. MAD (rear boom) and external sonobuoy launch tubes (grid of place spots toward the rear)[202]

Second Gulf War (Iraq) (2003-2011)

The second Gulf War lasted from March 2003 until December 2011.

Second Gulf War Veterans Listing

SECOND GULF WAR VETERANS	ENLISTED	BRANCH
Tyrone Samuel Henry – See Ford family feature		
Anthony Thompson – See Afghanistan War	1994-2014	Navy

New Jersey Army National Guard

The Army National Guard's mission is to maintain well-trained, well-equipped units available for prompt mobilization by a state governor for local and statewide emergencies or by the President of the United States during national emergencies.

The National Guard is composed of civilians who train one weekend each month and two weeks each summer. They may be activated during wartimes or provide assistance during national emergencies such as natural disasters or civil disturbances.

A New Jersey State Army National Guard armory was located at 18th Street and Bay Avenue in Ocean City. Battery B became Battery C, 308AA Anti-Aircraft Artillery Battalion became 286th Armored Field Artillery Battalion in 1955.

The 386th was equipped with 105mm Howitzers on track or tank chassis. It was home of Battery C, 6th Howitzer Battalion, 112th Artillery Unit. When the Ocean City facility closed, the unit relocated to the Atlantic City armory at 1008 Absecon Boulevard where they became part of the 157th Field Artillery Battalion.

New Jersey Army National Guard Listing

NEW JERSEY ARMY NATIONAL GUARD VETERANS

William Griffin
James Hannah
Joseph Hannah
Carl Leroy Henry
Joseph Henry
Bernard W. Morris, Jr.
Sylvester Willis Thompson, Jr.
Wayne Thompson, Sr.

New Jersey Army National Guard Photo Gallery

Ocean City native S. Willis Thompson enrolled in Officer Candidate School at Temple University and completed officer field training at the New Jersey Military Academy Officer Candidate School of the New Jersey National Guard at Sea Girt, New Jersey. He completed training at The Artillery and Missile School at Fort Sill, Oklahoma.

Thompson served as 2nd Lieutenant at the Ocean City armory. His placement in Field Artillery was a perfect match as Howitzer artillery fire required operating heavy equipment and calculating missile ranges, skills he learned in his civilian occupation as a crane operator, surveyor, and estimator. Thompson advanced to Commander of the Atlantic City Armory when the Ocean City armory closed.

Lt. S. W. Thompson Completes Army Course

FORT SILL, OKLA. (AHTNC)— Army 2nd Lt. Sylvester W. Thompson Jr., 24, whose wife, Martha, and parents live at 624 Haven av., Ocean City, N. J., completed the 17-week field artillery officer basic course October 14 at The Artillery and Missile School, Fort Sill, Okla.

The course, designed for newly-commissioner officers, trained Lieutenant Thompson in communications, artillery transport, tactics and target acquisition.

Lieutenant Thompson was graduated from Ocean City High School in 1953 and attended Temple University.

Sylvester Willis Thompson, Jr. (1935-2006)

OFFICIAL VISITORS. First Lieutenant avid Bicknell and Second Lt. Sylvester. hompson, of the Ocean City unit, Army ational Guard, exhibit one of the unit's tanks for Mayor Nathaniel C. Smith (right) and Safety Director D. Allen Stretch at the Muster Day activities at the local armory on Sunday.—Senior Studio Photo.

Second Lt. Sylvester Willis Thompson, Jr., 18th Street National Guard Armory.
Ocean City Sentinel Ledger.

Commander
Sylvester Willis Thompson, Jr.

National Guard Limits Recruits

Battery Nearing Membership Quota

Membership in B Battery of the New Jersey National Guard is now limited to high school graduates and veterans of the military services, Capt. T. R. Sweigart, Battery commander, announced this week.

The limitation was imposed because of the rapid growth of the Battery in the past year, which has increased the roster almost to its strength limit.

Between January 1, 1954, and the same date this year, Capt. Sweigart reported, the Battery has increased from 45 men to 71 men and two officers. He said future applicants will be screened carefully.

Meanwhile, the Battery sections continue weekly drills at the armory, 18th st. and Haven av. In addition to section training last week, the Battery was briefed on explosives, booby traps and land mines. Section training included drills in communications, mess, formation, motor maintenance, 88 MM AA gun firing and maintenance drills, and practice fire and maintenance on 50 calibre machine guns.

Three new recruits were sworn in. They were Thomas C. Fox, Ira Charmichael and Fred Burroughs.

Following drills, members participate in target practice with .22 rifles, or shoot darts and watch television in quarters.

National Guard Limits Recruits,
Ocean City Sentinel Ledger, 1955

Local Guardsmen Win Rifle Championship

Battery B of the New Jersey National Guard, with headquarters in Ocean City, last week annexed the 308th AAA Battalion rifle championship by outshooting rival Battalion marksmen at Wildwood.

Battery B's sharpshooters boast an average of 1,160 points a match, and will now engage in competition with National Guard teams throughout the state.

Meantime, the Battery basketball team is playing each Tuesday night at the Convention Hall here, and to date has won one and lost on in competition against other Battalion teams.

Local Guardsmen Win Rifle Championship,
Ocean City Sentinel Ledger, 1955

Resort Guardsmen Win Over Battery C, 68-50

Ocean City's B Battery outgunned Wildwood C Battery, 68-50, in a 308th AAA Battalion basketball game last week at Convention Hall here.

The contest was a close one through the first two periods, with the local unit coming off at half time with a 28-24 edge. Ocean City applied the pressure in the third period to build its lead by 10 points and added a four-point margin in the final period.

Joe Hannah was the big gun of the evening, pacing Ocean City with 30 points on 13 field goals and four fouls. James Hannah added 17 and Lou Addario 15 to the B Battery total. Laricks topped C Battery with 21 points.

Twins Joseph Hannah (1936-1986)
and James Hannah (1936-1991)
National Guards basketball, Ocean City
Convention Center, February 3, 1955
Ocean City Sentinel Ledger

Atlantic City Press

ATLANTIC CITY, N.J., TUESDAY, JULY 8, 1958

ATTEND OFFICERS' COURSE—Eight area men returned Saturday from Sea Girt, where they participated in the second summer field training session of the N. J. Military Academy Officer Candidate School of the N. J. Army National Guard. From left are Sylvester W. Thompson Jr., 624 Haven Ave., Ocean City; Barnett H. Strickler, 6802 Ventnor Ave., Ventnor; Daniel Modiano. 817 Atlantic Ave., this city; Thomas L. Glenn Jr., 11 N. Quincy Ave., Margate; Louis Germanio, Maple Shade Lane. Beesley's Point; David H. Singer. 3529 Pacific Ave., this city; William H. Walls, 223 W. Pleasant Ave., Pleasantville and (sighting through 81 MM mortar) William L. Donnelly, 218 Washington Ave., Ventnor.

New Jersey Army National Guard. Atlantic City Press, 1958.

'Hey, Where Did That Wheel Go?'

Private Charles Evernisen (left) and Sergeant Wayne Thompson, both of Ocean City, are bogged down in downpour during field training at Camp Drum, N.Y. Both are New Jersey Army National Guardsmen.

The Evening Bulletin
NEW JERSEY NEWS

54   PHILADELPHIA TUESDAY, JULY 18, 1961   FS

Wayne Thompson on right. New Jersey Army National Guard. Camp Drum, New York. July 1961. The Evening Bulletin, New Jersey News, July 18, 1961.

Wayne Thompson on right

In March 1964, Battery B was on maneuvers at Camp Pickett in Virginia when Lieutenant S. Willis Thompson was advised that his grandfather, Joseph Armour Thompson, had passed away.

The troop commander was more than surprised when five men (S. Willis Thompson, Wayne Thompson, Carl Henry, Joseph Henry, and William Griffin) all requested leave each claiming their grandfather had died. The commander had no idea five first cousins belonged to the unit.

William Gilbert Griffin, OCHS Class of 1963
Photo courtesy William Griffin

Carl Leroy Henry
Photo courtesy Sonia Henry, sister

Honoring Their Service and Sacrifice

Operation Recognition

In a special 2002 ceremony, representatives of Ocean City High School and the State of New Jersey presented long awaited diplomas to fourteen Ocean City students who left high school to serve in the military during World War II. Among those receiving diplomas were brothers Dewitt and Oscar Harmon.

NOVEMBER 13, 2002   *Ocean City's Only Locally Owned New..*

Ocean City World War Two vets win battle to receive high school diploma

By ANN RICHARDSON
Correspondent

For a dozen veterans at Ocean City High School on Monday morning, another battle was won. At a special ceremony held in their honor, these brave men, who risked their lives to serve their country during World War II, were awarded the one thing they nearly earned but were never able to obtain despite their sacrifice - a genuine high school diploma.

Addressing the nations "Greatest Generation," those who left home and school to defend their ideals of freedom and liberty across the globe, the veteran's received their long overdue diplomas through a state-wide program called Operation Recognition. Most of the veteran's went on to live success-ful, fulfilling lives. They had varied careers, some in the military, and others were teachers, firefighters, businessmen and entrepreneurs. However, they all had one thing in common-they sacrificed their education and put themselves in harms way to preserve freedom for future generations.

Planned by Ocean City Board of
continued on Page 14

Also honored at Monday's ceremony were Roland "Rocky" Gannon, who served in the military in WWII, Korea and Vietnam; James Flanagan, a Seaville resident who served in the Army; Charles Shropshire, Navy, who served on the USS Intrepid; Marco Smigliani, Marines, a Vietnam War veteran; Andrew Allegretto, of OCHS, Air Force and member of the Flying Tigers; the late Ancilo Florentino, of OCHS, accepted by his daughter Susan; Oscar Harmon, Air Force, of OCHS and his brother Dewitt Harmon; John West, Navy, of OCHS; and James Shropshire, of OCHS, accepted by his wife.

"It's really nice to have this," said Oscar Harmon, who went on to be the first black American to join the Ocean City Fire Department. "I was in the Fifth Air Force, I served in the South Pacific under General MacArthur. They took me into the service at the tail end of 1941. I wanted ...this diploma so badly when I came home. But...

Operation Recognition:
Veterans Get Long Awaited Diplomas.
Ocean City Sentinel, November 14, 2002

312

"Friends Richard Barton, Lawrence Motley, Edward Harvey and myself all volunteered to be drafted. We wanted to stay together but we didn't. Richard Barton could not go. He was only 17. The rest of us went and we were separated. I was sent to Fort Ord, Calif. From there I went to British New Guinea and there I ran into my homeboy Richard Barton. I received a transfer to his company, Heavy Truck Engineering Co. From there we went to the Philippines. After Japan's surrender, I left Richard and went to Yokohama, Japan and from there back to the states, Fort Dix, and discharge. I later learned Richard Barton had become a career soldier for over twenty years."

Excerpt from biography sheet Dewitt Harmon submitted to Ocean City Board of Education

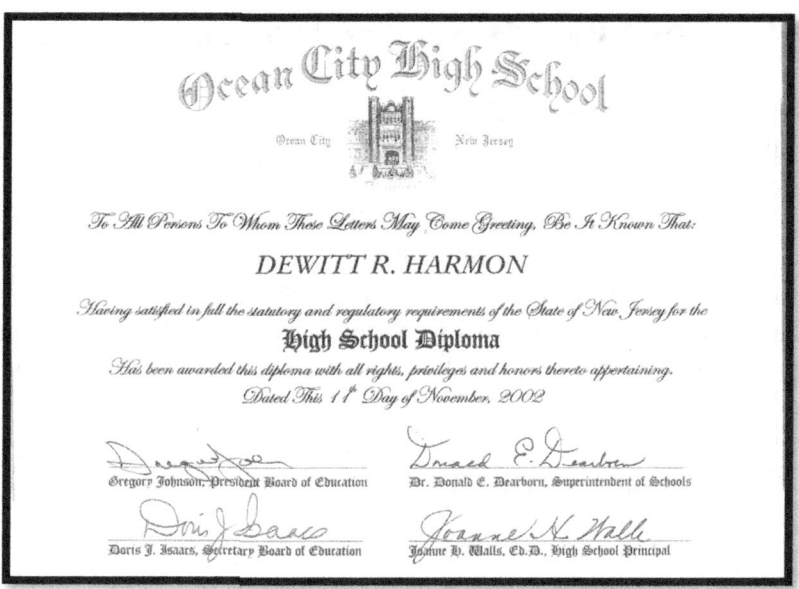

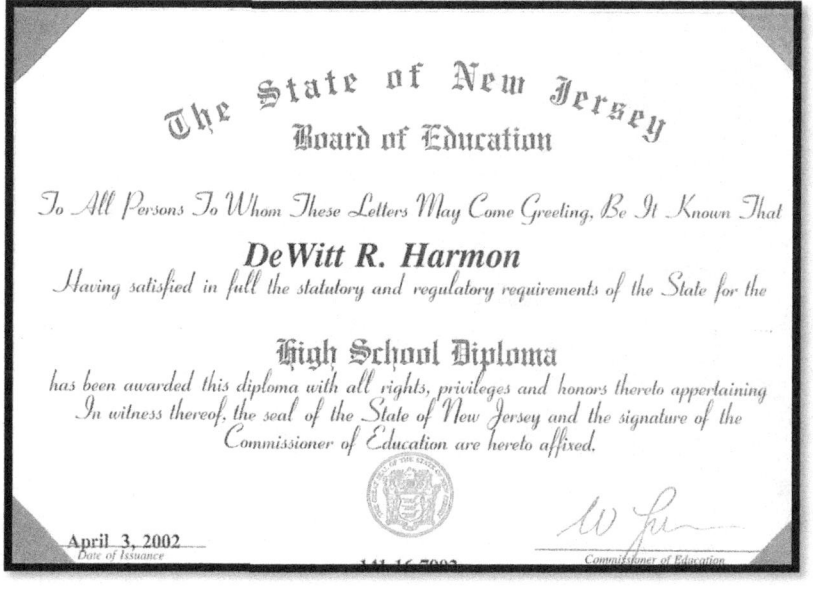

The Ford Family: Heroes and Sheroes
"I've never seen anything like it.
So much from one family."
S. John Loeper, President
Ocean City Historical Museum, Feb. 2019
Black History Month Exhibit

FEATURE: Ford Family Service Record

Ruby Wallace Wheatley Ford came to Ocean City as a young girl. She attended Central Avenue Elementary School and Ocean City High School. Ruby married Samuel Ellis Ford, Sr., a horse trainer who followed the horse racing circuit. While working as a domestic at King Manor for Judge Franklin King, she reared three sons who all forged laudable careers in the military. The oldest son, Samuel Ellis Ford, Jr. started a long family tradition when he joined the military. His two brothers and four more generations followed in his footsteps going on to become quiet heroes and heroines. In all, thirteen members of this family, male and female, pursued military careers amassing nearly 200 years of service to the country.

Ford family photos courtesy Samuel Ellis Ford, III

L-R: Unidentified friend, Norman Ford, Ruby Ford, and Theodore Ford.

Veteran	Military	Federal Gov't.
Samuel Ellis Ford, Jr.	19+ yrs.	
Norman Kenneth Ford	22 yrs. 9 mos.	28 yrs.
Theodore Charles Ford	22 yrs.	21 yrs.
Samuel Ellis Ford, III	4 yrs.	
Donald Carl Ford, Sr.	20 yrs.	
Norman Kenneth Ford, Jr.	Unk.	
Marilyn Harvey Hill	4 yrs.	
Dianne Ford-Goodwin	20 yrs.	
Donald Carl Ford, Jr.		1 yr.
Tyrone Samuel Henry		4 yrs.
Genaia Hill	20 yrs.	
Imani Hubbard	7 yrs.	
Camaron Savage, Jr. ROTC		
Subtotal	138+ yrs. 9 mos.	54 yrs.
Total Years of Service:	192+ yrs. 9 mos.	

Samuel Ellis Ford, (1931-1972). OCHS Class of 1949. U.S. Air Force.

United States Air Force   **Years of Service: 19+**

Samuel Ellis Ford, Jr. enlisted in the United States Air Force at Fort Dix in Burlington County, New Jersey after graduating with the OCHS Class of '49. After basic training and radar training, he was stationed at the now defunct 770 Radar Squadron, Sage, Palermo Air Force Station, a radar site in Upper Township, New Jersey.

In 1951, Airman Ford was assigned to Thule, Greenland for an eighteen-month tour to help carry out the USAF plan to construct an air base and radar site. The young man from a summer resort island was on his way to the Arctic frontiers. The selected site was 750 miles north of the Arctic Circle, 947 miles from the North Pole, and near an indigenous settlement called Pituffik (the place where dogs are tied). Amidst the Arctic's icebergs, polar ice sheets, and Fjords, Thule Air Base would be the United States Air Force's northernmost installation. The Arctic weather presented challenges that required snowshoes and skis. The troops lived in tents during construction. Airplanes were the only way in or out.

Thule, Greenland c. 1951
Communications, 770 Radar Squadron

Thule Air Base became home to the 21st Space Wing's global network of sensors providing missile warning, space surveillance, and space control to North American Aerospace Defense Command (NORAD) and Air Force Space Command (AFSPC). Thule was to become home to the 821st Air Base Group. The base hosted the 12th Space Warning Squadron which operated a Ballistic Missile Early Warning System designed to detect and track ICBMs launched against North America and part of the 50th Space Wing's global satellite control network. Reconnaissance missions were flown across the Arctic Ocean from Thule AFB to the former Soviet Union. F-89 Fighter-Interceptor Squadrons were based at Thule.

United States Air National Guard   **Years of Service: Not available**

Following service in the Air Force, Mr. Ford joined the Air National guard at Willow Grove, PA. Sergeant Ford died in 1972 from injuries sustained in a car accident while still active in the Air National Guard.

Norman Kenneth Ford, Sr. U.S. Army, 1952. Career Field: Infantry, Helicopter Maintenance.

United States Army   Years of Service: 22 yrs. 9 mo.

In 1952 Norman Kenneth Ford enlisted in the United States Army at Fort Dix. His career fields included Infantry and Helicopter Maintenance. Following basic training at Fort Dix and airborne training at Fort Benning, Georgia, he was assigned to the 43rd Infantry Division at Fort Washington, Alaska. Norman tallied many jumps as a paratrooper before severely injuring a knee. From Harleys to big cars to helicopters, Norman seemed always on the road to being a mechanic. He re-enlisted in 1956 for helicopter training. His skills on various helicopters took him to Texas, Alabama, Hawaii, Kansas, and Germany. He trained on the maintenance of CH47 Tandem Rotor Cargo helicopters and was a crew member transporting CH47s before being assigned to Phu Loi, Vietnam where he remained 20 months supporting the 25th Infantry Division. Following another re-up and a year as an instructor at the Helicopter Maintenance School, he was sent to Chu Li, Vietnam, this time as a Flight Engineer in the 178th ASHC supporting Marine and Infantry units. After another year as an instructor, he was sent to Korea as Maintenance Supervisor at various CH47 shops. MSgt. Ford retired from military service at Fort Dix in 1974.

Federal Aviation Administration   Years of Service: 13 yrs.

From 1974 to 1987, Norman worked as a Police Officer at the Federal Aviation Administration's Police Department at Washington National and Dulles International Airports. After completing Coast Guard studies for Smallboat Operator, he worked as Police Sergeant responsible for the River Patrol Section supervising boat patrols on the river side of the airport property.

Metro Washington Authority Airports   **Years of Service: 15 years**

When Maryland, Virginia and Washington, D.C. took control of Washington National and Dulles International Airports in 1987, changing its name to Metropolitan Washington Authority Airports, Mr. Ford was named Police Sergeant (Detective) investigating violations of federal and airport laws. Later, he was promoted to Police Lieutenant in charge of Professional Standards overseeing training and background investigations for police and civilians. In 1995 Lieutenant Ford moved to Dulles International Airport and was promoted to Police Major Station Commander in charge of all police activities on the airport. His last three years between 1999 and 2002 were spent back at Washington National as

Pfc Ford Takes Part in Alaskan Maneuver

Army Pfc Kenneth N. Ford, son of Mr. and Mrs. Samuel E. Ford, 611 Simpson av., Ocean City, is participating in "Exercise Snow Bird", a joint Army-Air Force training maneuver, in Alaska.

Airborne units, ground troops and equipment are being tested in the exercise for operation in temperatures as low as 50 degrees below zero.

Ford, a 1954 graduate of the University of Alaska, has been in the Army since October, 1952. He is a vehicle driver in the Service Company of the 71st Infantry Division's 53rd Regiment.

Norman Kenneth Ford, Exercise Snow Bird, Alaska. Ocean City Sentinel-Ledger, February 3, 1955

Police Major Station Commander in charge of all police activities. It was during this last stint that Commander Ford was summoned to respond to the September 11, 2001 terrorist attack on the Pentagon. Commander Ford and close friend, Lt. William Parker of The Parker K9 Group, LLC, were among the first to arrive on scene. Together they helped six people escape the fire. Commander Ford retired from Washington National Airport in 2002 having amassed a total of 50 years 9 months of federal government service.

CH-47 tandem rotor cargo helicopter lifting jeep.

Cell phone photo of Norman Ford, Police Major Station Commander at Washington National Airport, directing rescue operations following the September 11, 2001 attack on the Pentagon. Terrorists hijacked American Airlines Flight 77 and deliberately crashed the airplane into the Pentagon, killing all 64 people on the plane and 125 people in the Pentagon. Ford and canine officer William Parker helped save six people.[203]

United States Air Force   **Years of service: 22 years**

Theodore Charles Ford,
OCHS Class of 1955
Career Field: U.S. Air Police.

Theodore Charles Ford graduated in the Ocean City High School Class of '55 and immediately joined the Air Force where he was assigned to the Air Police. Following basic training at Lackland AFB, Texas, he was sent to California and then back to McGuire AFB and Andrews AFB on the east coast. His next tour was to Kamaka, Japan and on to Thailand where he was part of the Special 56th Air Command at Nakhon Phanom Royal Thai Navy Base (NKP) along the Mekong River in Thailand. After serving in Australia with the 5th Defense Communications Squadron, he returned stateside to the 509 Bomb Wing Pease AFB, New Hampshire and then Andrews AFB and Bowling AFB, both in Washington, D.C. During his career, his assignments included Flight Commander, Non-Commissioned Officer in Charge of Airman Training, and protection of the Presidential executive vehicle fleet including Air Force One planes and other vehicles used by the U.S. Secretary of State and foreign dignitaries. His work required completion of the Flight Guard program, Secret Service, Diplomatic and explosive device training. Msgt. Ford retired from Bolling AFB, Washington, D.C. in 1977.

United States Department of Treasury   **Years of Service: 21 years**

After serving with the Air Police, Theodore became a Secret Service agent and traveled around the world with Presidents, Vice Presidents and other top U.S. officials and foreign dignitaries.

Department of State Diplomatic Security Service

Mr. Ford's military career provided the basis for a smooth transition into the Law Enforcement and Security arm of the U.S. Department of State in 1978. As a Special Agent (Secret Service), he was a sworn federal officer responsible for ensuring a safe environment for the conduct of U.S. foreign policy and for the security of Foreign Service personnel, property, and sensitive information throughout the world. He was stationed in Plains, Georgia at the Carter House.

Department of State Dignitary and Protection Division

Between 1978 and 1987, Mr. Ford coordinated all aspects of protective security details for cabinet-level foreign dignitaries visiting the United States, i.e., foreign ministers, former heads of state, British royal family, Secretaries General of the United Nations and NATO, and His Holiness the Dalai Lama of Tibet. Mr. Ford was based at Andrews AFB, Washington, D.C. but traveled worldwide. His assignments included Dignitary Protection Program Manager and Supervisor General Services Administration vehicles. A few of his security details included Ronald Reagan, Alexander Haig, Gerald Ford, George Schultz, Prince Charles of Wales and Princess Dianna, and the Philippines President.

Department of State Protection of Foreign Mission and Officials

From 1987 until retirement, Mr. Ford protected foreign missions and officials. These years allowed him to meet and work with George H. W. and Barbara Bush, Bill Clinton, and Gen. Colin Powell who recognized the Ford family for their many years of service. Mr. Ford retired from the Diplomatic Security Service in 1998 but continued to work in the field as a contractor with the D.C. Metropolitan Police Department and other security forces. He was in Washington, D.C. when Barack Obama was installed as the first Black President of the United States (POTUS).

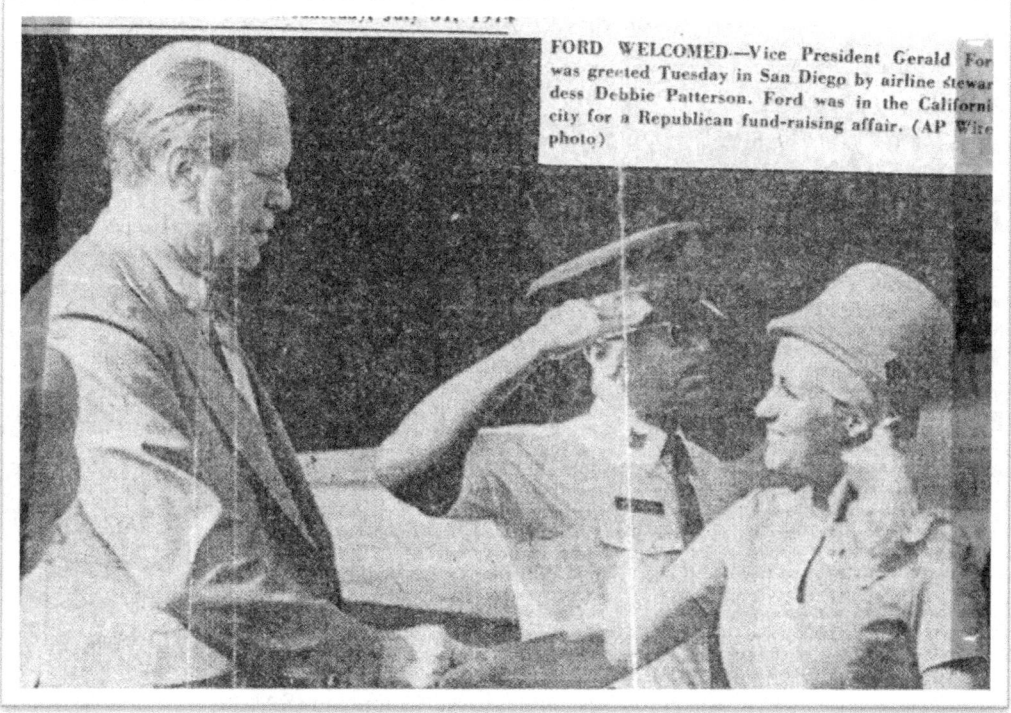

FORD WELCOMED—Vice President Gerald For was greeted Tuesday in San Diego by airline stewar dess Debbie Patterson. Ford was in the Californi city for a Republican fund-raising affair. (AP Wire photo)

President Gerald Ford greeted by an airline stewardess.
Theodore Ford salutes as the President arrives in San Diego.

Theodore Ford far left. Prince Charles and Princess Diana center. c. 1980s.

Theodore Ford has been featured in the Ocean City Historical Museum's OCHS Alumni All Star Exhibit.

Samuel Ellis Ford, III, OCHS Class of 1968
U.S. Air Force 307 Strategic Air Command (SAC)

Don Carl Ford, Sr. OCHS Class of 1970
U.S. Air Force 16th Special Operations Squadron, 8th Tactical Fighter Wing Flight Engineer

Spectre AC-130 gunship.

Norman Kenneth Ford, Jr.

Marilyn Harvey Hill. OCHS Class of 1970.

Dianne Ford-Goodwin, U.S. Navy
Chief Petty Officer

Don Carl Ford, Jr., U.S. Arm

Tyrone Samuel Henry,
OCHS Class of 1987. U.S. Marines Special
Security Forces. Infantry. Operation Desert
Shield and Operation Desert Storm. Liberation
of Kuwait and removal of Saddam Hussein.

Genaia Hill
U.S. Navy Chief Petty Officer
Industrial Hygienist Medical Services Corps.

Imani S. Hubbard
U.S. Air Force MOS 92M Mortuary Affairs Unit 67
3rd QM Co.

Camaron Savage
U.S. Army Junior ROTC

In 2019, the Ford family was the subject of a month-long exhibit celebrating Black History Month at the Ocean City Historical Museum. Ocean City Historical Society Museum president John Loeper and exhibit curator Loretta Thompson Harris review Ford family exhibit. February 2019.

Veterans' Memorial Park

Veterans' Memorial Park at 6th Street and Wesley Avenue occupies one full block and is dedicated to all men and women from Ocean City who served in the military. Veterans are memorialized through flags, artifacts, monuments, a dedication wall, plaques, and engraved brick walkways.

First Honor Roll Dedicated in 1942

First local tribute by the resort to men in service in the present conflict was paid on Memorial Day 1942, when the original honor roll was dedicated at city hall and then placed indoors on the wall of the entrance vestibule.

No fewer than 22 local civic patriotic and fraternal organizations joined with the American Legion in this program by placing floral tributes at the World War Memorial Monument, honoring the "boys" of 1917-18. The honor roll of the present conflict was unveiled by John H. Wood, 5-year-old son of Lieutenant-Commander (now Commander) John L. Wood, of the Navy. The dedicatory address was by the late Mayor George D. Richards.

First Honor Roll Dedicated in 1942.
Ocean City Sentinel Ledger, August 1942

Morgan-Ranck Post No. 137 monument honoring World War I veterans was dedicated to veterans of World War I in 1920. It stood in front of Ocean City's City Hall until 1947 when it was relocated to Memorial Park at 6th Street and Wesley Avenue. On Memorial Day 1942, organizations gathered to lay flowers at the base of the monument. That same day, the honor roll for veterans of World War II was unveiled and hung in the vestibule of City Hall.

Ocean City All Wars Memorial Plaque.

Monument honoring World War I veterans
in place at Memorial Park

The monument honoring World War I veterans is in place at Memorial Park after relocation from the corner of 9th Street and Asbury Avenue in front of City Hall. Newlin Turner and Otto Thompson are Westside residents honored on the City's World War I memorial plaque. Newlin was a member of Morgan-Ranck Post No. 137.

City officials watch as Thompson & Sons' work crew relocates the monument from City Hall property to Memorial Park. Sylvester Thompson, Sr. seated in foreground. Thompson employee Charlie Patton far right. Photo c. 1947. Photo courtesy Ocean City Historical Museum.

***

You Can't Afford to Miss Any of These Bargains

Check every item in this advertisement and then think it over. If you are not now an AMERICAN STORES CUSTOMER you will be amazed at the big savings. Prove to yourself it pays to deal at an "Asco" Store, where quality counts and your dollars go the farthest.

745 ASBURY AVENUE

Reg. 7c Quality — **Blue Rose Rice** lb **5c**

B. G. Crisp lb 18c	Gold Seal Oats pkg 8c	Tender Peas can 12½c

Special Combination Sale for This Week Only

ASCO
Buckwheat
Pancake Flour
Golden Syrup
3 for 25c

Regular 31c N. B. C. Marshmallow Creams lb 29c	"Quality Counts" ASCO	"Asco" Oleomargarine lb 20c

Corned Beef lb can 8c	"Asco" Pork & Beans 3 cans for 25c

Makes the Best Cup You Ever Drank

"Asco" Coffee lb 25c

Victor Bread 6c	Quality Fruits

Regular 20c can Colburn's Mustard 17c	"Asco" TEAS lb 45c — ½ lb pkg 23c; ¼ lb pkg 12c

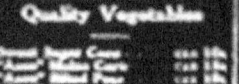
Today—Try a Pound of the Delicious Louella Butter Known as the Finest Butter in America

Rich Creamy Cheese lb 23c	Quality Vegetables	Fancy Norway Mackerel each 7c, 15c

FINAL THOUGHTS

Westside residents came to Ocean City for all the same reasons everybody else did. They were people looking for an opportunity to improve their lot in life and religious souls bent on making a better world by building up this coastal town. It was a chance to grab the golden ring - a new life, a hope fulfilled, a dream they dared to dream come true.

There in the center of town they made a house a home amidst the railroads and trains that rumbled through daily, laundries that belched out clouds of insidious smoke, and all those environmental detractors no one else in the town wanted to tolerate. It took fortitude, true grit to break through barriers and build bridges, not always physical barriers, and not always physical bridges.

With fits and jolts of progress restrained by witting and unwitting societal norms, people of the Westside persevered. They survived. They thrived. They even found joy. Despite the odds, or perhaps because of the odds, Westside residents broke Emma Marie Trusty's ties that bound.

To those who walked with us, marched with us, stood with us and for us, I simply say, "Thank you."

***

ENDNOTES

[1] New Jersey State Census 1885, 1895, 1905, 1915

[2] United States Federal Census 1900, 1910, 1920, 1930, 1940, 1950, 1960, 1970

[3] New Jersey Characteristics of the Population, 1960 census, Page 32-108, Table 22

[4] New Jersey Characteristics of the Population, 1970 census, Page 32-117, Table 58

[5] Census of Population, New Jersey State Library 1980, 1990

[6] https://www.newjersey-demographics.com/ocean-city-demographics

[7] https://oceancitynj.areaconnect.com/statistics.htm

[8] www.census.gov

[9] https://www.facebook.com/groups/1328899257169456/posts/2512320848827285/

[10] Facebook.com

[11] U.S., School Yearbooks, 1880-2012"; School Name: Philadelphia High School For Girls; Year: 1946

[12] https://www.facebook.com/ocnjmuseum/photos

[13] Police Dept./Postal Service, Government Services 7.2. Ocean City Historical Museum. Senior Studios Photo

[14] Police Dept./Postal Service, Government Services Book 7.2. Ocean City Historical Museum

[15] https://ocnjdaily.com/three-new-ocean-city-officers-graduate-in-police-academy-class/

[16] Fires/Fire Dept., Government Services 7.1. Courtesy Ocean City Historical Museum

[17] ocnjdaily.com

[18] https://somerspoint.com/2022/02/05/somers-point-says-final-goodbye-firefighter-eric-jones/

[19] 1950 United States Federal Census. Ancestry.com

[20] Nathan Davis, 2022

[21] Municipal Employees Book, Pg. 16B. Courtesy Ocean City Historical Museum

[22] 1900 Federal census

[23] 1900 Federal census

[24] Polk's Ocean City Directory, 1928

[25] Ocean City Sentinel Ledger, 1953

[26] Ancestry.com. U.S., School Yearbooks, 1900-2016 [database on-line]. Lehi, UT, USA: Ancestry.com Operations, Inc., 2010.

[27] Janet Motley Kline

[28] Janet Motley Kline and Nathan Davis, Jr.

[29] Richard "Dick" Grimes,

[30] Ocean City Old Timers program booklet, 1971

[31] High Seas Cause OC Beachfront Loss. Cumberland County Edition, Atlantic City Press

[32] What All The Excitement Was About. Ocean City Sentinel Ledger, April 10, 1958

[33] Spindly Forest. Ocean City Sentinel Ledger, July 1960

[34] OCNJ Daily. Staff writer Donald Wittkowski, January 10, 2021

[35] https://www.facebook.com/ocnjmuseum/photos

[36] https://www.yelp.com/biz_photos/port-o-call-hotel-ocean-city?select=yZsOuOLskeo699OG4aj32A

[37] O.C. to Try Nylon Bags To Slow Beach Erosion. Atlantic City Press, August 1967

[38] https://brigantinenow.com/looking-back-the-popular-infamous-brigantine-castle/

[39] https://www.google.com/search?tbs=lf:1,lf_ui:1&tbm=lcl&sxsrf=ALiCzsb4dSFi7W mjVUj PYY7GpOVhsy3PHA:1657804168964&q=manayunk+biking+trails&rflfq

[40] https://www.inquirer.com/news/manayunk-canal-history-expressway-schuylkill-river-philadelphia-20190313.html

[41] https://www.inquirer.com/news/manayunk-canal-history-expressway-schuylkill-river-philadelphia-20190313.html

[42] https://hiddencityphila.org/2012/02/restoration-of-manayunk-canal/

[43] https://www.google.com/search?q=manayunk+canal+history&sxsrf=

[44] https://www.google.com/search?q=manayunk+canal+history&sxsrf=

[45] https://manayunkmag.com/2021/05/tales-from-the-towpath/

[46] https://manayunk.com/visit-us/dsr/plans-and-projects/manayunk.html

[47] https://en.wikipedia.org/wiki/Manayunk_Canal_Towpath

[48] https://www.phillytrib.com/lifestyles/manayunk-rich-in-history-the-arts/article_0e840e68-d36b-50b7-a7a1-80196cdbed24.html. Accessed 9/7/2023

[49] Local firm receives $4 million contract. The Sentinel Ledger, Business/Finance, February 6, 1986

[50] https://en.wikipedia.org/wiki/Roland_Wiggins

[51] Charlottesville's News and Arts Weekly, September 2019

[52] Theodore Ford telephone interview, 2018

[53] Nathan Davis interview, September 2022.

[54] https://d33byq9npfy6u9.cloudfront.net/2/2019/09/Wiggins_personal1-e1568751599366.jpg

[55] https://www.c-ville.com/hitting-the-right-note-jazz-legend-roland-wiggins-reflects-on-a-lifetime-of-musical-expression/

[56] https://www.facebook.com/events/574056006453984?ref=newsfeed

[57] https://www.facebook.com/rolandawiggins/photos/a.1131850200271200/2796652800457590/?type=3

[58] Ancestry.com. Andrew Gold originally shared this on 25 Aug 2022

[59] Grimes 1999 newspaper article

[60] https://library.princeton.edu/libraries/firestone/rbsc/aids/sanborn/cape-may/ocean-city.html accessed Aug 17, 2023

[61] https://library.princeton.edu/libraries/firestone/rbsc/aids/sanborn/cape-may/ocean-city.html accessed Aug 17, 2023

[62] Green, Facebook, Dec. 2020

[63] Facebook photo.

[64] Ocean City's Alice Peterson is 108 years old. Photo courtesy of Ocean City Sentinel Ledger, 2003/

[65] Ancestry.com

[66] Firemen Felled Fighting Blaze. Ocean City Sentinel Ledger, April 28, 1966

[67] Clarence Motley, The Afro American, 1935

[68] Ancestry.com

[69] Sylvester Thompson, Sr. as told to William Griffin

[70] Donald Wittkowski, OCNJ Daily

[71] https://www.bumc.bu.edu/centenarian/statistics/

[72] Ocean City Historical Museum Transportation Bk. 29 Pg. 23C

[73] https://aoghs.org/petroleum-in-war/oil-pipelines-big-inch/. Accessed Sept. 6, 2023.

[74] Telephone interview with Barbara Potts Bonaparte

[75] Boyd's Ocean City Directory, 1922

[76] Polk's Ocean City Directory, 1928-1929

[77] Richard Grimes, Ocean City Gazette, Oct 1999

[78] Sally Nania Huff, September 2021

[79] Vivian M. Strawberry, 2021

[80] Vivian M. Strawberry, 2021

[81] Dr. Townsend is Chairman of Unit to Survey Area. Sentinel-Ledger, 1955

[82] https://www.constructionjournal.com/projects/details/bfc213119abd4db59e3dbb40ad156b7e.html. Accessed 2/5/2024.

[83] Donald Wittkowski, Apr 13, 2022. https://ocnjdaily.com/old-homes-demolished-make-room-new-housing-development/

[84] Richard Kabat remembered for men's shop. David Nahan/Sentinel Staff. https://ocnjsentinel.com/richard-kabat-remembered-for-mens-shop/

[85] https://www.facebook.com/thechatterboxoc/

[86] https://songlyricdesigns.com/elvis-presley-walk-a-mile-in-my-shoes-vintage-script-song-lyric-quote-music-print/

[87] https://www.cdc.gov/healthequity/racism-disparities/index.html. Accessed online 3/18/2023

[88] https://www.pinterest.com/pin/291326669627331797/. Accessed online 2/4/24.

[89] Wikipedia: tokenism

[90] https://www.merriam-webster.com/dictionary/tokenism#dictionary-entry-1

[91] Janet Motley Cline

[92] https://www.blackpast.org/african-american-history/graves-jocko-1764-1776/

[93] https://www.blackpast.org/african-american-history/jim-crow/

[94] https://img.lelivrescolaire.fr/anglais-3e-2017/i-want-to-break-free/stolen-from-africa/3000.ang3.6.03.mis.jimcrow.jpg

[95] https://www.history.com/news/blackface-history-racism-origins

[96] https://www.history.com/news/blackface-history-racism-origins

[97] https://picryl.com/amp/topics/blackface

[98] https://www.fhwa.dot.gov/highwayhistory/green.cfm

[99] https://www.google.com/search?q=victor+hugo+green&sxsrf

[100] https://en.wikipedia.org/wiki/Wesleyan Grove

[101] Atlantic City Free Public Library

[102] https://www.blackpast.org

[103] And Now, A Lily-White Ocean. Clarence Motley, Newspaper columnist and printer, Afro Banner, 1934.

[104] https://www.theflandershotel.com/history/

[105] https://www.waymarking.com/gallery/image.aspx

[106] http://www.shorelocalnews.com/remembering-staintons-department-store/

[107] https://en.wikipedia.org/wiki/Greensboro sit-ins

[108] https://www.britannica.com/event/sit-in-movement

[109] Photo: https://www.britannica.com/biography/Thomas-Dartmouth-Rice

[110] https://www.google.com/search?q=greensboro+lunch+counter+sit+in&tbm

[111] https://www.history.com/topics/black-history/civil-rights-movement-timeline

[112] https://www.history.com/topics/black-history/civil-rights-act

[113] https://www.archives.gov/milestone-documents/13th-amendment#

[114] https://www.archives.gov/milestone-documents/13th-amendment

[115] https://www.archives.gov/milestone-documents/15th-amendment. National Archives. Accessed 5/23/2023

[116] https://www.archives.gov/milestone-documents/plessy-v-ferguson#

[117] https://www.history.com/topics/black-history/civil-rights-movement#civil-rights-act-of-1957

[118] https://www.history.com/topics/black-history/civil-rights-movement#civil-rights-act-of-1964

[119] https://www.nytimes.com/2013/06/26/us/supreme-court-ruling.html

[120] https://nj.gov/state/historical/his-2021-juneteenth.shtml#:~:text=Slavery's%20final%20 legal%20death%20in,to%20slavery%20in%20the%20state

[121] https://www.britannica.com/place/Ocean-City-resort-New-Jersey

[122] https://www.facebook.com/ocnjmuseum/photos

[123] Richard Grimes, Ocean City Old Timers Historian

[124] Fred Miller, *Ocean City Beach Patrol,* Arcadia Publishing 2004, Charleston, South Carolina; Chicago, Illinois; Portsmouth, New Hampshire; San Francisco, California

[125] bundya51 originally shared photos on Facebook 01 May 2012 and 25 Apr 2012

[126] bundya51 originally shared photo on Facebook 28 Jun 2012

[127] https://www.facebook.com/ocnjmuseum/photos

[128] https://click.e.inquirer.com/?qs=6d842cb793e2224d28b5d5793f60c04baba1b15ac658f8d5e73 98e25618e901852744545f9c5497f1e1fe5a9cd6bec4bdc98e87a9c8f287d80b46e169a4ae18e

[129] https://ocnjdaily.com/ocean-city-begins-pesticide-free-experiment/

[130] https://ocnjdaily.com/one-of-ocean-citys-historic-buildings-to-get-makeover/, 2018

[131] Photo originally shared by Charles Lounsberry, Facebook, July 16, 2022

[132] https://www.pinterest.com/erodriguez1295/the-civil-war/

[133] http://righttofightexhibit.org › during-war › navy

[134] https://www.wikiwand.com/en/Military_history_of_African_Americans#

[135] Historical Society of Pennsylvania

[136] https://www.bridgemanimages.com/en-US/douglass/union-civil-war

[137] https://www.usct.org/2016/06/10/camp-william-penn-headquarters/

[138] https://www.usct.org/2016/06/10/camp-william-penn-headquarters/

[139] History.net

[140] Ancestry.com - 1890 Veterans Schedule

[141] Find-A-Grave.com

[142] "Freedom To All", Joseph G. Bixby, 2011

[143] Seaside Cemetery Burial Records

[144] Ancestry.com

[145] https://en.wikipedia.org/wiki/Causes_of_World_War_I

[146] Photo credit Buyenlarge/Archive Photos/Getty Images

[147] Ancestry.com

[148] U.S. Naval History and Heritage Command Photograph. USS Pocahontas Reunion Association Collection, 1974.

[149] U.S., Army Transport Service Arriving and Departing Passenger Lists, 1910-1939, Ancestry.com

[150] U.S., Veterans Administration Master Index, 1917-1940

[151] U.S., Headstone Applications for Military Veterans, 1925-1963

[152] U.S., Department of Veterans Affairs BIRLS Death File, 1850-2010

[153] U.S. Federal Census, 1930

[154] Ancestry.com. petejim_originally shared this on 04 Oct 2015

[155] Ancestry.com. petejim_originally shared this on 04 Oct 2015

[156] https://www.history.navy.mil/content/history/nhhc

[157] Ancestry.com

[158] https://www.blacksoldiersmattered.com/unit?id=813%20Pion%20Inf

[159] https://www.ibiblio.org/hyperwar/OnlineLibrary/photos/sh-usn/usnsh-p/id3014.htm

[160] https://www.ancestry.com/imageviewer/collections/61464

[161] Ancestry.com

[162] Ancestry.com

[163] https://commons.wikimedia.org/w/index.php?curid=75200975 Public Domain

[164] U.S., Army Transport Service, Passenger Lists, 1910-1939, Ancestry.com

[165] Ancestry.com

[166] https://www.familysearch.org/en/wiki/African_American_Military_Records#
World_War_I_.281917-1918.29

[167] https://www.ancestry.com/imageviewer/collections

[168] Ancestry.com. Copyrighted I.F.S. from N. Moser N.Y.

[169] Ancestry.com

[170] https://www.britannica.com/event/Spanish-American-War

[171] https://worldpopulationreview.com/us-cities/ocean-city-nj-population

[172] https://www.history.com/topics/world-war-ii

[173] https://www.trumanlibraryinstitute.org/tru-history-4-2/

[174] https://www.history.com/news/harry-truman-executive-order-9981-desegration-military-1948

[175] https://www.history.com/topics/world-war-ii/world-war-ii-history#section_8

[176] https://iloveancestry.com/topics/ancestry/historical-events/20th-century/tuskegee-institute-
tuskegee-airmen/

[177] https://njmonthly.com/articles/jersey-living/double-victory/

[178] https://www.dav.org/learn-more/news/2015/black-history-month-2015-remembering-red-ball-
express/

[179] www.army.mil, Public Domain, https://commons.wikimedia.org/w/index.php? curid=247543

[180] https://en.wikipedia.org/wiki/Red_Ball_Express#/media/File: Red_Ball_Express_-
_Truck_in_the_mud.jpg

[181] https://www.history.com/news/761st-tank-battalion-black-panthers-liberators-battle-of-the-bulge

[182] army.mil

[183] www.history.com

[184] https://www.nationalww2museum.org/war/articles/black-panthers-761st-tank-battalion

[185] https://ancestralfindings.com/761st-tank-battalion-black-panthers/

[186] https://www.blackpast.org/african-american-history/92nd-infantry-division-1917-1919-1942-
1945-0/

[187] https://www.blackpast.org/african-american-history/92nd-infantry-division-1917-1919-1942-
1945-0/

[188] By US_92nd_Infantry_Division.png: Nocladorderivative work: Asiela (talk) -
US_92nd_Infantry_Division.png, Public Domain

[189] https://commons.wikimedia.org/w/index.php?curid=11327784

[190] https://www.historynet.com/how-the-buffalo-soldiers-helped-turn-the-tide-in-italy-during-world-war-ii/

[191] https://www.sfasu.edu/heritagecenter/9795.asp

[192] https://www.sfasu.edu/heritagecenter/9795.asp

[193] U.S. World War II Army Enlistment Records, 1938-1946

[194] U.S. World War II Navy Muster Rolls, 1938-1949

[195] Big Game Hunter, Atlantic City Press, June 12, 1961

[196] Ocean City, NJ Veterans Memorial Park And The Wall of Honor, James E. Houck, undated.

[197] https://www.c-ville.com/hitting-the-right-note-jazz-legend-roland-wiggins-reflects-on-a-lifetime-of-musical-expression/

[198] https://www.usmilitariaforum.com/forums/index.php?/topic/231375-cold-war-certificate-of-recognition/

[199] https://nonpartisanpedicab.com/things-to-do-in-dc-visit-the-vietnam-war-memorial/

[200] https://www.historynet.com/the-vietnam-war-a-history-of-americas-controversial-war/

[201] https://en.wikipedia.org/wiki/82nd_Airborne_Division

[202] https://en.wikipedia.org/wiki/Lockheed_P-3_Orion

[203] http://www.dodmedia.osd.mil/Assets/Still/2004/Air_Force/DF-SD-04-12734.JPEG

BIBLIOGRAPHY

Abstract of the eighth Annual Report of the President of the Ocean City Association, 1889.

Bilby, Joseph G. *Freedom to All – New Jersey's African American Civil War Soldiers*, Hightstown, NJ, Longstreet House, 2011.

Boyd's Ocean City Directory, C. E. Howe Addressing and Printing Co. Publishers, 1922.

Boyd's Atlantic City Directory Including... Ocean City. C. E. Howe Company, Phila., PA publisher, 1911.

Cape May County Records Room. *Incorporation Book 3*, County of Cape May, Cape May Court House, NJ.

Darby, Bertram, *The Cape May County New Jersey Magazine of History and Genealogy*, June 1952.

Dorwart, Jeffrey M., *Cape May County, New Jersey, The Making of an American Community Resort,* New Brunswick, Rutgers University Press, 1992.

Gopsill's 1902 Directory for Atlantic City, Ventnor, South Atlantic, Longport and Ocean City.

Gopsills Philadelphia City Directory, Philadelphia, 1894. U.S. City Directories (Beta), Ancestry.com.

Miller, Fred and Susan, *Images of America, Ocean City's Historic Hotels,* Arcadia Publishing, 2014.

National Archives. *Death Records, Veterans' Service Records*, National Archives and Records Administration. Washington, DC

New Jersey Characteristics of the Population, Census 1960, 1970, Table 58.

New Jersey Marriage Records 1670-1965. Ancestry.com Operations, Inc., 2016.

New Jersey State Archive; Trenton, NJ, USA; *State Census of New Jersey, 1915.* Ancestry.com.

New Jersey State Census 1885, 1895, 1905, 1915.

New Jersey State Library Census of Population, 1980, 1990.

Polk's Ocean City (Cape May County Directory), R. L. Polk & Co. Publishers, 1948, Ancestry.com online

Polk's Ocean City (New Jersey) Directory, R. L. Polk & Co. publishers, 1918-1919.

Polk's Ocean City (New Jersey) Directory, R. L. Polk & Co. publishers, 1924.

Polk's Ocean City (New Jersey) Directory, R. L. Polk & Co. publishers, 1928.

Polk's Ocean City (New Jersey) Directory, R. L. Polk & Co. publishers, 1937.

Polk's Ocean City Guide Book and Directory, 1892.

Rizzo, Dennis. *Parallel Communities. The Underground Railroad in New Jersey.* Published by The History Press, Charleston, SC, 2008.

Roberson, Alice Jones. *Whitesboro, New Jersey. Pioneers, Early Settlers, New Town.* Published by BookMasters, Inc., Mansfield, Ohio, 2002.

Rush, Mary Townsend. Ocean City Guide Book and Directory, 1893.

Salem County Clerk's Office, *Death Records,* County of Salem, Salem, NJ

Scott, J. D. *Map of Ocean City New Jersey from Actual Surveys and Official Records.* Published by J. D. Scott. 1896.

Shaw, John T. and Gardener. *U.S. City Directories (Beta),* 1928, Ancestry.com online.

Trusty, Emma Marie, *The Underground Railroad Unveiled – Ties That Bound,* Amed Literary, 1999

United States Federal Census 1900, 1910, 1920, 1930, 1940, 1950, 1960, 1970.

Wood, William B., *First Annual Report of the Ocean City Association,* October 28, 1880.

Woodson, Carter G. Ph.D, *Free Negro Heads of Families in the United States in 1830,* The Association for the Study of Negro Life and History, Inc., Washington D.C., 1925

William G. Griffin Private Collection

Funeral Program Collection (1964-1981)	
Newspaper Clippings	Various
Homer Jones Obituary	Not dated
Obituary Album	
Photograph Albums	
Program Booklets	
I.B.P.O.E. of W. Geranium Temple No. 469	
45th Anniversary	1972
Bacchus, Davis, Mack Appreciation Dinner	1975
48th Anniversary	1975
49th Anniversary	1976
50th Anniversary	1977
57th Anniversary	1984
Ocean City High School Baccalaureate Service	1963
Ocean City High School Commencement Exercises	1963
Ocean City Old Timers (OCOT)	
Annual Reunion and Homecoming, St. James A.M.E.	1968
Annual Awards Banquet & Scholarship Presentations	1969
Annual Memorial Service, Shiloh Baptist Church	1969
Oliver W. O'Farrell Scholarship Presentations & Awards	1970
Program, Macedonia UMC,	1970
Oliver W. O'Farrell Scholarship Club Awards Banquet	1971
8th Annual Church Service, St. James A.M.E. Church	1972
Service, Shiloh Baptist Church	1973
Annual Reunion, Macedonia UMC	1974
Service, Macedonia UMC	1978
Program, Tabernacle Baptist Church	1979
OCOT Memorial Service, Shiloh Baptist Church	1981
Oliver W. O'Farrell Scholarship Club, Macedonia UMC	1994
St. James A.M.E. Church	
Annual Easter Program	1967
Annual Men's Day	1969
Appreciation Mr. & Mrs. Conquest, Joseph Mitchell	1972

Appreciation Hour Sister Carrie B. Scott   1972
Dedication Services for Church Furniture   1975
Annual Men's Day   1975
65th Annual Men's Day   1976
65th Annual Women's Day   1976
66th Annual Women's Day   1978
Sara E. Banks Ordained Local Elder   1977
67th Annual Women's Day   1977
68th Annual Women's Day, Rev. Mrs. Sara Banks   1978
Salute to Service: Senior Choir & Six Senior Missionaries   1979
73rd Annual Women's Day   1984

INDEX

ABOUT THE AUTHOR

THE WESTSIDE Series

Ocean City in True Color

Breaking Barriers, Building Bridges

Loretta Thompson Harris. c. 2023

Loretta Thompson Harris is a fourth generation Ocean City native and retired Atlantic Electric executive who served on numerous boards and charitable organizations during her working years. She is Past President of the National Association of Negro Business and Professional Women, Past President of the Atlantic County Women's Hall of Fame, former United Way allocator and member of the Summit Bank Advisory Council. She currently serves as a volunteer researcher, exhibitor, and lecturer for the Ocean City Historical Museum and is a member of OCNJ AARP Chapter 1062 and Richard Somers Chapter #1148, Questers International.

Loretta's formative years were spent growing up in a medina-like atmosphere behind the invisible walls of the small area called the Westside. Under the watchful eyes of parents and neighbors, the inquisitive little Daddy's girl quickly learned the ways of her world. She relished the stories and friendly banter of neighborhood men at the local gas station and next-door barber shop. Though never destined for the kitchen, she enjoyed being with the women of the family as they cooked and cleaned and reminisced about their southern upbringing.

For more than thirty years, Loretta has been researching her family history and documenting the untold story of Ocean City's African American and Native American neighborhood. Loretta enjoys antiquing along South Jersey's back roads, preserving cemeteries, traveling, and Newport jazz. The Westside**Error! Bookmark not defined.** Series is the history of Ocean City's African American community told by one of its own.

Made in the USA
Columbia, SC
04 September 2024

41584300R00193